T0386492

FREE WILL AND HUMAN AGENCY: 50 PUZZLES, PARADOXES, AND THOUGHT EXPERIMENTS

In this new kind of entrée to contemporary discussions of free will and human agency, Garrett Pendergraft collects and illuminates 50 of the most relevant puzzles, paradoxes, and thought experiments. Assuming no familiarity with the philosophical literature on free will, each chapter describes a case, explains the questions that it raises, briefly summarizes some of the key responses to the case, and provides a list of suggested readings. Every chapter is accessible, succinct, and self-contained. The puzzles are divided into five broad categories: the threat from fatalism, the threat from determinism, practical reason, social dimensions, and moral luck. Entries cover topics such as the grandfather paradox, theological fatalism, the consequence argument, manipulation arguments, luck arguments, weakness of will, action explanation, addiction, blame and punishment, situationism in moral psychology, and Huckleberry Finn. *Free Will and Human Agency* is an effective and engaging teaching tool as well as a handy resource for anyone interested in exploring the questions that have made human agency a topic of perennial philosophical interest.

Key Features:

- Though concise overall, offers broad coverage of the key areas of free will and human agency.
- Describes each imaginative case directly and in a memorable way, making the cases accessible and easy to remember.
- Provides a list of suggested readings for each case.

Garrett Pendergraft is Blanche E. Seaver Professor of Philosophy at Pepperdine University. His research focuses on understanding and responding to various threats to free will and moral responsibility.

PUZZLES, PARADOXES, AND THOUGHT EXPERIMENTS IN PHILOSOPHY

Imaginative cases—or what might be called puzzles, paradoxes, and other thought experiments—play a central role in philosophy. This series offers students and researchers a wide range of such imaginative cases, with each volume devoted to fifty such cases in a major subfield of philosophy. Every book in the series includes: some initial background information on each case, a clear and detailed description of the case, and an explanation of the issue(s) to which the case is relevant. Key responses to the case and suggested reading lists are also included.

Recently published volumes:

EPISTEMOLOGY
KEVIN MCCAIN

FREE WILL AND HUMAN AGENCY
GARRETT PENDERGRAFT

Forthcoming volumes:

AESTHETICS
MICHEL-ANTOINE XHIGNESSE

PHILOSOPHY OF LANGUAGE
MICHAEL P. WOLF

ETHICS
SARAH STROUD AND DANIEL MUÑOZ

PHILOSOPHY OF MIND
TORIN ALTER, AMY KIND, AND CHASE B. WRENN

BIOETHICS
SEAN AAS, COLLIN O'NEIL, AND CHIARA LEPORA

METAPHYSICS
SAM COWLING, WESLEY D. CRAY, AND KELLY TROGDON

For a full list of published volumes in **Puzzles, Paradoxes, and Thought Experiments in Philosophy**, please visit www.routledge. com/Puzzles, Paradoxes, andThoughtExperimentsinPhilosophy/ book-series/PPTEP

FREE WILL AND HUMAN AGENCY: 50 PUZZLES, PARADOXES, AND THOUGHT EXPERIMENTS

Garrett Pendergraft

Routledge
Taylor & Francis Group

NEW YORK AND LONDON

Cover image: Anselm Schwietzke / EyeEm / Getty Images

First published 2023
by Routledge
605 Third Avenue, New York, NY 10158

and by Routledge
4 Park Square, Milton Park, Abingdon, Oxon, OX14 4RN

Routledge is an imprint of the Taylor & Francis Group, an informa business

Library of Congress Cataloging-in-Publication Data
A catalog record for this title has been requested

ISBN: 978-0-367-64757-5 (hbk)
ISBN: 978-0-367-64194-8 (pbk)
ISBN: 978-1-003-12611-9 (ebk)

DOI: 10.4324/9781003126119

Typeset in Bembo
by codeMantra

CONTENTS

PREFACE

Reflection upon free will (and human agency more broadly) is almost guaranteed to produce puzzlement and consternation. It is one of the most accessible subjects of philosophical reflection, and yet at the same time one that remains mysterious even to experts. Thus it is only appropriate that we examine free will and human agency in light of this natural and persistent puzzlement. This book brings together 50 puzzles, paradoxes, and thought experiments, each of which represents both the satisfactions and struggles of thinking about human agency. The entries are grouped thematically, but they can be read in any order. Each chapter stands alone, but there are also numerous cross-references so that readers can pursue a particular interest or pick up additional context as needed.

Each chapter begins with an accessible presentation of the puzzle, paradox, or thought experiment and also includes a brief discussion of some of the different engagements with it in the philosophical literature. The chapter then ends with a short list of recommended readings for those who want to dive a little deeper.

This book is designed to be useful both as a textbook and for individual study. It could serve as the primary text in a course focused on free will, or as one of several texts in an introductory course. In a lower-level course, the chapters themselves might be enough; in an upper-level course, individual chapters could be fruitfully paired with one or more of the reading suggestions to provide a more advanced experience. Each chapter is designed to be accessible to beginning students, but also informative enough—especially when coupled with the recommended readings—to be a useful resource for professional scholars.

As we'll see in Chapter 38, gratitude is an important example of the reactive emotions. It's also a fitting attitude for me to express here, in light of all of the help and support I've received while working on this project. I would like to thank Andy Beck for the opportunity to undertake the project, and for his enthusiastic support along the way. I am grateful to Justin Coates, Taylor Cyr, Andrew Eshleman, Andrew Law, Ben Mitchell-Yellin, Dan Speak, Philip Swenson, Patrick Todd, and Neal Tognazzini for numerous ideas and comments that helped shape the book. And I would like to thank John Martin Fischer for his essential role in shaping the career of which this book is a part. I am grateful to Julianne Carter for the alacrity with which she accepted and executed the various research tasks that I sent her way, and especially for her assistance in tracking down some important primary sources. Thanks also to Jackson Felkins for additional research assistance. And finally, I would like to thank Amy, Sage, Curran, and Cardiff for their unfailing love and support—without which this project probably wouldn't have been possible, but definitely wouldn't have been worthwhile.

One of the themes of this book is that human agency is valuable but flawed. My own human agency is certainly no exception, and as a result there are no doubt errors that remain despite my best efforts to eliminate them. Praise for any admirable features of this book must be shared with those mentioned above (among others), but blame for the flaws rests entirely with me.

PART I

FATALISM AND OTHER SOURCES OF EXISTENTIAL ANGST

Chapters 1–9 group together a set of challenges to free will that can all loosely be described as *fatalist* challenges. (Although of course many of these challenges could be categorized in other ways as well.) In Chapter 1 we begin with an intuitively compelling picture of our freedom: the idea that our choices take place in the context of a (metaphorical) "garden of forking paths." The notion of fatalism encapsulates a set of concerns that cause us to wonder whether this picture is an accurate representation of reality.

Chapter 2 ("Tomorrow's Sea Battle") refers to a famous passage from Aristotle, in which he considers arguments that begin with very simple ingredients (apparently true predictions) and end with a disturbing conclusion about a lack of control. Aristotle doesn't seem to endorse the fatalistic conclusion, but the third chapter ("A Date with Destiny") features a thought experiment told by someone—Richard Taylor—who does endorse fatalism. Taylor's thought experiment involves an individual named Osmo, who discovers a book that accurately describes his entire life.

Chapter 4 (*"Stranger than Fiction"*), inspired in part by the movie of the same name, features a similar type of story, i.e., one in which the main character (Harold Crick) discovers that his life is the subject

DOI: 10.4324/9781003126119-1

of a book. Unlike Osmo, however, Crick's story is still being written (albeit not by him), which gives him the opportunity to lobby the author for a better ending. The fifth chapter ("The Trouble with Time Travel") also involves someone trying to rewrite a narrative. In this case, however, the protagonist, Tim, is trying to travel back in time and rewrite his family's history by killing his own grandfather.

One common feature of the fatalistic stories in Chapters 3–5 is a knowledge of what's going to happen (or what has already happened, in Tim's case). Some philosophers (Taylor included) have thought that knowledge of what's going to happen makes it impossible to *deliberate* about what's going to happen. Chapter 6 ("Does Deliberation Require Uncertainty?") puts this claim under the microscope.

Two recurring themes, then, are predictions (which can give rise to fatalist concerns) and deliberation (which seems to be threatened by those fatalist concerns). Chapter 7 ("One Box or Two?") takes up the prediction concern by examining Newcomb's problem. The predictor in Newcomb's problem can be described as more or less accurate, depending on which variation of the problem we're considering, but there's one particular predictor who is supposed to be infallible: the God of traditional Christian theism. Chapter 8 ("Does Divine Foreknowledge Undermine Our Freedom?") examines the theological version of the fatalist challenge.

The final chapter in this part ("Fatalism in the Courtroom") borrows from Clarence Darrow's famous defense of Leopold and Loeb. We'll extract an argument from Darrow's wide-ranging plea to the effect that free will is not just non-existent, but perhaps even *impossible*.

THE GARDEN OF FORKING PATHS

GETTING STARTED IN OUR THINKING ABOUT FREE WILL

Jorge Luis Borges made a name for himself primarily in literature, but he has also shaped contemporary discussions of free will and moral responsibility. His influence on the free will discussion comes from a very simple thought experiment, which helps us get a handle on one way of thinking about free choice. In Borges's short story "The Garden of Forking Paths," the character Stephen Albert says the following: "In all fictions, each time a man meets diverse alternatives, he chooses one and eliminates the others" (Borges 1998 [1941], 125).

Encountering "diverse alternatives" is like walking through a garden and coming to a fork in the path; making a choice is like choosing between the different forks. Borges's character describes this as what happens in fiction, but various philosophers have been willing to use the description for reality as well. John Martin Fischer, for example, introduces the commonsense notion of freedom as the view that "the future is a garden of forking paths" (1994, 3).

One reason why this picture has become one of the dominant metaphors for thinking about free will is that it captures a sense in which the future, unlike the past, seems to be open. (For more on statements about the future, see Chapter 2.) The path we have already traversed

DOI: 10.4324/9781003126119-2

has been written into our journey, but the path we take into the future has yet to be decided.

Robert Kane captures the importance of this metaphor by asking us to consider a recent law school graduate, Molly, who is deciding between two different job offers:

> If Molly believes her choice is a *free* choice (made "of her own free will"), she must believe both options are "open" to her while she is deliberating. She could choose either one. (If she did not believe this, what would be the point of deliberating?) But that means she must believe there is more than one possible path into the future available to her and it is "up to her" which of these paths will be taken. Such a picture of an open future with forking paths—a "garden of forking paths," we might call it—is essential to our understanding of free will. Such a picture of different possible paths into the future is also essential, we might even say, to what it means to be a person and to live a human life.
>
> (Kane 2005, 6–7)

As Kane points out, the way that we think about our choices is fundamental to the way that we think about ourselves as human persons.

Our ability to reflect on our own freedom, however, often gives rise to various concerns. We might wonder whether our future path is up to us in the way it seems to be. Do we really have the choices between different paths that we think we have? Are we really the one writing our own story? Perhaps our story has already been written—by someone else, or perhaps by impersonal forces—and we are merely living it out.

If you've ever pondered possibilities such as these, then you've encountered the philosophical problem of *fatalism*. And you're joining a venerable tradition of philosophers who have been thinking about this problem, and passing it along, for thousands of years. In fact, Daniel Dennett speculates that the problem of fatalism might be the original philosophical problem: "The idea of Fate is older than philosophy itself" (1984, 1). One of the core movements of philosophical thought is to wonder whether things really are as they seem to be, and one of our first and strongest seemings is the impression that we are making free choices on a regular basis.

Over the next few chapters, we'll be sharpening the challenge of fatalism by examining its various facets and examining in detail their potential implications for our freedom. We will also be working to increase our understanding of numerous crucial concepts. The central concept of this book is, as you may have guessed, the concept of *free will*. But rather than spending a lot of time up front trying to define free will in a comprehensive way, we will instead highlight various ways of understanding the concept as they become relevant. We will also note how these different ways of understanding free will align or conflict with each other.

For now, we can simply say that Borges's garden of forking paths is one influential and intuitively plausible way of understanding free will: to have free will is to have the ability to choose between different paths into the future. Free will is a type of control over what we do.

RESPONSES

As you might imagine, not everyone has bought into the idea of a garden of forking paths as the right way to think about free will. (It is, after all, only a picture (van Inwagen 1989, 410).) As Kane acknowledges, some would argue that the forking paths metaphor "hides a multitude of puzzles and confusions" (2005, 7). Unfortunately, however, there hasn't been a lot of discussion of how exactly the metaphor is obscure or confusing. (Although see Waller and Waller 2015 for an argument that the forking paths metaphor is inconsistent with a different, but equally plausible, way of thinking about free choice.)

Since the garden of forking paths is a strongly anti-fatalist metaphor, one way to look for alternatives is to look for metaphors that have a better chance of being consistent with fatalism. John Martin Fischer, though not a fatalist himself, has offered a couple of promising examples of this strategy. (See Chapter 25 for an additional example.) One of Fischer's suggestions is that we could shift our focus from the path we choose to the way we choose to walk it:

> Even if there is just one available path into the future, I may be held accountable for *how I walk down this path*. I can be blamed for taking the path of cruelty, negligence, or cowardice. And I can be praised for walking with sensitivity, attentiveness, and courage. Even if I somehow discovered there is but one path into the future, I would still care deeply how I walk down this path. I would aspire to walk with grace and dignity.

I would want to have a sense of humor. Most of all, I would want to do it my way.

(Fischer 1994, 216)

And for those who want to get away from talk of garden paths entirely, they could explore the idea that exercising agency is like playing the cards that you've been dealt. Fischer develops this idea in an article discussing some of Joel Feinberg's work:

Our behavior may well be "in the cards" in the sense that we simply have to play the cards that are dealt us. Further, just as an astronaut may still control the lift-off of the rocket, even though she did not build the platform that makes the launch possible (or ever have any control over the platform), we can be accountable for playing the cards that are dealt us, even if we did not manufacture the cards, write the rules of the game, and so forth. ... It is a kind of wisdom—a wisdom found in Feinberg—to recognize that, when you play the cards that are dealt you (in a certain distinctive way), you can exercise a robust sort of control, even in the absence of the power to make the cards, to own the factory that makes the cards, to make up the rules of the game, and so forth (to infinity) ...

(Fischer 2006, 129)

Choosing between paths is a powerful idea that seems to capture something about the type of freedom that we, as humans, appear to enjoy. Whether it ends up being the *best* way to think about free will remains an open question that we will continue to examine throughout this book.

RECOMMENDED READING

Borges, Jorge Luis. 1998 [1941]. "The Garden of Forking Paths." In *Collected Fictions*, translated by Andrew Hurley, 119–28. New York: Penguin Books.

Fischer, John Martin. 1994. *The Metaphysics of Free Will: An Essay on Control.* Oxford: Blackwell.

Kane, Robert. 2005. *A Contemporary Introduction to Free Will*, chapter 1. New York: Oxford University Press.

Rice, Hugh. 2018. "Fatalism." In *The Stanford Encyclopedia of Philosophy*, edited by Edward N. Zalta, Winter 2018. https://plato.stanford.edu/archives/win2018/entries/fatalism.

WORKS CITED

Dennett, Daniel C. 1984. *Elbow Room: The Varieties of Free Will Worth Wanting.* Oxford: Clarendon Press.

Fischer, John Martin. 2006. "The Cards That Are Dealt You." *The Journal of Ethics* 10: 107–29.

Van Inwagen, Peter. 1989. "When Is the Will Free?" *Philosophical Perspectives* 3: 399–422.

Waller, Robyn Repko, and Russell L. Waller. 2015. "Forking Paths and Freedom: A Challenge to Libertarian Accounts of Free Will." *Philosophia* 43: 1199–1212.

TOMORROW'S SEA BATTLE

THE MOST IMPORTANT SEA BATTLE IN HISTORY?

The Battle of Salamis, which took place in 480 B.C., is widely regarded as one of the most important naval battles in the history of western civilization (Strauss 2004). Not only did an outnumbered Greek navy defeat the Persian armada in the face of what seemed like an unstoppable advance (thus preserving Greek independence); but it also enabled Athens to become the dominant political and cultural power in Greece.

Aristotle wrote *De Interpretatione* more than a century later, in 350 B.C., but the Greek victory loomed large enough in his culture's historical consciousness that any reference to a "sea battle" would no doubt bring to mind the Battle of Salamis. Aristotle uses just such a reference, in *De Interpretatione* 9, in his discussion of some puzzles having to do with the way we talk about the future. As it turns out, parts of Aristotle's discussion are also relevant to our understanding of free will.

A comprehensive treatment of Aristotle's discussion would require much more space than is available here. Not only are we going to be focusing narrowly on the implications for free will (ignoring broader questions involving how we talk about the future), but we will also be

DOI: 10.4324/9781003126119-3

setting aside numerous scholarly disputes over Aristotle's stance toward the arguments he considers in *De Interpretatione* 9. So this chapter will have to oversimplify and gloss over lots of interesting details; but the hope is that by extracting and discussing one simple argument, it will still serve as a good introduction to one type of fatalist challenge to free will.

Historical records tell us that the Battle of Salamis took place on September 25. Suppose that on the 24th, Themistocles utters the sentence, "There will be a sea battle tomorrow." (Themistocles was the architect and chief advocate of the Greek naval strategy.) This type of statement is called a *future contingent statement* because it's about a contingent event in the future. (A contingent event, unlike a necessary event and unlike an impossible event, may or may not happen; it's possible for it to happen but also possible for it not to happen.)

Future contingent statements, or just "future contingents" for short, appear to be different from statements about the past. Once a contingent event occurs, and at every point after it occurs, there is a type of necessity that attaches to it in virtue of its occurrence. (This type of necessity is sometimes called the *necessity of the past*.) For example, "There will be a sea battle tomorrow" seems to be alterable in a way that "There was a sea battle yesterday" isn't. (For more on this asymmetry, see Torre 2011.)

Aristotle acknowledges the intuitive plausibility of this point at the beginning of chapter 9: "With regard to what is and what has been it is necessary for the affirmation or the negation to be true or false. ... But with particulars that are going to be it is different" (18a27–34; Barnes 1984). He then proceeds, however, to give us some reasons why this apparent distinction between past statements and future statements might be illusory. When Themistocles predicts that there will be a sea battle tomorrow, it's plausible to assume that this prediction, like all predictions, must be either true or false: it can't be neither, and it can't be both. Every prediction will either correspond with the way reality turns out or it will fail to correspond with reality. If the sea battle occurs, then Themistocles' prediction was true; if it doesn't occur, then it was false.

If this way of thinking about predictions is right, then we might start to worry that there isn't that much difference between the past and future after all; maybe there's a type of necessity that attaches to the future as well. Here's how Aristotle expresses the worry: "Now if this be so, nothing is or takes place fortuitously, either in the present or in the future, and there are no real alternatives; everything takes place of necessity and is fixed" (18b5–6; McKeon 2001).

It's important to keep in mind that the necessity Aristotle references here is not the same as *logical* necessity or *physical* necessity. (Physical necessity is governed by the laws of nature, whereas logical necessity is governed by the laws of logic.) Future contingent events wouldn't be necessary in the way that "A square cannot be a circle" is logically necessary or in the way that "Nothing travels faster than the speed of light" is physically necessary. Nevertheless, just thinking about the sea battle prediction (and predictions in general) has given us reason to wonder whether *some* type of necessity attaches to everything that happens. (One word that philosophers often use to capture this type of necessity is *inevitability*.)

Aristotle strengthens the worry by generalizing a little bit:

> For there is nothing to prevent someone's having said ten thousand years beforehand that this would be the case, and another's having denied it; so that whichever of the two was true to say then, will be the case of necessity. ... Hence, if in the whole of time the state of things was such that one or the other was true, it was necessary for this to happen, and for the state of things always to be such that everything that happens happens of necessity. For what anyone has truly said would be the case cannot not happen; and of what happens it was always true to say that it would be the case.
>
> (18b33–19a6; Barnes 1984)

A true prediction from yesterday is one thing, but a true prediction from *10,000 years ago* is another. A prediction from that long ago seems to put control over the event even farther out of our reach. But it's not the prediction itself that's making things happen; there has to be something about the world (something about "the state of things," as Aristotle says) that's generating the necessity—that's making the event inevitable. And whatever it is about reality that's making these statements true, it's arguably not something we have any control over.

This particular fatalist argument, then, comes in three stages: a true prediction, which implies inevitability, which implies a lack of control. The end result might not seem too troubling at first. A sea battle is a pretty complex event that depends upon a lot of factors. We don't have to work too hard to imagine that an event like the Battle of Salamis was inevitable, in the sense that there were forces at work pushing it forward in a way that overwhelmed any one person's individual contribution. (Although on the other hand it also seems as though there were at least *some* people who were capable of doing things that would have prevented the battle from occurring.) But we can insert any event whatsoever into this argument pattern. Even if we pick an action that we seem to have maximum control over (a basic bodily movement, perhaps), we can run a parallel argument, to the effect that we actually don't have control over that action. Indeed, every event that occurs—which includes every action that occurs—seems to be threatened by this argument pattern. This lack of control would mean that we don't have the freedom that we appear to have.

RESPONSES

Although there are various points at which someone might resist this fatalist argument, most of the responses have focused on the first two stages. For example, some have taken seriously the idea that a true prediction would imply inevitability, and then used a rejection of inevitability to reverse the order of argument (cf. Prior 1967). On Prior's view, "There will be a sea battle" actually *means* "It is necessary that there be a sea battle tomorrow." To say that something *will* happen is the same as saying that it *must* happen. And since not everything is inevitable, there will be lots of predictions that turn out false, even though the event predicted actually occurs. On this view, *all* future contingent statements are false. (For a comprehensive contemporary treatment of this view, see Todd 2021.)

Another solution, which Aristotle himself suggests, focuses on the first stage of the argument. This solution rejects the very first step of the argument, namely the assumption that every prediction is either true or false. Aristotle allows that *some* predictions can be true or false; for example, a disjunctive (either/or) prediction, "There either will or will not be a sea battle tomorrow" must be true. The two possibilities covered in the disjunctive prediction are exhaustive, so there's no other way for reality to turn out. Thus the prediction, which in effect says that reality will turn out in one of the only two possible ways it can turn out, must be true. *But*, Aristotle says, if we separate the disjunctive prediction into its individual disjuncts, it doesn't follow that either of the individual predictions has to be true:

> Everything necessarily is or is not, and will be or will not be; but one cannot divide and say that one or the other is necessary. I mean, for example: it is necessary for there to be or not be a sea battle tomorrow; but it is not necessary for a sea-battle to take place tomorrow, nor for one not to take place—though it is necessary for one to take place or not to take place.
>
> (19a29–32; Barnes 1984)

His claim then, appears to be that for statements about contingent events in the future, there may not be any fact of the matter about whether the event will occur. And in that case a prediction that the event will occur is neither true nor false.

A contemporary variation on this response comes from MacFarlane (2003), who defends the possibility that the truth value of future contingents might vary according to the context in which they are assessed. The details of his proposal are complex, but the basic idea is that we should distinguish between the moment at which a statement is uttered and the moment at which it's assessed for truth value. When Themistocles says (on the 24th), "There will be a sea battle," there are some possible futures in which the sea battle occurs and other possible futures in which it doesn't; so if we assess the statement immediately upon utterance, it's neither true nor false. But as time passes, the battle becomes more and more likely (there are fewer and fewer possible futures that *don't* contain a battle), until at some point it becomes inevitable. At this point, whenever it may be, if we were to assess the utterance then it would be true. If we are considering a different possible world, in which the battle doesn't occur, then the utterance is assessed as neither true nor false until its nonoccurrence becomes inevitable, at which point it can be assessed as false.

RECOMMENDED READING

Aristotle. 350 B.C. *De Interpretatione*.
Iacona, Andrea. n.d. "Future Contingents." In *Internet Encyclopedia of Philosophy*. https://iep.utm.edu/fut-cont.

MacFarlane, John. 2003. "Future Contingents and Relative Truth." *The Philosophical Quarterly* 53: 321–36.

Øhrstrøm, Peter, and Per Hasle. 2020. "Future Contingents." In *The Stanford Encyclopedia of Philosophy*, edited by Edward N. Zalta, Summer 2020. https://plato.stanford.edu/archives/sum2020/entries/future-contingents.

WORKS CITED

Barnes, Jonathan, ed. 1984. *Complete Works of Aristotle: The Revised Oxford Translation.* Vol. 1. Princeton, NJ: Princeton University Press.

McKeon, Richard, ed. 2001. *The Basic Works of Aristotle.* Revised ed. New York: Modern Library.

Prior, Arthur N. 1967. *Past, Present and Future.* Oxford: Oxford University Press.

Strauss, Barry. 2004. *The Battle of Salamis.* New York: Simon & Schuster.

Todd, Patrick. 2021. *The Open Future: Why Future Contingents Are All False.* Oxford: Oxford University Press.

Torre, Stephan. 2011. "The Open Future." *Philosophy Compass* 6: 360–73.

A DATE WITH DESTINY

A MORBID THOUGHT EXPERIMENT

John O'Hara's novel, *Appointment in Samarra* (1934), contains an epigraph written by W. Somerset Maugham, which is a retelling of an ancient Mesopotamian fable. Here is the story in full, as narrated by Death herself:

> There was a merchant in Baghdad who sent his servant to market to buy provisions and in a little while the servant came back, white and trembling, and said, Master, just now when I was in the marketplace I was jostled by a woman in the crowd and when I turned I saw it was Death that jostled me. She looked at me and made a threatening gesture; now, lend me your horse, and I will ride away from this city and avoid my fate. I will go to Samarra and there Death will not find me. The merchant lent him his horse, and the servant mounted it, and he dug his spurs in its flanks and as fast as the horse could gallop he went. Then the merchant went down to the marketplace and he saw me standing in the crowd and he came to me and said, Why did you make a threatening gesture to my servant when you saw him this morning? That was not a threatening gesture, I said, it was only a start of surprise. I was astonished to see him in Baghdad, for I had an appointment with him tonight in Samarra.

The servant, in trying to avoid his fate, unwittingly brought it upon himself.

DOI: 10.4324/9781003126119-4

We saw in Chapter 2 that the way we talk about the future can raise fatalist concerns. The truth of a prediction (especially a prediction far in advance) seems to imply a type of inevitability that threatens our freedom. But it takes a few steps to work out this threat, and even with the argument in front of us it might be hard to feel the force of it. Stories like the Mesopotamian fable above lead to a similar argument, and thus represent a similar threat; but the way such stories are told tends to make the threat more real.

Richard Taylor (1992, ch. 6), for example, tells the story of Osmo, an ordinary man who discovers a book that recounts "all the more or less significant episodes" in his life. Unbeknownst to Osmo, the contents of this book were given to a scribe by God, who dutifully recorded them, assembled them, and had them published. Osmo discovers the book as an adult. He is mesmerized by the recounting of his childhood, and shocked at its inerrancy regarding more recent events, but dismissive of what it has to say about his death. The book says that he will die in a plane crash in Fort Wayne, so he simply resolves not to get on the flight.

Here's how the story ends:

> (About three years later our hero, having boarded a flight for St. Paul, went berserk when the pilot announced they were going to land at Fort Wayne instead. According to one of the flight attendants, he tried to hijack the aircraft and divert it to another airfield. The Civil Aeronautics Board cited the resulting disruptions as contributing to the crash that followed as the plane tried to land.)
>
> (Taylor 1992, 60)

Here again we see the same pattern: the actions designed to avoid one's fate become the very actions that contribute to bringing it about. (This pattern is instantiated in various places in popular culture as well; in the movie *Kung Fu Panda*, for example.) It's not that Osmo's failure (or the servant's failure) to avoid his fate supports fatalism directly; instead, these stories support the argument for fatalism indirectly, by illustrating in a vivid way how feelings of control can be illusory. Setting aside the dramatic endings, Taylor explains how stories like Osmo's might lead to us to doubt our own freedom:

> Osmo's extraordinary circumstances led him to embrace the doctrine of fatalism. Not quite completely, perhaps, for there he was, right up to the

end, trying vainly to buck his fate—trying, in effect, to make a fool of God, though he did not know this, because he had no idea of the book's source. Still, he had the overwhelming evidence of his whole past life to make him think that everything was going to work out exactly as described in the book. It always had. It was, in fact, precisely this conviction that terrified him so.

But now let us ask these questions, in order to make Osmo's experiences more relevant to our own. First, why did he become, or nearly become, a fatalist? Second, just what did his fatalism amount to? Third, was his belief justified in terms of the evidence he had? And finally, is that belief justified in terms of the evidence *we* have—or in other words, should we be fatalists too?

This last, of course, is the important metaphysical question, but we have to approach it through the others.

(Taylor 1992, 60)

As Taylor points out (1992, 61), all of us are fatalists about some things, like the rising of the sun. Full-blown philosophical fatalism generalizes these local fatalist thoughts into the view that *everything that occurs* is similarly inevitable for us. If philosophical fatalism is true, then our sense that some things are avoidable is simply an illusion.

Taylor goes on to argue that, not only was Osmo justified in becoming a fatalist, but we should become fatalists too. He points out that Osmo became a fatalist because he read the relevant propositions in a book, and discovered one by one that all of them were true. But neither the book nor the discovery is essential to the fatalist argument: the book would be just as threatening if it were never discovered, and the *contents* of the book would be just as threatening even if they were never written down. All it takes is for there to be a set of true propositions that accurately describe every event that constitutes our life. And since, for every event that occurs, there is a truth about it ahead of time, it would seem that our fate is sealed; our future is unavoidable.

A simple regimentation of this argument might run as follows:

(1)   For every action we perform, there already exists a true proposition specifying that we'll perform that action.
(2)   If there already exists a true proposition specifying that we'll perform an action, then the action isn't free.
(3)   Therefore, none of our actions are free.

Regimenting the argument this way helps us see that the two primary components of the fatalist challenge are (1) true propositions that (2) we have no control over. We'll look at a response that rejects (1), a response that rejects (2), and a bonus response that refrains from specifying which component should be rejected.

RESPONSES

The first response, discussed in more detail in Chapter 2, is to reject premise (1). Perhaps propositions specifying our actions are neither true nor false until we make them that way, or perhaps they are simply false until the action really does become inevitable. We've all experienced the phenomenon of trying to make it somewhere on time but cutting it close. While you're en route, there's a sense in which it seems false that you will (or won't) make it; it just depends on how much traffic there is, or on whether you catch a green light, or on some other detail. But sometimes, unfortunately, it becomes clear that you're not going to make it; "You won't make it" has become true because it's no longer possible for you to make it. Before that, though, it would have been false to say that you wouldn't make it (but also false to say that you would make it).

Another response borrows from the Ockhamist response to the argument for *theological* fatalism (cf. Chapter 8). According to the Ockhamist, some facts (which we might call "soft facts") are about the past but also about the future. Thus, the truth of these facts depends in part on how things turn out in the future. If we were to apply these insights to the fatalist argument, we could try to reject (2) by saying that our actions *can* be free even if they are accurately described by a true proposition that already exists. It may be true that I'm going to perform an action later, but I'm still free to refrain; and if I *had* refrained, then that true proposition would have been false instead. (For additional connections between the story of Osmo and theological fatalism, see Hunt 1993.)

The final solution we'll consider borrows from a famous move in epistemology, namely G. E. Moore's response to skepticism. One of Moore's responses to the skeptical argument is, roughly, that he is more certain that the conclusion is false than he is certain that any of the premises are true (1953). Even if he can't say *which* premise is false, he has good reason to believe that one of them is indeed false. So we could try to make a similar move with respect to the fatalist argument above. We could say, in other words, that we are more certain that some of our actions are free than we are certain that either of the premises are true. We have lots of evidence that we are free, but not as much evidence supporting esoteric claims about the truth value of past propositions or the relation between truths in the past and actions in the future. Advocates of this response have to be careful not to slip into casual dogmatism, but it's a type of move that many of us have made in the past. We encounter something that seems well supported, but we're so confident that it's wrong that we're willing to resist that support even if we can't yet figure out where it goes wrong. This approach doesn't always pay off, but sometimes our resistance is vindicated.

RECOMMENDED READING

Finch, Alicia. 2017. "Logical Fatalism." In *The Routledge Companion to Free Will*, edited by Kevin Timpe, Meghan Griffith, and Neil Levy, 191–202. New York: Routledge.

Hunt, David P. 1993. "Divine Providence and Simple Foreknowledge." *Faith and Philosophy* 10: 394–414.

Rice, Hugh. 2018. "Fatalism." In *The Stanford Encyclopedia of Philosophy*, edited by Edward N. Zalta, Winter 2018. https://plato.stanford.edu/archives/win2018/entries/fatalism.

Taylor, Richard. 1992. *Metaphysics*, 4th edition, chapter 6. Englewood Cliffs, NJ: Prentice Hall.

WORKS CITED

Moore, G. E. 1953. "Hume's Theory Examined." In *Some Main Problems of Philosophy*, 108–26. London: Allen & Unwin.

O'Hara, John. 2013 [1934]. *Appointment in Samarra*. New York: Penguin Classics.

STRANGER THAN FICTION

THE VALUE OF NARRATIVE

"Little did he know that this simple, seemingly innocuous act would result in his imminent death."

This is one of the most important lines in the movie *Stranger than Fiction*, in which the main character (Harold Crick, played by Will Ferrell) discovers that he is the protagonist in a novel that someone else is in the process of writing. One day he starts to hear a narrator in his head, describing the events in his life with perfect accuracy (and "with a better vocabulary," as he acknowledges). This accuracy eventually convinces him that the mysterious narrator is actually an *author*, orchestrating the events of his life. (So he is understandably upset when he hears the author utter the line above, foreshadowing his demise.) Crick thus finds himself in the strange position of living a life whose narrative originates with someone else.

Pondering Harold Crick's plight reveals some tensions in our concept of ourselves as free and responsible agents. On one hand, we all want to think of our life as following some sort of narrative arc, whether it includes overcoming obstacles, finding redemption, or simply growing and improving steadily over time. (And of course there are dozens of other identifiable narrative arcs that someone might

DOI: 10.4324/9781003126119-5

want to traverse.) On the other hand, we don't want to discover that our life follows a narrative arc *too* closely, or that someone else is the author of that narrative arc, lest we start to lose our sense of autonomy. We can't be *complete* authors of our own narrative, in the sense that we are unaffected by external factors, but we do want to maintain a significant degree of creative control.

In previous chapters we have seen how we tend to view ourselves as the author of our own story (see Chapter 1), but also how the discovery of a certain type of story—a comprehensive story of our life—might push us toward becoming fatalists (see Chapter 3). Although the *Stranger than Fiction* thought experiment does resemble the story of Osmo because both include the discovery of a book, the philosophical implications diverge sharply. Taylor uses the story of Osmo to introduce the idea that a complete, accurate description of our life already exists, even if it has never been recorded. And this idea, in turn, might push us toward an acceptance of fatalism. The story of Harold Crick, on the other hand, is not intended to push us toward fatalism by making us think that there might be an author out there currently in the process of writing each of our stories. Instead, Harold's story has philosophical relevance because it opens up a lot of interesting questions about the importance of narrative to our understanding (and our valuing) of ourselves as individuals and as free agents.

One particularly insightful treatment of narrative value comes from David Velleman (1991), who points out that the value of someone's life depends on the ordering or structure of events in that life—"on what might be called their narrative or dramatic relations":

> Consider two different lives that you might live. One life begins in the depths but takes an upward trend: a childhood of deprivation, a troubled youth, struggles and setbacks in early adulthood, followed finally by success and satisfaction in middle age and a peaceful retirement. Another life begins at the heights but slides downhill: a blissful childhood and youth, precocious triumphs and rewards in early adulthood, followed by a midlife strewn with disasters that lead to misery in old age. Surely, we can imagine two such lives as containing equal sums of momentary well-being. Your retirement is as blessed in one life as your childhood is in the other; your nonage is as blighted in one life as your dotage is in the other.
>
> (Velleman 1991, 58)

Velleman invites us to agree with him that the first life has more value than the second life, even though we can stipulate that both lives contain the same overall amount of well-being. His explanation of this judgment is that the meaning and value of an event depend on more than just the goods (or evils) that it brings about; the event's meaning and value also depend on the *narrative relations* between that event and other events in a person's life:

> A particular [event], providing a particular boost to one's current welfare, can mean either that one's early frustrations were finally over or that one's subsequent failures were not yet foreshadowed, that one enjoyed either fleeting good luck or lasting success—all depending on its placement in the trend of one's well-being. And the event's meaning is what determines its contribution to the value of one's life.
>
> (Velleman 1991, 63)

One implication of this view is that there are some lives in which an earlier death would be better. For example, someone might opt to forego an experimental treatment of a fatal illness on the grounds that even if the treatment is successful, it will only add a few months of life and those months will involve a lot of pain and suffering. We can imagine someone deciding that they are content with the narrative arc of their life, and that they would rather end it peacefully and naturally instead of desperately groping for a few more months. As Velleman puts it, on this view someone's attitude toward death "depends on whether an earlier or later death would make a better ending to his life story" (1991, 74).

Let's briefly look at some of the ways in which *Stranger than Fiction* illustrates a narrative theory of life's value. After Crick hears his death predicted by the narrator, he consults with a professor of literature, Dr. Jules Hilbert, who helps him figure out the type of story he's in (with the ultimate goal of identifying the author). Hilbert also advises him, in light of his imminent demise, to *live his life*: to make his life the one he's always wanted it to be. Through a stroke of luck, they eventually realize that Karen Eiffel is the author; the bad news, though, is that she's notorious for killing her protagonists. Crick manages to locate Eiffel, and visits her to plead for his life. (She is thoroughly shaken by the experience of meeting one of her fictional characters in the flesh.) Eiffel has completed the story, including

Harold's death, but hasn't typed it out yet. She gives it to Harold to read. He can't bring himself to read it, so he asks Professor Hilbert to read it for him: "You have to read it. You—You have to tell me what to do or what not to do. You—If I can avoid it. If—If I have a chance. Please."

After Hilbert reads it, he delivers the bad news to Crick:

> Hilbert: Harold, I'm sorry. You have to die.
> Crick: What?
> Hilbert: It's her masterpiece. It's possibly the most important novel in her already stunning career, and it's absolutely no good unless you die at the end. [pauses] I've been over it again and again, and I know how hard this is for you to hear.
> Crick: You're asking me to knowingly face my death?
> Hilbert: Yes.
> Crick: Really?
> Hilbert: Yes.
> Crick: I thought you'd, uh—I thought you'd find something.
> Hilbert: I'm sorry, Harold.
> Crick: Can't we just try and—just see if she can change it?
> Hilbert: No.
> Crick: No?
> Hilbert: Harold ... in the grand scheme, it wouldn't matter.
> Crick: Yes it would.
> Hilbert: No.
> Crick: I could change. I could quit my job. I could—I could go away with Ana. I could be someone else.
> Hilbert: Harold, listen to me.
> Crick [now in tears]: I can't die right now. It's just really bad timing.
> Hilbert: No one wants to die, Harold, but unfortunately we do. Harold. Harold, listen to me. Harold, you will die someday, sometime ... You will die. You will absolutely die. Even if you avoid this death, another will find you. And I guarantee that it won't be nearly as poetic or meaningful as what she's written.

The sentiments that Hilbert expresses here line up almost perfectly with the theory that Velleman proposes. Harold "has to" die in the way that the author, Eiffel, has envisioned because of the meaning that his death would contribute to the overall story of his life.

To be sure, there's something unsettling about hearing Hilbert tell Harold that he has to die, even if he doesn't want to. As it turns out, however, Harold himself comes to a similar realization. After reading the story himself, he tells Eiffel that he endorses the narrative:

> I read it, and I loved it. And there's only one way it can end. I mean, I don't have much background in literary anything, but this seems simple enough. I love your book. And I think you should finish it.

Harold has decided to embrace his fate. (You'll have to watch the movie to see what happens next.)

RESPONSES

There hasn't been much philosophical discussion of *Stranger than Fiction*, but Velleman's (1991) narrative theory has been quite influential. Among many other places, it is discussed in Broome (2004), Fischer (2005), and Metz (2013). For more general discussion of narrative theories, see the positive arguments in Wong (2008) and the criticisms in Vice (2003).

Perhaps the primary complaint against Velleman's view is that more needs to be said in order for his suggestive remarks to count as a complete theory (cf. Metz 2013, 38). Fischer (2005, 386–87), for example, points out that we would want such a theory to render a judgment about the value that death contributes to a narrative in a wide range of possible situations. But there are lots of cases in which it won't be clear what to say about the relative value of different ways (and times) of dying. What should we say about someone who has accomplished a significant amount in his life, but who has also been recently incapacitated so that he is no longer able to undertake any significant pursuits or projects? He still enjoys simple pursuits like watching television and reading the news. Are those interests enough to justify extending the narrative, or would it be better for him to end the story sooner rather than later? More detail is needed before we can answer that question with any degree of certainty. Not to mention that even asking such questions produces a little bit of discomfort, causing one to wonder whether it might be impertinent to make such theoretical judgments about someone else's life.

RECOMMENDED READING (OR VIEWING)

Fischer, John Martin. 2005. "Free Will, Death, and Immortality: The Role of Narrative." *Philosophical Papers* 34: 349–403.
Forster, Marc. 2006. *Stranger than Fiction*.
Metz, Thaddeus. 2007. "New Developments in the Meaning of Life." *Philosophy Compass* 2: 196–217.
Velleman, J. David. 1991. "Well-Being and Time." *Pacific Philosophical Quarterly* 72: 48–77.

WORKS CITED

Broome, John. 2004. *Weighing Lives*. New York: Oxford University Press.
Metz, Thaddeus. 2013. *Meaning in Life*. New York: Oxford University Press.
Vice, Samantha. 2003. "Literature and the Narrative Self." *Philosophy* 78: 93–108.
Wong, Wai-hung. 2008. "Meaningfulness and Identities." *Ethical Theory and Moral Practice* 11: 123–48.

THE TROUBLE WITH TIME TRAVEL

5

THE GRANDFATHER PARADOX

Time travel has served as a plot device for numerous films, novels, and short stories. Philosophers, never shy about ruining a good story, have sometimes asked whether these time travel stories are *consistent*—whether it's even possible that they are true. Fictional stories typically describe a world that is not our own, but is more or less similar to our own. Barring some surprising developments, worlds in which time travel occurs are radically dissimilar to our own world. Some have worried, though, that time travel is not just unlikely but *impossible*, which is to say that there is no possible world, fictional or otherwise, in which time travel occurs. If these worries hold up, then time travel stories are not just far-fetched but literally inconsistent: the situations that they describe could not possibly occur in *any* world, much less in a world similar to our own.

There's no requirement, of course, that a novelist or screenwriter tell a consistent story; lots of good stories have minor inconsistencies. But, other things being equal, it seems that if you're telling a story, then it's better for it to at least be *possible* that the story might occur.

DOI: 10.4324/9781003126119-6

There are various ways to articulate the concern that time travel stories are not possible; one of the most popular ways has been via the *grandfather paradox*. David Lewis sets up the paradox as follows:

> Consider Tim. He detests his grandfather, whose success in the munitions trade built the family fortune that paid for Tim's time machine. Tim would like nothing so much as to kill Grandfather, but alas he is too late. Grandfather died in his bed in 1957, while Tim was a young boy. But when Tim has built his time machine and traveled to 1920, suddenly he realizes that he is not too late after all. He buys a rifle; he spends long hours in target practice; he shadows Grandfather to learn the route of his daily walk to the munitions works; he rents a room along the route; and there he lurks, one winter day in 1921, rifle loaded, hate in his heart, as Grandfather walks closer, closer ...
>
> (Lewis 1976, 149)

The problem with this story arises when we consider what would happen if Tim were to be successful in his attempt to kill Grandfather in 1920. If he succeeds, making it so that Grandfather died before Tim's father was conceived, then his father never would have been born. And if Tim's father had never been born, then Tim himself never would have been born. And if Tim had never been born, then of course he could not have traveled back in time to kill his grandfather. Thus, Tim's killing his own grandfather requires that Tim exist, but it would also guarantee that Tim *doesn't* exist. Since it's impossible for Tim to both exist and not exist, it's impossible for Tim to kill his own grandfather. And yet time travel, if it were possible, would seem to allow Tim to do the impossible, namely to kill his own grandfather. This is the basic idea behind the grandfather paradox.

(Of course, there's nothing about Tim's grandfather that makes him essential to the story. We could also tell the story so that it involves Tim killing himself as a baby, or killing his father before he was born, or doing anything else that would guarantee that Tim is never born. For a large-scale portrayal of this paradox, see the movie *Tenet*.)

Lewis's story about Tim and his grandfather can be converted into an argument that time travel is impossible:

(1)   If time travel is possible, then Tim can kill Grandfather in 1920.
(2)   Tim cannot kill Grandfather in 1920.
(3)   Therefore, time travel is impossible.

It seems, then, that we have a sound argument for the conclusion that time travel is impossible. But not everyone has been happy with this conclusion. Lewis himself, for example, claimed that if we are careful about how we think about Tim and his abilities, then we can see that the argument doesn't work.

Lewis makes his case by focusing on the meaning of the word *can,* and the ways in which that meaning can shift according to the context in which the word is used. (See also Chapter 28.) Lewis points out that there are various facts that help determine the meaning of statements involving "can," and which facts are relevant to that determination depends on the context. In typical cases, when we ask whether someone can kill someone else, we focus on facts about motives, weapons, proximity, and the like. If we focus on these types of facts, then it seems as though Tim satisfies all the conditions required for being able to kill someone:

> He has what it takes. Conditions are perfect in every way: the best rifle money could buy, Grandfather an easy target only twenty yards away, not a breeze, door securely locked against intruders. Tim is a good shot to begin with and now at the peak of training, and so on. What's to stop him? The forces of logic will not stay his hand! No powerful chaperone stands by to defend the past from interference ... In short, Tim is as much able to kill Grandfather as anyone ever is to kill anyone.
>
> (Lewis 1976, p. 149)

If we focus on these typical facts—on ordinary contexts—then we see that there is a legitimate sense in which it is true to say that Tim can kill his grandfather.

Of course, the addition of Tim's time travel makes it so that his context is not an ordinary context. There are other facts that are relevant to evaluating can-claims in this context, like the fact that Grandfather cannot be killed because that would prevent Tim's existence. When we add *that* fact to the set of facts that helps determine the meaning of can-claims, it becomes clear that Tim cannot kill his grandfather.

In short, Lewis's first point is that both of these ways of using the term "can" are correct, relative to the appropriate context. His second point is that the first premise of the argument against time travel relies on one way of using "can," whereas the second premise relies on a different way of using "can." If we hold fixed the meaning throughout the course of the argument (which is what we ought to do), then either the first premise is false or the second is false. If we focus on ordinary contexts, then the first premise is true but the second premise is false: Tim *can* in fact kill his grandfather, it's just that we already know he *won't*. If we focus on Tim's special context, which includes the fact that Grandfather doesn't die in 1920, then the second premise is true but the first premise is false: even if Tim were to travel back in time, he cannot kill Grandfather in 1920 because it's a fact that Grandfather doesn't die in 1920.

According to Lewis, then, the lesson of the grandfather paradox is not that time travel is impossible; instead, the lesson is that the meaning of the term "can" is context-sensitive.

RESPONSES

There are some philosophers who respond to the grandfather paradox (and the argument against time travel) simply by accepting the conclusion. Of those who reject the conclusion, though, it seems fair to say that Lewis's way of doing it is the most popular. Nevertheless, there have been other proposals for rejecting the conclusion. Kadri Vihvelin (1996), for example, agrees with Lewis that the argument against time travel is unsound, but she provides an influential objection to his solution to the paradox.

Some have claimed that time travel would generate (or presuppose) a branching structure in time. According to this understanding of time travel, if Tim were to travel back in time, then he would actually be traveling back to a different timeline. If he kills Grandfather on that timeline, then there are still no contradictions, because the version of Grandfather on the original timeline is still alive. (The branching timeline model has been more popular with scientists than it has with philosophers; for one endorsement, see Greene 2004.)

Others have appealed to the notion of *hypertime*, which is an additional dimension within which time itself changes. (Things change over time, whereas time changes over hyper time.) See Wasserman (2018, 78–99) for a comprehensive and insightful discussion of the branching response and the hypertime response.

RECOMMENDED READING (OR VIEWING)

Lewis, David. 1976. "The Paradoxes of Time Travel." *American Philosophical Quarterly* 13: 145–52.

Nolan, Christopher. 2020. *Tenet*.

Tognazzini, Neal A. 2017. "Free Will and Time Travel." In *The Routledge Companion to Free Will*, edited by Kevin Timpe, Meghan Griffith, and Neil Levy, 680–90. New York: Routledge.

Wasserman, Ryan. 2018. *Paradoxes of Time Travel*, chapter 3. Oxford University Press.

WORKS CITED

Greene, Brian. 2004. *The Fabric of the Cosmos: Space, Time, and the Texture of Reality*. A.A. Knopf.

Vihvelin, Kadri. 1996. "What Time Travelers Cannot Do." *Philosophical Studies* 81: 315–30.

DOES DELIBERATION REQUIRE UNCERTAINTY?

A CLASS-ACTION THOUGHT EXPERIMENT

All of us deliberate on a regular basis, but we don't often think about deliberation itself: what exactly it involves, what it requires, and when it is or isn't possible. Among those who *have* thought about these issues, many of them have argued (or simply assumed) that deliberation requires uncertainty: that deliberation is possible only if you don't already know what you're going to do. Deliberation, they might say, is just the process of figuring out what to do when you have more than one option. If you already know what you're going to do, then deliberation loses its point. Something could, however, be pointless but still possible; so why do some people think that deliberation is not even *possible* given that you already know what you're going to do?

Carl Ginet is one of those who thinks that deliberation requires uncertainty, because the notion of deliberating while knowing what you're going to do is incoherent:

> For a person to claim that he knows what he will decide to do ... and *then* to begin the process of making up his mind what he will do—trying to persuade himself one way or another by offering himself reasons for and

DOI: 10.4324/9781003126119-7

against the various alternatives—would surely be a procedure of which we could make no sense. Either his undertaking to make a decision belies his prior claim to knowledge, or his prior claim makes a farce of his undertaking to make a decision.

(Ginet 1962, 51)

Here Ginet talks about deliberation in terms of "undertaking to make a decision" by offering reasons for and against various alternatives. Thus, implicit in Ginet's argument is an assumption that there are two necessary conditions for deliberation: available alternatives and a genuine weighing of those alternatives. And then he argues that uncertainty (or at least a lack of knowledge) about the result of deliberation is a necessary condition for a *genuine* weighing of alternatives. Otherwise, says Ginet, your deliberation is a farce.

Richard Taylor takes up this point, arguing that deliberation presupposes ignorance, and that without ignorance it can only be a sham: "If [anyone] does already know what he is going to do, there is nothing there for him to decide, and hence nothing to deliberate about" (Taylor 1964, 75). In support of this claim, he provides an example of a groom thinking about his upcoming wedding:

For example, it might be possible for a group of observers to infer reliably from certain signs that a certain man is about to be married. They see the flowers, witnesses assembled, preacher waiting, music playing, groom suitably attired, and so on. From the same evidence, which is apparent to the groom himself, he too can gather that he is about to be married, though for him, unless he doesn't realize what he has gotten himself into, such signs and portents are superfluous. If, however, he regards these signs as reliable evidence of what he is about to do, he cannot deliberate about what to do—he is past deliberation and the die is cast. If, on the other hand, he still does deliberate about whether to get married—if he has last minute misgivings and second thoughts—then he obviously does not regard the signs as reliable evidence of what he is going to do. He is, in fact, contemplating confuting the very thing those signs point to, by walking right out of the church.

(Taylor 1964, 75)

(Taylor's argument doesn't rest entirely on examples like this one, but they do carry a significant amount of argumentative weight for him.)

Ginet and Taylor, then, argue for something like the following deliberation restriction:

> **Deliberation restriction:** If someone already knows whether or not they are going to do something, then it is not possible for them to deliberate about doing that thing.

Despite the intuitive appeal of the deliberation restriction (not to mention the endorsement of numerous contemporary philosophers), there are some reasons to doubt whether what it's claiming is actually true.

RESPONSES

The seeds of doubt are actually sown in Taylor's article itself, where he discusses in more detail the process by which we come to know what we are going to do:

> There seem, in fact, to be only these two ways in which one could know what he is going to do; namely, by *inferring* what he is going to do, or by *deciding* what he is going to do. In neither case can one deliberate about what he is going to do.
>
> (Taylor 1964, 75)

Once you know what you're going to do, the matter is settled. But there are two ways of settling it, corresponding to the inferences and the decisions that Taylor mentions above. Let's call the process of inferring what you'll be doing *epistemic settling:* you are looking at evidence and using that evidence to make an inference about what you'll do. And let's call the process of deciding what you'll do *practical settling.* The process of deciding what you'll do, of course, is just deliberation; you gain knowledge of what you'll do at the terminus of your deliberation.

What seems to be missing in most discussions of the deliberation restriction is an argument for why these two types of settling, epistemic and practical, must always accompany each other. If there is even just one case in which epistemic settling can occur independently of practical settling, then that case will serve as a counterexample to the deliberation restriction. Here is a pair of cases (borrowed from

Pendergraft 2014) in which epistemic settling seems to occur prior to practical settling. The cases also involve the groom from Taylor's example, whom we will call Gavin:

> Let us imagine that Gavin (the indecision of the wedding now behind him) is one of the plaintiffs in a knockdown class-action lawsuit. The defendants, anxious to get this business behind them, invite each of the plaintiffs, in turn, to consider a now-or-never settlement offer. As it happens, Gavin is the last to receive the offer, and as such is able to benefit from his knowledge of the choices of the previous plaintiffs. Oddly enough, each and every individual before him accepts the settlement (though they are bound by oath not to disclose the terms). Gavin, who is not particularly interested in the details of the case or even the amount of money at stake, has no reason to believe that his response will be any different than the numerous other plaintiffs who have gone before. Hence, Gavin eventually comes by the knowledge that he, too, will accept the offer of settlement. Now consider him in the negotiating room: upon receiving the offer, will he still be able to deliberate about what to do? It seems that he will indeed. There is no real barrier to him weighing the relevant alternatives (accept the settlement, or reject it) while at the same time retaining his knowledge that he will in fact accept the settlement.
>
> Or consider a variation on the case. This time Gavin doesn't know what the others in the plaintiff class have decided, and he has been given twenty-four hours to think about whether he wants to accept the settlement offer. He shares the terms with his wife (to whom he's been married for some years now), and she, in some ways knowing him better than he knows himself, tells him that he will accept the offer. He thus comes to know, on the basis of testimony, that he will accept the settlement. And yet, again, it does not seem as though any sort of barrier has been erected that now prevents him from (practically) deliberating. The issue may have been settled epistemically (through his coming to know what he will do), but this is different from practically settling the issue.
>
> (Pendergraft 2014, 348–49)

Epistemic settling and practical settling almost always go together, and we have all experienced them in tandem countless times throughout our lives. But nothing about these experiences establishes that they *must* go together. What these examples help us realize is that there are some cases in which the two types of settling come from different sources. And when the types of settling come from different sources, there's nothing preventing the epistemic settling from happening prior to the practical settling. So perhaps we can, after all, deliberate while already knowing the results of that deliberation.

For additional recent discussion of what deliberation requires and involves, see Clarke (1992), Coffman and Warfield (2005), Nelkin (2011), Nielsen (2011), and Pereboom (2008).

RECOMMENDED READING

Coffman, E. J., and Ted A. Warfield. 2005. "Deliberation and Metaphysical Freedom." *Midwest Studies in Philosophy* 29: 25–44.

Ginet, Carl. 1962. "Can the Will Be Caused?" *The Philosophical Review* 71: 49–55.

Nelkin, Dana Kay. 2011. *Making Sense of Freedom and Responsibility*, chapter 6. Oxford University Press.

Taylor, Richard. 1964. "Deliberation and Foreknowledge." *American Philosophical Quarterly* 1: 73–80.

WORKS CITED

Clarke, Randolph. 1992. "Deliberation and Beliefs About One's Abilities." *Pacific Philosophical Quarterly* 73: 101–13.

Nielsen, Karen Margrethe. 2011. "Deliberation as Inquiry: Aristotle's Alternative to the Presumption of Open Alternatives." *The Philosophical Review* 120: 383–421.

Pendergraft, Garrett. 2014. "Against Deliberation Restrictions." *Religious Studies* 50: 341–57.

Pereboom, Derk. 2008. "A Compatibilist Account of the Epistemic Conditions on Rational Deliberation." *The Journal of Ethics* 12: 287–306.

ONE BOX OR TWO?

NEWCOMB'S PROBLEM

Newcomb's problem was popularized by Robert Nozick, who presented it (in his 1969) as a dilemma for decision theory. Discussion of the problem can get pretty technical, but the basic idea is relatively simple. The thought experiment begins with a predictor whom you know to be reliable:

> Suppose a being in whose power to predict your choices you have enormous confidence. (One might tell a science-fiction story about a being from another planet, with an advanced technology and science, who you know to be friendly, etc.) You know that this being has often correctly predicted your choices in the past (and has never, so far as you know, made an incorrect prediction about your choices), and furthermore you know that this being has often correctly predicted the choices of other people, many of whom are similar to you, in the particular situation to be described below. One might tell a longer story, but all this leads you to believe that almost certainly this being's prediction about your choice in the situation to be discussed will be correct.
>
> (Nozick 1969, 114)

DOI: 10.4324/9781003126119-8

With this predictor in place, you now face a difficult choice:

- There are two boxes, B1 and B2.
- You have two options:
  - Take what's in both boxes.
  - Take only what's in B2.
- B1 contains $1,000; B2 contains $0 or $1,000,000, depending on what you choose:
  - If the being predicts that you will take what's in both boxes, then she will put nothing in B2.
  - If the being predicts that you will take only what's in B2, then she will put $1,000,000 in B2.

What makes this problem so paradoxical, as Nozick points out (1969, 115–16), is that there appear to be compelling arguments in favor of both choices being the best choice; but of course they can't both be the best choice.

Here's a quick argument for taking what's in B2 only (call this option "one-boxing"): You should make the choice that yields the most money. If you choose both boxes, then it is almost certain that the being will have predicted this and thus will have put nothing in B2. If, on the other hand, you choose B2 only, then it is almost certain that the being will have predicted this and thus will have put $1,000,000 in B2. (Moreover, you know that numerous other people have been given the same choice; and everyone who chose one box ended up with $1,000,000, whereas everyone who chose two boxes ended up with only $1,000.) So you should choose box B2 only, because that will yield more money.

That seems like a pretty strong argument. But now consider this argument for taking what's in both boxes (call this option "two-boxing"): You should make the choice that yields the most money. The being has already put the $1,000,000 in B2 or not. (Suppose that she made her prediction last week, and that the boxes have been sitting, untouched, since then.) If you choose B2 only, then you'll either get $0 (if the being predicted that you would two-box) or $1,000,000 (if she predicted that you would one-box). If you choose both boxes, then you'll either get $1,000 or $1,001,000, depending on the prediction. (Moreover, your friend was able to take a look in B2 yesterday.

She can't tell you what she saw, but it doesn't matter—because either way she is hoping you'll take both boxes and get the extra $1,000.) Thus, no matter what the prediction was, you'll get $1,000 more by choosing both boxes. So you should choose both boxes.

It would seem, then, that the person trying to make the rational choice is stuck with conflicting arguments, both of which appear to be roughly equally compelling. One-boxing appears to deliver the most value, whereas two-boxing appears to be the better choice no matter what the predictor has done. In the language of decision theory, we can say that the principle of expected utility maximization supports one-boxing, whereas the principle of dominance supports two-boxing (Weirich 2020). Perhaps the fact that these two principles render opposing verdicts in this case helps explain why people's responses to the problem tend to diverge so sharply: "To almost everyone it is perfectly clear and obvious what should be done. The difficulty is that these people seem to divide almost evenly on the problem, with large numbers thinking that the opposing half is just being silly." (Nozick 1969, 117)

Nozick gives each side a fair hearing, but in the end he comes down on the side of two-boxing. When professional philosophers were surveyed about this puzzle (among lots of other puzzles; see Bourget and Chalmers 2021), 39% endorsed two-boxing, whereas only 31% endorsed one-boxing. (Presumably the 30% who chose "Other" aren't quite sure what to say about this problem.)

RESPONSES

Perhaps you're wondering what exactly Newcomb's problem, interesting as it may be, has to do with free will. Admittedly, free will doesn't show up at the surface level of the problem. But there are several ways of responding to the problem that involve free will in some way or another.

For example, as you deliberate about what choice to make in Newcomb's problem, you might start to wonder whether the predictor can predict *all* of your actions—not just your choice of boxes—and then start to wonder whether such a comprehensive predictive ability would undermine your free will. If the predictor is accurate enough (perfectly accurate or almost perfectly accurate), then you might wonder what it is that's grounding her knowledge of the future. Is she able to somehow look into the future and perceive what you're going to choose? If so, then you might also wonder whether deliberating about what to do will make a difference to your choice, and indeed you might wonder whether your choice of which box(es) to take could even be free. In short, depending on how the predictor is described, Newcomb's problem might naturally lead to a general freedom and foreknowledge problem. (See Chapter 8 for a discussion of this latter problem, which is sometimes called the problem of theological fatalism.)

Alternatively, Paul Weirich (2020) points out that we might try to resolve the problem by appealing to the need for a freely developed disposition to choose box B2 only:

> A way of reconciling the two sides of the debate about Newcomb's problem acknowledges that a rational person should prepare for the problem by cultivating a disposition to one-box. Then whenever the problem arises, the disposition will prompt a prediction of one-boxing and afterwards the act of one-boxing (still freely chosen).

So the rational person would two-box (following the principle of expected utility maximization), if encountering Newcomb's problem without any prior knowledge of it. But once someone becomes aware of the problem, the rational thing to do is cultivate a disposition to one-box. This disposition would be rational because it would produce more utility; and, other things being equal, a choice flowing from a rational disposition is presumably rational as well.

Huemer (2018, chapter 5) discusses an alternative way of resolving the problem. He thinks that principles of rationality (e.g., the principle of expected utility maximization and the principle of dominance) should not be in conflict, so he recommends a reinterpretation of the principle of expected utility maximization. The basic idea is that the likelihood of getting $1,000,000 does not depend on the chance that the predictor was correct, but on the chance that the world (including, most importantly, our brain) was in the right state at the time that the prediction was made. The chance that the world was in the right state could very well be 50% or less than 50%, in which case the principle of expected utility maximization could point toward two-boxing.

Huemer (2018, 126) also endorses the solution that says we should cultivate a disposition to choose both boxes, but he emphasizes that this solution in effect splits the problem into two: (i) Should I choose one box or two boxes, and (ii) Should I be a one-boxer or a two-boxer? Huemer maintains that "two boxes" is the correct answer to (i), even if "one-boxer" is the correct answer to (ii).

RECOMMENDED READING

Huemer, Michael. 2018. *Paradox Lost: Logical Solutions to Ten Puzzles of Philosophy*, chapter 5. Palgrave Macmillan.

Lewis, David. 1979. "Prisoners' Dilemma Is a Newcomb Problem." *Philosophy & Public Affairs* 8: 235–40.

Nozick, Robert. 1969. "Newcomb's Problem and Two Principles of Choice." In *Essays in Honor of Carl G. Hempel: A Tribute on the Occasion of His Sixty-Fifth Birthday*, edited by Nicholas Rescher, 114–46. Dordrecht: Springer Netherlands.

WORKS CITED

Bourget, David, and David Chalmers. 2021. "Philosophers on Philosophy: The 2020 PhilPapers Survey." Unpublished manuscript, Nov. 3, 2021.

Weirich, Paul. 2020. "Causal Decision Theory." In *The Stanford Encyclopedia of Philosophy*, edited by Edward N. Zalta, Winter 2020. https://plato.stanford.edu/archives/win2020/entries/decision-causal.

DOES DIVINE FOREKNOWLEDGE UNDERMINE OUR FREEDOM?

A PUZZLE ABOUT FOREKNOWLEDGE

In previous chapters (e.g., Chapter 3), we have seen how truths in the past (about what we're going to do in the future) can give rise to fatalist concerns. These concerns fall into a category that we could label as "logical fatalism." Now it's time to look at a related threat to freedom— *theo*logical fatalism—which comes from the theological doctrine of divine omniscience. (To be omniscient, roughly speaking, is to know all of the true propositions while believing none of the false ones.) This attribute is an important part of the traditional perfect-being conception of God according to which he is all-powerful, all-knowing, and morally perfect. But taking omniscience seriously raises a puzzle about free will: If God knows all the truths about the future, and his knowledge is infallible, then how can our actions be free? If we assume that exhaustive divine foreknowledge exists, then we can pick any apparently free action at random and generate an argument to the effect that that action is, contrary to appearances, not free after all.

Discussion of the apparent tension between freedom and foreknowledge dates back to Augustine (if not earlier), but the currently

DOI: 10.4324/9781003126119-9

standard version of the argument for theological fatalism was introduced into contemporary philosophical discussion by Nelson Pike (1965). Since then, the argument has been examined and discussed by a host of philosophers, who have together produced a voluminous literature on the subject. One particularly clear treatment of the argument can be found in Zagzebski (2021), so we will use (a simplified version of) her regimentation as our starting point.

There are three primary ingredients in the contemporary argument for theological fatalism: *God's infallible foreknowledge*, the *necessity of the past*, and a *transfer of necessity* principle. We will look at each ingredient in turn.

Suppose it's true that you will answer the telephone tomorrow, and let T represent the proposition expressing that truth. Suppose also that God has complete foreknowledge. Given these suppositions, we can conclude that every truth will be one that God believed, and indeed believed ahead of time. Whether we are talking about yesterday, last week, or a million years ago, God will at that time have a belief corresponding to every truth. Also, it is commonly assumed that past events are necessary in virtue of having already occurred: once something has happened, it is fixed and unalterable, even if at the time of its occurrence it didn't have to happen. (This *necessity of the past* is sometimes also called accidental necessity or temporal necessity; see Chapter 27 for discussion.) Since God's beliefs are in the past, the necessity of the past presumably applies just as much to them as to anything else. We can summarize these considerations in the following premise:

(1)   It is necessary that God believed that T.

We are supposing that God's foreknowledge is not just exhaustive (complete) but infallible, which means that it can't fail to be accurate: there is no possible circumstance in which God believes some proposition P but P is false. This licenses us to assert a second premise stating that God's believing something necessarily implies its truth:

(2)   It is necessary that if God believed T, then T.

The third and final main ingredient is the *transfer of necessity* principle. The basic idea behind this principle is that if nobody can do anything about some state of affairs, and that state of affairs leads to another state of affairs (in a way that nobody can do anything about), then it follows that nobody can do anything about the second state of affairs either. For example: If nobody can do anything about the occurrence of an earthquake, and if the earthquake necessarily leads to an avalanche, then nobody can do anything about the avalanche either. We will express this principle as follows:

(3)   If it's necessary that P, and it's necessary that P implies Q, then it's necessary that Q.

Premises (1) and (2) claim that God's belief is necessary and that his belief necessarily implies the truth of what he believes. Premise (3) then tells us that the necessity of God's belief transfers to the truth he believes. Together these premises deliver the fatalistic conclusion:

(4)   It's necessary that T.

If it's necessary that you will answer the phone tomorrow, then it seems that you're not free with respect to that action. And there's nothing special about that action, so the point generalizes to any action whatsoever. Thus we can see how the traditional doctrine of divine omniscience leads to theological fatalism.

RESPONSES

According to the argument for theological fatalism, then, there is a fundamental incompatibility between divine foreknowledge and human freedom. As is the case with any incompatibility argument, there are going to be two main ways of responding. One could accept the argument, and as a result abandon the idea that we have free will or abandon the idea that God has foreknowledge. For theists who want to endorse a traditional conception of God, this first way of responding will be costly.

The second way of responding to the argument is to attempt to show that foreknowledge and free will are compatible. Rather than trying to cover all of these attempts, we will just look briefly at a handful of representative examples—most of which involve denying premise (1) ("It is necessary that God believed that T").

First, someone who inclines toward an Aristotelian view of future contingents (see Chapter 2) will probably deny (1). If "You will answer the telephone tomorrow" isn't true (because it's neither true nor false), then God would not have believed it at all, much less *necessarily* believed it. The view that God doesn't have beliefs about future contingents is often called *open theism*. (Open theists differ on *why* God doesn't have beliefs about future contingents: because they don't have a truth value, or because they're all false, or because it's not logically possible to know in advance what someone will freely do.)

A different reason for denying (1) stems from the idea that we should conceive of God as existing outside of time, in a sort of eternal present. If God is outside of time, then (as Boethius pointed out in Book V of *The Consolation of Philosophy*) it will not be correct to say that he believed something yesterday or at any other time. According to the Boethian picture, God's knowledge of the world's timeline is analogous to a lookout's knowledge of a road below her. She can see the relative positions of the various travelers, but her knowledge of their positions doesn't impose any necessity on them. Similarly, says the Boethian, God's knowledge of our positions on the timeline, as he looks out on us from his eternal present, doesn't impose any necessity on us.

An alternative way, perhaps a less radical way, of rejecting premise (1) is called *Ockhamism* because it traces back to William of Ockham (1324). The Ockhamist solution recognizes a distinction between propositions that are about the past alone and propositions that are about the past *and* the future. Facts that are only about the past are sometimes called *hard facts*; facts that are about both the past and the future are sometimes called *soft facts*. For example, "I woke up early this morning" is a hard fact, whereas "I woke up early this morning, 12 hours before my meeting this afternoon" is a soft fact. Someone making the latter statement is referencing the past ("this morning") but also referencing the future ("this afternoon").

Although it has proven exceedingly difficult to provide a satisfactory account of exactly what makes something a soft fact, one key feature of soft facts is that they exhibit what is sometimes called *counterfactual dependence*. Consider again the statement, "I woke up early this morning, 12 hours before my meeting this afternoon," and suppose that I utter it at noon. At that point its truth seems to be not yet fixed: the meeting's start time could be moved, or it could be canceled altogether. Given that the meeting occurs as scheduled, the statement is true; but if—counter to fact—the meeting were to be canceled, then the statement would be false. Thus, the truth of this particular soft fact seems to depend on how things turn out this afternoon. It's (partly) about the past, but it also seems to depend on, rather than dictate, the future.

This dependence is what appears to provide a way out of the argument for theological fatalism. It's true that you will answer the telephone tomorrow; but you are free to refrain from answering the telephone, and if you *had* refrained in that way, then God *would have* believed something other than what he actually believed. (See Adams 1967 for a response to Pike 1965 along these lines; Plantinga 1986 also offers a helpful treatment of the Ockhamist response.)

Another response accepts (1) but rejects the transfer of necessity principle in (3). According to this response, there's a *type* of necessity that gets transferred, with the result that we are unable to do otherwise. But this type of necessity does not rule out moral responsibility. The basis for this response comes from a famous set of examples devised by Harry Frankfurt and subsequently developed by a host of philosophers. (See Chapter 16 for a discussion of these examples.) David Hunt (1999) attributes this response to Augustine.

The final response we'll consider comes from Merricks (2009), who rejects the argument for theological fatalism (and also the argument for logical fatalism) on the grounds that it begs the question. According to Merricks, the only way the argument can establish that we have no choice about the action foreknown by God is if it illicitly *presupposes* that we have no choice about the action. (For a response to Merricks, see Fischer and Todd 2011.)

RECOMMENDED READING

Hunt, David P. 1999. "On Augustine's Way out." *Faith and Philosophy* 16: 3–26. Reprinted in Fischer and Todd (2015).

Merricks, Trenton. 2009. "Truth and Freedom." *The Philosophical Review* 118: 29–57. Reprinted in Fischer and Todd (2015).

Pike, Nelson. 1965. "Divine Omniscience and Voluntary Action." *The Philosophical Review* 74: 27–46.

Plantinga, Alvin. 1986. "On Ockham's Way Out." *Faith and Philosophy* 3: 235–69.

Todd, Patrick, and John Martin Fischer. 2015. "Introduction." In *Freedom, Fatalism, and Foreknowledge*, 1–38. Oxford: Oxford University Press.

Zagzebski, Linda. 2021. "Foreknowledge and Free Will." In *The Stanford Encyclopedia of Philosophy*, edited by Edward N. Zalta, Spring 2021. https://plato.stanford.edu/archives/spr2021/entries/free-will-foreknowledge.

WORKS CITED

Adams, Marilyn McCord. 1967. "Is the Existence of God a 'Hard' Fact?" *The Philosophical Review* 76: 492–503.

Boethius. 524. *The Consolation of Philosophy*.

Fischer, John Martin, and Patrick Todd. 2011. "The Truth About Freedom: A Reply to Merricks." *The Philosophical Review* 120: 97–115. Reprinted in Fischer and Todd (2015)

Fischer, John Martin, and Patrick Todd, eds. 2015. *Freedom, Fatalism, and Foreknowledge*. Oxford: Oxford University Press.

Ockham, William. 1983 [c. 1324]. *Predestination, God's Foreknowledge, and Future Contingents*, 2nd edition. Translated by Marilyn McCord Adams and Norman Kretzmann. Indianapolis, IN: Hackett.

FATALISM IN THE COURTROOM

A SHOCKING CRIME

In May of 1924, Nathan Leopold and Richard Loeb were arrested for the kidnapping and murder of 14-year-old Bobby Franks. Leopold and Loeb's crime was particularly shocking because they chose their victim at random and had no apparent motive, other than a desire to demonstrate their belief that morality had no claim on them. (For a detailed treatment of the Leopold and Loeb case, see Baatz 2008, which is reviewed and briefly summarized in Gordon 2008.)

Clarence Darrow, who would later become famous for his role in the Scopes trial, took on the unenviable task of defending Leopold and Loeb in court. His basic argument was that their actions were the result of their character (the type of person they had become), but their character was not up to them. Instead, their character had been given to them by a variety of external circumstances and influences that were outside of their control. Here's what he had to say about Loeb:

> What has this boy to do with it? He was not his own father; he was not his own mother; he was not his own grandparents. All of this was handed to him. He did not surround himself with governesses and wealth. He did not make himself. And yet he is to be compelled to pay.
>
> (Darrow 1924, 71)

DOI: 10.4324/9781003126119-10

The argument, in other words, is that the death penalty is not justified for Loeb (or Leopold) because "he did not make himself." Darrow later expands on the argument:

> There is something else in this case, Your Honor, that is stronger still. There is a large element of chance in life. I know I will die. I don't know when; I don't know how; I don't know where; and I don't want to know. I know it will come. I know that it depends on infinite chances. Did I make myself? And control my fate? I cannot fix my death unless I commit suicide, and I cannot do that because the will to live is too strong; I know it depends on infinite chances.
>
> (Darrow 1924, 86)

Here Darrow also introduces the element of chance, which would seem to lead to a different argument; so let's set aside that notion and maintain our focus on the idea of making oneself. Presumably Darrow's point about making oneself would apply to various other kinds of punishment as well, and maybe even moral responsibility in general. Thus we can abstract away from the specific details of the Leopold and Loeb case and consider a Darrow-style argument against free will. Kadri Vihvelin (2013, 50) provides a helpful regimentation of the general argument:

(1)   We have free will (of the kind necessary for moral responsibility and justified blame and punishment) only if we make our selves.

(2)   We don't make our selves.

(3)   Therefore we don't have free will.

Although we are discussing Darrow's argument(s) in the context of fatalism, we should acknowledge that this argument doesn't fit perfectly into the fatalist pattern. It doesn't appeal to past truths, or divine foreknowledge, or mysterious authors of one's story. And even though Darrow's view about free will is sometimes referred to as hard determinism (see, e.g., Kane 2005, 70), this argument doesn't make a direct appeal to determinism (or even causation). In fact, the references to chance might even point *away* from determinism, since chanciness is typically treated as the opposite of determinism. As Vihvelin has pointed out (2013, 53–54), on at least one plausible way of interpreting

Darrow's argument, it is actually an argument that free will is *impossible*. (So perhaps a view built on the argument above should be referred to as *impossibilism*, rather than fatalism or hard determinism.) On this interpretation of the argument, to have free will is to have *ultimate control* over one's self; to be able to choose, without any external or prior influences, the type of self that one is going to have.

RESPONSES

If we interpret "making our selves" as having ultimate control over our selves, then it seems pretty clear that free will would be impossible. Even if we were able to choose every aspect of our self, we would have to make that choice on the basis of our desires and values. And those desires and values have to come from outside of our selves, in some sense. If my choice of self depends on desires and values that were given to me, then my control over how my self is made falls short of ultimate control. (A contemporary version of this interpretation can be found in Galen Strawson's 1994; for a response to Strawson, see Clarke 2005.)

One way to respond to this argument is to question the standard for free will that it puts forward. The self-making criterion is quite literally an impossibly high standard, which should prompt us to wonder what reasons we have for thinking that it's the correct standard. It seems intuitively obvious that we have free will, so we have at least some initial reason to doubt a standard that renders that intuition not just false, but not even *possibly* true.

If we are going to reject the ultimate control standard, then it seems that we should try to say a little bit about what kind of standard should replace the impossible standard. One option is to downgrade the control requirement from ultimate control to merely *significant* control (Vihvelin 2013, 52–53): We have free will only if we have significant control over the type of selves that we become. (The term "significant" covers a wide range of degrees of control, so if we were to pursue this option then we would of course need to say more about what counts as significant.) Interpreting the argument in this way would render the condition in (1) more plausible, but it would at the same time render the claim in (2) *less* plausible. Clearly we don't have ultimate control over the making of our selves, but why can't we have significant control?

A related question, which we can only mention in passing, is whether a Darrow-type view would be dangerous if it were universally (or even just generally) accepted. (We can ask this same question about any view that denies the existence of free will.) In other words, suppose that philosophers and other experts somehow reached a consensus that free will is impossible because it would require that we make our selves. Supposing that they did reach such a consensus, should they try to share that consensus with the general public? (These are important issues on which people deserve to be informed!) Or, on the contrary, should they try to cover up the consensus and instead put forward a "noble lie" to the effect that we are in fact free and responsible? After all, some studies (e.g., the studies reported in Vohs and Schooler 2008) have shown that people who come to believe that they don't have free will tend to engage in more wrongdoing than they would have otherwise. (But see Nadelhoffer et al. 2020 for some reasons to be skeptical of these empirical findings.) Answering this question would require input not only from philosophers, but also from social scientists and political theorists.

RECOMMENDED READING

Darrow, Clarence. 1989 [1924]. "Compulsion." In *Philosophical Explorations*, edited by Steven M. Cahn, 97–105. Buffalo, NY: Prometheus Books.

Vihvelin, Kadri. 2013. *Causes, Laws, and Free Will: Why Determinism Doesn't Matter*, chapter 2. New York: Oxford University Press.

WORKS CITED

Baatz, Simon. 2008. *For the Thrill of It: Leopold, Loeb, and the Murder That Shocked Jazz Age Chicago*. New York: HarperCollins.

Clarke, Randolph. 2005. "On an Argument for the Impossibility of Moral Responsibility." *Midwest Studies in Philosophy* 29: 13–24.

Darrow, Clarence. 1924. *The Plea of Clarence Darrow, August 22nd, 23rd & 25th, MCMXXIII, in Defense of Richard Loeb and Nathan Leopold, Jr., on Trial for Murder*. Chicago, IL: Ralph Fletcher Seymour.

Gordon, John Steele. 2008. "Murder Most Rational and Confounding." *The New York Times*, August 17.

Kane, Robert. 2005. *A Contemporary Introduction to Free Will*. New York: Oxford University Press.

Nadelhoffer, Thomas, Jason Shepard, Damien L. Crone, Jim A. C. Everett, Brian D. Earp, and Neil Levy. 2020. "Does Encouraging a Belief in Determinism Increase Cheating? Reconsidering the Value of Believing in Free Will." *Cognition* 203: 1–13.

Strawson, Galen. 1994. "The Impossibility of Moral Responsibility." *Philosophical Studies* 75: 5–24.

Vohs, Kathleen D., and Jonathan W. Schooler. 2008. "The Value of Believing in Free Will: Encouraging a Belief in Determinism Increases Cheating." *Psychological Science* 19: 49–54.

PART II

THE THREAT FROM DETERMINISM(S)

The next fifteen chapters address various ways in which our access to free will may (or may not) be impacted by the truth (or falsity) of determinism. This is the largest part of the book, reflecting the centrality of the debate over whether free will is compatible with determinism. For better or worse, the apparent threat from determinism has dominated the free will discussion for hundreds of years.

Let's start by looking at a few of the most relevant terms and concepts. First, the notion of free will itself. We have been operating with the intuitive picture of the garden of forking paths, but now it's time to specify what we mean with a little more precision. There are two different but partially overlapping ways of understanding free will: it can be understood as the *ability to do otherwise*, or as the feature of our agency that *makes us eligible for moral responsibility*. (We'll look at both of these characterizations in more detail in the chapters that follow.) And the second important concept is, of course, that of determinism. At the most basic level of description, determinism is just the idea that the past determines the future: the way the past was entails everything about the way the future will be. (And it's important to note that "the way the past was" includes the laws of nature. So it's the past and the laws working together, so to speak, that dictate how the future will go.)

DOI: 10.4324/9781003126119-11

We will look at the idea of determinism in much more detail in Chapter 10 ("The Genesis Tub"). We will then (in Chapter 11, "Swerving Atoms") look at some of the first recorded concerns about determinism and its implications for free will.

Although there are countless different approaches to free will, most of them can be categorized according to a fairly straightforward taxonomy. First, we can divide them into *compatibilist* approaches and *incompatibilist* approaches. As you might have suspected, compatibilists believe that free will is compatible with determinism whereas incompatibilists believe that free will is incompatible with determinism. In fact, for any apparent threat to free will, there will be compatibilist approaches and incompatibilist approaches. For example, there are also compatibilist and incompatibilist approaches to divine foreknowledge (see Chapter 8).

Strictly speaking, one can be a compatibilist or incompatibilist without taking a stand on whether we have free will or whether determinism is true. But most theorists do want to take some sort of stand on these questions. An incompatibilist who believes that we have free will (and therefore that determinism is false) is a *libertarian*; an incompatibilist who believes that determinism is true (and therefore that we don't have free will) is a *hard determinist*. Most contemporary compatibilists affirm the existence of freedom, but would prefer to stay agnostic on the truth of determinism. Those compatibilists who do affirm determinism are *soft determinists*. (So both hard and soft determinists believe that determinism is true, but they disagree about whether we have free will due to their disagreement on the compatibility question.)

As the debate over the compatibility question took shape in the seventeenth and eighteenth centuries, most compatibilists had a pretty straightforward view about free will: on their view, it mainly involved doing what one wanted, without hindrance or undue influence. In the middle of the twentieth century, however, this conception of free will came under attack; these developments are covered in Chapter 12 ("Fear of Snakes"). Chapter 13 ("Incompatibilist Mountain") brings us to the contemporary discussion and introduces (among other things), the famous *consequence argument* for incompatibilism. Two prominent ways of responding to the consequence argument are covered in Chapter 14 ("An Impossible Feat of Engineering") and 15 ("Can Elwood Buy an Edsel?"), respectively.

These first few chapters of Part II largely focus on free will as the ability to do otherwise—as the possession of alternative possibilities. In Chapter 16, ("The Nefarious Neurosurgeon"), however, we look at an influential challenge to the importance of alternative possibilities. That challenge sets the stage for a look at how determinism might threaten free will and moral responsibility without any appeal to the presence or absence of alternative possibilities (Chapter 17, "The Avalanche").

Whether or not moral responsibility requires alternative possibilities, it definitely requires some sort of control. Chapter 18 ("The Broken Steering Wheel") examines some different notions of control in detail and explores their relevance to moral responsibility.

We are mostly interested in control over *actions,* but sometimes we are morally responsible in virtue of *omitting* to act. Chapter 19 ("Shark-Infested Waters") expands our examination of control by looking at some thought experiments involving omissions.

The next two chapters introduce an important challenge to compatibilism and an important challenge to incompatibilism, respectively. Chapter 20 ("Professor Plum's Unfortunate Upbringing") presents a manipulation argument against compatibilism and then Chapter 21 ("Rolling Back and Replaying the Universe") presents a luck argument against libertarianism.

We close Part II by looking at some higher-level methodological issues. We ask whether we can gain insight into our theorizing by examining commonsense intuitions (Chapter 22, "Surveying the Folk"), we ask whether our theorizing should be sensitive to the possibility of future empirical discoveries (Chapter 23, "Metaphysical Flip-Flopping"), and then we take a step back (Chapter 24, "The Fundamental Free Will Puzzle?") so that we can look at some general characterizations of the fundamental problem of free will.

"THE GENESIS TUB"

LISA SIMPSON'S SCIENCE EXPERIMENT

In Season 8 of *The Simpsons*, there's an episode ("The Genesis Tub") in which Lisa puts one of her baby teeth in a bowl of soda so she can demonstrate the deleterious effect of soda on teeth. (She says to herself, "Science has already proven the dangers of smoking, alcohol, and Chinese food; but I can still ruin soft drinks for everyone!") Bart shocks her with static electricity (to demonstrate "that nerds conduct electricity"), which she then inadvertently transfers to the tooth sitting in the soda. As it turns out, that electric shock somehow generates a miniature version of human civilization. As Lisa watches through her microscope, this mini-civilization develops along the same lines as our own, including the Renaissance and the Reformation ("I've created Lutherans!"). Bart tries to destroy it, prompting the residents of the bowl to shrink Lisa down to their size so that she (whom they consider to be a god) can protect them from Bart. Unfortunately, they haven't developed the technology for restoring her to original size, so she is resigned to remaining with them as their leader for the rest of her days.

Let's now imagine a modified version of this story in which Bart is removed; as a result, Lisa gets to watch the civilization develop from start to finish. She's curious whether it would develop the same way if restarted, so she rinses off her tooth, pours more soda into the bowl, and initiates a new civilization with another jolt of static electricity.

DOI: 10.4324/9781003126119-12

As it turns out, the civilization develops exactly as before, down to the last detail. Ever the scrupulous scientist, she resolves to record more observations. Over the course of the next year, she initiates and observes 1,000 different miniature universes. Every single time, the mini-universe follows the development of our own civilization, down to the last detail.

The more times that she sees things turn out exactly the same way, the more likely she is to believe that the way things actually turn out is the only way they could have turned out. This is the essential characteristic of *determinism*: at any given point in history, there's only one possible future.

Let's flesh out this definition of determinism a bit. Imagine that the entire history of the world can be completely and accurately described in a single gargantuan proposition; call this proposition H. Imagine also that the laws of nature can be completely specified in another single gargantuan proposition; call this proposition L. If determinism is true, then the conjunction of H and L entails everything that will happen in the future. One implication of determinism, then, is that if some person (or machine) knew H and L, they could deduce everything that will happen in the future *on the basis of that knowledge alone.* (Marquis de Laplace, in his *Essai philosophique sur les probabilités* (1814), developed a thought experiment including such a being, who knows everything about the history and the laws of the world and as a result can predict every detail of the future.)

Although this way of defining determinism appeals to entailment between propositions, the idea of *causation* is under the surface, doing the work (so to speak). The type of determinism that is most relevant to the free will problem is *causal* determinism: not just causal determinism here and there, but *universal* causal determinism. Another way of saying that an event is determined is to say that it's *completely caused*. If all events (including all of our actions) are completely caused, then we have at least some reason to doubt that we have free will. (As we will see in subsequent chapters, whether those doubts can be adequately assuaged is one of the primary controversies in the philosophical discussion of free will.)

Although the fatalist challenge to free will (see Part I) is conceptually distinct from the determinist challenge, it might be helpful to think of fatalism as a species of determinism: we might even call it *logical determinism.* Whereas causal determinism prompts the worry that we don't have any control over our actions because they are completely caused by something else, logical determinism prompts the worry that we don't have any control over our actions because truths about what we will or won't do are already in existence.

Logical determinism and causal determinism are the most widely discussed types of determinism, but they are not the only types. For example, some interesting recent work discusses *many-brothers determinism* and *mirror determinism* (Law and Tognazzini 2019, who are building on Hudson 2001, 2005). The metaphysical details of these types of determinism can get pretty arcane, but the basic ideas are relatively straightforward. Let's look at many-brothers determinism first.

On some views about the way things (including persons) are composed, all it takes to compose something is to combine some particles. So let's suppose that a man named Ewan is composed of a number of simple particles. (They are simple in the sense that they cannot be divided into smaller parts.) Let's number all of the particles from 1 to n, where n is the total number of particles that Ewan is made of. Now imagine a bunch of Ewans—Ewan 1, Ewan 2, and so on—where each numbered Ewan consists of all the particles of the original Ewan, *minus* a single particle (particle 1, particle 2, etc.) So Ewan 7, for example, consists of all of Ewan's particles except for particle 7.) This gives us a lot of Ewans, and even this number n is a mere fraction of all of the possible Ewans that we could get by subtracting particles. (Since removing a few particles doesn't destroy someone, there will be quite a few particle combinations that will still count as Ewan.)

The point of this somewhat abstruse composition exercise is that the actions of each of the Ewans appear to be determined by the actions of all the other Ewans. And if one person's actions are determined by another person's actions, then we have reason to doubt that the first person's actions are free. If Ewan 7 performs a certain action, then his performing of that action entails that Ewan 77 will also perform that same action, and vice versa. So if composition consists of combining particles, then it seems that everyone will have many metaphysical siblings, each and every one of whom determines what they do! Thus we have a problem for free will that's analogous to the problem of causal determinism. Causal determinism is probably less controversial than this view of composition, so maybe there's an overall sense in which many-brothers determinism is less of a threat; but the possibility of its truth, just like the possibility of the truth of causal determinism, still threatens free will.

To get a handle on mirror determinism, think about your reflection in a mirror. Everything you do entails everything that your reflection does. Given that you do something, your reflection will do it too. Your reflection, of course, exists in two dimensions, whereas you exist in (at least) three. But now consider the possibility (endorsed by some metaphysicians) that we, as three-dimensional objects, exist within a higher-level reality called hyperspace, which contains (at least) four dimensions. Since our mirror reflections are two dimensional entities that represent three-dimensional objects, we can imagine the possibility that *we* are merely three-dimensional reflections of some four-dimensional object. This possibility turns the tables on us, making our actions the mere reflection of some other higher-level person. And if our actions are merely a reflection of this other person's actions, then we might start to wonder whether our actions are free.

The final view we'll consider here is not explicitly a deterministic view, but it has seemed to many to have deterministic implications. In the philosophy of time, *presentists* believe that only the present moment is real, whereas *eternalists* (or *four-dimensionalists*) believe that all times are equally real. On the eternalist view, the universe is like a four-dimensional block that we (or parts of us) are somehow moving through. (See Sider 2001, ch. 1 for an introduction to four-dimensionalism.) If the future already exists, then it's easy to see why we might start to doubt whether the details of our journey to that future are up to us.

RESPONSES

Although the definition of determinism that we started with above is relatively widely used, not everyone agrees that it's the best way to characterize determinism. For a comprehensive recent treatment, see Hoefer (2016). For more on the distinction between fatalism and determinism, see Bernstein (2002). (For various ways of responding to the threat of determinism, see the other chapters in this section.)

As we were imagining subtracting particles from persons, you might have started wondering whether such entities really count as persons, as agents who can exercise free will; and you might have also wondered how far this subtraction process can go without destroying the agent. For an interesting recent discussion that touches on some of these issues, see Dietz (2020).

RECOMMENDED READING

Law, Andrew, and Neal A. Tognazzini. 2019. "Free Will and Two Local Determinisms." *Erkenntnis* 84: 1011–23.

Werndl, Charlotte. 2017. "Determinism." In *The Routledge Companion to Free Will*, edited by Kevin Timpe, Meghan Griffith, and Neil Levy, 669–79. New York: Routledge.

WORKS CITED

Bernstein, Mark. 2002. "Fatalism." In *The Oxford Handbook of Free Will*, edited by Robert Kane, 65–81. New York: Oxford University Press.

Dietz, Alexander. 2020. "Are My Temporal Parts Agents?" *Philosophy and Phenomenological Research* 100: 362–79.

Hoefer, Carl. 2016. "Causal Determinism." In *The Stanford Encyclopedia of Philosophy*, edited by Edward N. Zalta, Spring 2016. http://plato.stanford.edu/archives/spr2016/entries/determinism-causal.

Hudson, Hud. 2001. *A Materialist Metaphysics of the Human Person*. Ithaca, NY: Cornell University Press.

Hudson, Hud. 2005. *The Metaphysics of Hyperspace*. Oxford: Oxford University Press.

Laplace, Pierre-Simon. 1814. *Essai Philosophique Sur Les Probabilités*. Paris.

Sider, Theodore. 2001. *Four-Dimensionalism: An Ontology of Persistence and Time*, chapter 1. Oxford: Clarendon Press.

11

SWERVING ATOMS

AN ANCIENT WORRY

In subsequent chapters, we will examine contemporary discussions of the apparent tension between free will and determinism. But concerns about determinism are not merely contemporary concerns. As far back at least as Lucretius in the first century B.C., philosophers were publicly ruminating about the threat of determinism. Lucretius, in *On the Nature of the Universe* (bk. 2, lines 251–55), famously describes what would need to happen in order for us to "snap the bonds of fate":

> Again, if all movement is always interconnected, the new arising from the old in a determinate order—if the atoms never swerve so as to originate some new movement that will snap the bonds of fate, the everlasting sequence of cause and effect—what is the source of the free will possessed by living things throughout the earth?

Here Lucretius appears to be embracing the incompatibilist idea that if determinism is true (if the new always arises from the old "in a determinate order") then we don't have free will. What's needed in order to make room for free will is some "new movement," made possible by a swerve of the atoms.

Although Lucretius doesn't explicitly describe these swerves as random, there does seem to be a chanciness implied by the notion of a swerve. A swerving of the atoms seems to imply that even if we knew

DOI: 10.4324/9781003126119-13

everything about the past history of the world, and everything about the laws of nature, we still wouldn't be able to reliably predict what happens next. This is just what it means for determinism to be false, and it also seems like a pretty good definition of randomness. (It's also worth noting, as Kane (1996, 17) points out, that these swerves need to happen somewhere in the vicinity of the brain, or at least the body; otherwise it's hard to see how they could be of any use to us.)

The problem, of course, is that it's not at all clear that introducing randomness helps secure free will. If we think about paradigm cases of random events, they are not what we would describe as free. For example, we've all experienced the occasional involuntary shiver or muscle spasm or twitch of the eyelid. (In my own case these are usually attributable to drinking too much coffee.) Upon introspection, these movements of ours appear to be random: they catch us by surprise, and they don't appear to be under our control (at least initially). So if that's what we're talking about when we talk about atoms swerving, then it doesn't appear to be much help for free will. Random swerves might snap the bonds of fate, but the resulting movements hardly seem free.

To give Lucretius' view of freedom a full hearing, we would need to say a lot more about his views on physics, and in particular the version of Epicurean atomism that he is famous for defending. In lieu of doing that (but see Berryman 2016 and Sedley 2018), let's look at two other perspectives on physics—one historical, one contemporary— that appeal to a swerving of atoms (in a very loose sense of the terms "atom" and "swerve").

RESPONSES

One way to address the threat of randomness is to consider the possibility that the atoms are swerving in a purposeful way. If some of the relevant atoms were somehow capable of swerving on purpose— breaking free from the bonds of fate and pursuing their own path— then we might be more inclined to recognize the resulting actions as free. There would still need to be some sort of organizing principle, though, to convert purposeful particle movements into a macro-level movement that deserves the label of free action.

These speculations sound pretty fanciful, but the resulting view is reminiscent of a theory associated with Leibniz, who flirted with ancient atomism before developing his own metaphysical system. (See, for example, one of his letters to Louis Remond, as quoted in Wilson 2008, 158.) Leibniz's theory replaced the concept of a material atom with the concept of a *monad*: an extensionless thinking substance that was, in effect, a soul. As Bertrand Russell puts it (2007 [1945], 583): "Thus Leibniz was led to deny the reality of matter, and to substitute an infinite family of souls." These monads operate according to a "pre-established harmony" which gives the illusion of interaction. Each human person is composed of numerous monads, each of which is a soul; but one of those constituent monads is dominant, controlling the others, and a person's actions are purposive in virtue of the purposes of this dominant monad. This dominant monad is what we would refer to as *the* soul of the person (Russell 2007 [1945], 584).

Thus Leibniz's view would seem to solve the problem of randomness, but at the cost of positing an infinite family of souls—too high of a price to pay for most philosophers.

Contemporary physicists go in for a different sort of swerving, not of atoms but of subatomic particles. According to most physicists, elementary particles behave in ways that are fundamentally indeterministic. (See Hodgson 2011 for a detailed treatment of quantum physics and its implications for free will.) Unfortunately, the same questions that plagued ancient atomism also apply to contemporary physics: How is this indeterminism different from mere randomness, and exactly how does it make room for free will? How does the presence of undetermined events at the quantum level contribute to free will at the macro level? (As we'll see in Chapter 13, answering these questions is an important task for contemporary libertarians.)

One influential (albeit speculative) treatment of these questions can be found in the work of Robert Kane (1996, 2007). On Kane's view, quantum indeterminacies *are* random (or close enough to random), but they don't play a direct role in free choices. Instead, they play an indirect role by providing a type of *resistance* that must be overcome in order for free choice to occur. If someone succeeds in overcoming this indeterministic resistance, then (assuming that the other conditions for freedom are met) they have made a free choice.

RECOMMENDED READING

Kane, Robert. 1996. *The Significance of Free Will*, chapter 1. Oxford: Oxford University Press.

O'Keefe, Tim. 2021. "Ancient Theories of Freedom and Determinism." In *The Stanford Encyclopedia of Philosophy*, edited by Edward N. Zalta, Spring 2021. https://plato.stanford.edu/archives/spr2021/entries/freedom-ancient.

WORKS CITED

Berryman, Sylvia. 2016. "Ancient Atomism." In *The Stanford Encyclopedia of Philosophy*, edited by Edward N. Zalta, Winter 2016. https://plato.stanford.edu/archives/win2016/entries/atomism-ancient.

Hodgson, David. 2011. "Quantum Physics, Consciousness, and Free Will." In *The Oxford Handbook of Free Will*, 2nd edition, edited by Robert Kane, 57–83. Oxford: Oxford University Press.

Kane, Robert. 2007. "Libertarianism." In *Four Views on Free Will*, by John Martin Fischer, Robert Kane, Derk Pereboom, and Manuel Vargas, 5–43. Malden, MA: Blackwell.

Lucretius Carus, Titus. 1994 [1st century B.C.]. *On the Nature of the Universe*. Translated by R. E. Latham. London: Penguin Books.

Russell, Bertrand. 2007 [1945]. *History of Western Philosophy*. New York: Simon & Schuster.

Sedley, David. 2018. "Lucretius." In *The Stanford Encyclopedia of Philosophy*, edited by Edward N. Zalta, Winter 2018. https://plato.stanford.edu/archives/win2018/entries/lucretius.

Wilson, Catherine. 2008. *Epicureanism at the Origins of Modernity*. Oxford: Oxford University Press.

12

FEAR OF SNAKES

A COUNTEREXAMPLE TO ONE TRADITIONAL WAY OF THINKING ABOUT FREEDOM

As we saw in the introduction to Part II, *free will* (or *freedom*, or *liberty*) is often understood as *the ability to do otherwise*. This is a helpful clarification of the term(s), but not as helpful as it could be—because it doesn't really help us distinguish between compatibilists and incompatibilists about free will and determinism. There are different ways of analyzing the ability to do otherwise, some of which render it consistent with determinism and some of which render it inconsistent with determinism. In this chapter we will look at a famous counterexample to one historically popular analysis of the ability to do otherwise.

As an introduction to the analysis, consider a representative passage from David Hume's *An Enquiry Concerning Human Understanding*:

> By liberty, then, we can only mean a power of acting or not acting, according to the determinations of the will; that is, if we choose to remain at rest, we remain at rest; if we choose to move, we also may. Now this hypothetical liberty is allowed to belong to everyone who is not a prisoner and in chains. Here, then, there is no subject of dispute.
>
> (Hume 1748, section VIII, 71)

Hume was operating within a tradition of theorizing about free will—often called "classical compatibilism"—that traces back at least

DOI: 10.4324/9781003126119-14

as far as the Stoics, and includes individuals such as Augustine, Thomas Hobbes, and Jonathan Edwards.

As McKenna and Pereboom (2016, 57) point out, Hume nicely summarizes three conditions that characterize classical compatibilism. First, acting freely requires doing what one wants to do ("acting according to the determinations of the will"). Second, acting freely requires acting without undue hindrance or external influence (as is done by someone who is "not a prisoner" and not "in chains"). Third, acting freely requires the ability to do otherwise: "if we choose to remain at rest, we remain at rest; if we choose to move, we also may." Hume's way of specifying the ability to do otherwise represents an analysis—the conditional analysis—that was widely subscribed to up through the middle of the twentieth century. Given that someone has performed an action, the conditional analysis says that their being able to do otherwise just means that had they *chosen* otherwise, they would have *done* otherwise. And although "choice" is the notion that Hume uses, we could substitute different notions: trying or wanting or deciding, among others. (The discussion below will focus on trying.)

Thus, for any action performed, we can test whether it's a free action by asking whether trying to do otherwise would have led to a different action. I pour myself a cup of coffee; if I had tried to make tea instead, would I have made tea? Yes. Therefore, other things being equal, my act of pouring myself a cup of coffee is free. But suppose instead that I was hypnotized to pour myself the cup of coffee. (Very little hypnotic suggestion would have been required.) In this case, if I had tried to make tea instead, I still would have poured myself a cup of coffee. Therefore, my act of pouring myself a cup of coffee while hypnotized is not free.

This analysis gets the right result in lots of ordinary cases, but unfortunately there are also numerous counterexamples involving impairments or obstacles to trying. Keith Lehrer (1976, 248) for example, asks us to "imagine that a man is pathologically afraid of snakes":

> He is taken before a large basket containing a placid python, but he cannot see the snake because a lid conceals the reptile from his view. The lid is then removed and he is asked to reach inside the box to touch the snake. ... Suppose that [he] is frozen with paralysis when the snake appears. ... The paralysis may, as I have suggested, completely incapacitate the man. He may, let us imagine, be stiff and rigid, his muscles exhibiting

contracture, rendering him unable to make any effort to move. It may be true, nevertheless, that he would have touched the snake if he had chosen to, or if he had tried to. The difference we must imagine, however, to accommodate such a choice or attempt is one that would alter the very state that prevents him from touching the snake, his pathological fear.

(Lehrer 1976, 248–49)

It seems intuitively obvious that this is a man who, in this case at least, is not able to do otherwise. And yet, if he had tried to touch the snake, he would have. So the conditional analysis gives us the wrong result in this case.

RESPONSES

A conditional analysis like the one we have been examining is one that describes someone (or something) as having a certain kind of *disposition*. Something that's fragile has a disposition to break when struck; something that's soluble has a disposition to dissolve in water. Similarly, we might say (in keeping with the conditional analysis) that someone who is able to do otherwise has a disposition to do otherwise upon trying to do otherwise.

Although the simple conditional analysis considered above is a failure, that doesn't rule out the possibility of some other, more complex dispositional analysis being more successful. In other words, we could maintain that free action involves some sort of disposition, while looking for a different kind of analysis of the relevant disposition. And several philosophers in recent years have pursued precisely this project, with Vihvelin (2004, 2013) and Fara (2005, 2008) serving as prime examples. (For critical discussion of the "new dispositionalism," see Clarke 2009, Franklin 2011, and Vetter and Jaster 2017.) The jury is still out on whether the new dispositionalism can overcome the problems of the classical conditional analysis without introducing too many new problems of its own.

One reason why it's so difficult to come up with a satisfying dispositional account of ability is that it's so difficult to come up with a satisfying account of dispositions in general. Consider the property of fragility, which we described above as a disposition to break when struck. It seems like we can turn this description into a simple analysis, saying that, for example, a piece of glass is fragile just in case it would break if it were struck. Unfortunately, there are some thought experiments that undermine this tidy definition. One such example comes from C. B. Martin (first published in 1994 but apparently devised long before that):

> The divine agent says, "I shall make the glass cease to be fragile, but whenever anything happens to it that would make it break if it were fragile, I shall, with my foreknowledge of the future, *make* it fragile again. So it will break whenever anything happens that breaks fragile glass—because it will *become* fragile on those occasions. At all other times I shall make it cease to be fragile." If I take the divine agent seriously, then when I crate up the piece of glass and attach the label reading "Fragile, handle with care," I may cross out the word "fragile" but retain the phrase "handle with care." This is absurd of me, but is the divine agent necessarily being absurd?
>
> (Martin 1994, 2)

This example creates a problem for the definition above, because the divinely altered piece of glass will break when struck, but it is *not* fragile. We could also imagine the opposite sort of intervention: one in which the glass remains fragile, but the divine agent intervenes to prevent it from breaking every time it's struck. In this case the glass is fragile but it will *not* break when struck. (For a canonical discussion of these "finkish" dispositions, see Lewis 1997.)

Thus it would seem that questions about how best to analyze abilities (and abilities to do otherwise) are intertwined with, and to a large extent dependent on, ongoing work on the metaphysics of dispositions.

RECOMMENDED READING

McKenna, Michael, and Derk Pereboom. 2016. *Free Will: A Contemporary Introduction*, chapter 3. New York: Routledge.

Choi, Sungho, and Michael Fara. 2021. "Dispositions." In *The Stanford Encyclopedia of Philosophy*, edited by Edward N. Zalta, Spring 2021. https://plato.stanford.edu/archives/spr2021/entries/dispositions.

Vihvelin, Kadri. 2017. "Dispositional Compatibilism." In *The Routledge Companion to Free Will*, edited by Kevin Timpe, Meghan Griffith, and Neil Levy, 52–61. New York: Routledge.

WORKS CITED

Clarke, Randolph. 2009. "Dispositions, Abilities to Act, and Free Will: The New Dispositionalism." *Mind* 118: 323–51.

Fara, Michael. 2005. "Dispositions and Habituals." *Noûs* 39: 43–82.

Fara, Michael. 2008. "Masked Abilities and Compatibilism." *Mind* 117: 843–65.

Franklin, Christopher Evan. 2011. "Masks, Abilities, and Opportunities: Why the New Dispositionalism Cannot Succeed." *The Modern Schoolman* 88: 89–103.

Hume, David. 1748. *An Enquiry Concerning Human Understanding*. London: A. Millar.

Lehrer, Keith. 1976. "'Can' in Theory and Practice: A Possible Worlds Analysis." In *Action Theory*, edited by Myles Brand and Douglas Walton, 241–70. Dordrecht: D. Reidel.

Lewis, David. 1997. "Finkish Dispositions." *The Philosophical Quarterly* 47: 143–58.

Martin, C. B. 1994. "Dispositions and Conditionals." *The Philosophical Quarterly* 44: 1–8.

Vetter, Barbara, and Romy Jaster. 2017. "Dispositional Accounts of Abilities." *Philosophy Compass* 12: 1–11.

Vihvelin, Kadri. 2004. "Free Will Demystified: A Dispositional Account." *Philosophical Topics* 32: 427–50.

Vihvelin, Kadri. 2013. *Causes, Laws, and Free Will: Why Determinism Doesn't Matter*. New York: Oxford University Press.

INCOMPATIBILIST MOUNTAIN

PHILOSOPHIZING AT ALTITUDE

Seasoned mountain climbers know that one of the dangers of mountain climbing is altitude sickness. If you go too high too fast, then you
might suffer from headaches, nausea, dizziness, or worse. Philosophers
aren't known for their mountain-climbing skills, but sometimes arguing for a philosophical position is kind of like the mental equivalent
of climbing a mountain—a sort of intellectual or conceptual ascent
to the summit. Robert Kane, who has had a significant influence on
theorizing about free will in recent decades (see for example Kane
1996), has taken this idea to heart with his construal (and defense) of
libertarianism about free will.

Determinism, as we have seen in earlier chapters, is the thesis that a
complete description of the past history of the world and a complete
specification of the laws of nature together entail every truth about
the future. In short: the past and the laws determine the future. Since
the events of the future include lots of human actions, the truth of
determinism would mean that every action in the future is guaranteed
by the combination of what happened in the past and how the laws
of nature are constituted.

Recall that a *libertarian* is someone who believes that (1) free will
is incompatible with determinism but also that (2) we have free will.
(From these two beliefs, of course, it follows that (3) determinism is
false.) The libertarian who wants to defend her view has at least two

DOI: 10.4324/9781003126119-15

tasks ahead of her. First, she must argue for her incompatibility claim: she must argue that free will is *in*compatible with determinism. She must argue, in other words, that there is no possible world in which determinism is true and free will exists. Second, though, she must also argue that free will is *com*patible with *in*determinism. (Note the shift in emphasis from the first argumentative task to the second.) In other words, she must argue that there is a possible world in which free will exists and determinism is false.

Kane (1996, 2005) has characterized this two-fold task using the mountain-climbing analogy. First the libertarian must make it to the top of Incompatibilist Mountain, and then she must make it safely back down the other side:

> Imagine that the task for libertarians in solving this dilemma is to ascend to the top of a mountain and get down the other side. (Call the mountain "Incompatibilist Mountain" ...). Getting to the top consists in showing that free will is incompatible with determinism. (Call it the Ascent Problem.) Getting down the other side (call it the Descent Problem) involves showing how one can make sense of a free will that requires indeterminism.
>
> (Kane 2005, 34)

The most popular path up Incompatibilist Mountain makes use of what has been called the *consequence argument* for incompatibilism. As van Inwagen (1983) puts it, determinism would mean that our actions are the mere *consequences* of the past and the laws. But we don't have any control over the past or the laws, so it would seem that we don't have any control over our actions either. It seems, in other words, that if determinism is true then we can't have free will; which is to say that determinism is incompatible with free will.

Even if this argument is successful, however, the libertarian's task is not done; she still faces the descent problem. It may not seem obvious why descending is a problem, but consider what the world would have to be like in order for determinism to be false. If determinism is false, then even a complete and total specification of the world (including the entire past and all the laws of nature) might not be enough to guarantee (much less help us predict) what happens next. Take, for example, someone's choice about whether to go to college. If the world is indeterministic, then the person who chose to go to college could have engaged in the exact same deliberations (down to the last mental state) and yet chosen not to go to college instead. And that seems perhaps too close to randomness to count as a free action. If we think of actions that are described as random—involuntary shivers, facial tics, and so on—those actions do not seem to be instances of free will. (For more on this challenge, see Chapter 11.)

So the libertarian has some work to do on the descent as well. And in some ways the descent problem is a harder problem, because it involves an explanatory component: it involves explaining *how* we can have free will even if indeterminism seems to be incompatible with freedom:

> Getting to the top of this mountain—demonstrating that free will and determinism are incompatible—is a difficult enough task for libertarians ... But many critics of libertarianism believe the Descent Problem—making sense of a free will that requires indeterminism—is even more difficult. Mountain climbers say that the descent from a mountain peak is often more difficult and dangerous than the ascent; and this may be the case for libertarians. The air is thin and cold up there on Incompatibilist Mountain; and if you stay up for any length of time, say critics of libertarianism, your mind gets foggy. You start having visions of fantastical ideas, such as transempirical power centers, noumenal selves, and unmoved movers, which libertarians have often invoked to explain their view.
>
> (Kane 2005, 34)

Kane is himself a libertarian (as mentioned above), but he clearly acknowledges that defending libertarianism requires more than just arguing that free will is incompatible with determinism. (See also Steward 2012, who uses the idea of Incompatibilist Mountain to structure her statement and defense of her version of libertarianism.)

RESPONSES

Not many people have engaged directly with the mountain-climbing metaphor in the literature, but it's not hard to imagine a few potential complaints. For example, an incompatibilist might think that this picture gives the wrong idea about who occupies the default position (or, on the other hand, who has the burden of proof). If the incompatibilist is the one who has to make her way up the mountain, then that suggests that the default view—the base camp, where we all have to start—is compatibilism. And someone might think that the default view should instead be incompatibilism, or at least that there's no reason to give the compatibilist the privilege of the default position.

There's a relatively easy way to respond to this objection, however. We can just say that anyone who's arguing for their view faces a mountain climb of sorts. So compatibilists have a mountain of their own to climb, involving an ascent (arguing that free will is compatible with determinism) and a descent (arguing that free will is compatible with *in*determinism). If someone believes that free will is not only compatible with determinism but *requires* the truth of determinism—i.e., if they are a soft determinist—then they will have to descend the mountain by arguing for the truth of determinism. (For a less irenic response to this objection see Lycan (2003, 109), who holds that "compatibilism, not just about free will but generally, on any topic, is the default.")

We will consider various ascent and descent problems in subsequent chapters. Responses to the consequence argument are covered in the chapters on local miracle compatibilism (Chapter 14) and backtracking compatibilism (Chapter 15), and reasons to doubt the compatibility of free will and indeterminism are covered in the chapter on the rollback argument (Chapter 21).

RECOMMENDED READING

Campbell, Joe. 2017. "The Consequence Argument." In *The Routledge Companion to Free Will*, edited by Kevin Timpe, Meghan Griffith, and Neil Levy, 151–65. New York: Routledge.

Kane, Robert. 2005. *A Contemporary Introduction to Free Will*, chapter 4. Oxford: Oxford University Press.

van Inwagen, Peter. 1983. *An Essay on Free Will*, chapter 3. Oxford: Clarendon Press.

Vihvelin, Kadri. 2018. "Arguments for Incompatibilism." In *The Stanford Encyclopedia of Philosophy*, edited by Edward N. Zalta, Fall 2018. https://plato.stanford.edu/archives/fall2018/entries/incompatibilism-arguments.

WORKS CITED

Kane, Robert. 1996. *The Significance of Free Will*. Oxford: Oxford University Press.

Lycan, William G. 2003. "Free Will and the Burden of Proof." *Royal Institute of Philosophy Supplements* 53: 107–22.

Steward, Helen. 2012. *A Metaphysics for Freedom*. Oxford: Oxford University Press.

AN IMPOSSIBLE FEAT OF ENGINEERING

FREEDOM TO BREAK THE LAWS (OF NATURE)

Have you heard the joke about the tachyon? (It is, admittedly, not a great joke.)

> The bartender says, "I'm sorry, but we don't serve faster-than-light particles here."
> A tachyon walks into a bar.

Tachyons are hypothetical particles that travel faster than light. According to Einstein (1907), tachyons could be used to travel (or at least communicate) backward in time. The reason why tachyons are merely hypothetical particles, rather than actual particles, is that traveling faster than light would violate the laws of nature. Peter van Inwagen (1983) appeals to this law of nature in his critique of compatibilism about freedom and determinism.

Crucial to van Inwagen's argumentation are the concepts of the *past history of the world* and the *laws of nature*. According to his argument (see Chapter 13), in a deterministic world the past and the laws entail the future; so changing the future would require altering the past or violating a law of nature; but nobody can alter the past and nobody can violate the laws of nature. Therefore, nobody can change the future; nobody can do anything other than what is already determined

DOI: 10.4324/9781003126119-16

to happen. (In other words, free will can't exist in a deterministic world.)

The claim that nobody can violate a law of nature may seem obvious, but van Inwagen still wants to provide some support for it. So he presents the following vignette:

> Suppose a bureaucrat of the future orders an engineer to build a spaceship capable of traveling faster than light. The engineer tells the bureaucrat that it's a law of nature that nothing travels faster than light. The bureaucrat concedes this difficulty, but counsels perseverance: "I'm sure," he says, "that if you work hard and are very clever, you'll find some way to go faster than light, even though it's a law of nature that nothing does." Clearly his demand is simply incoherent.
>
> (van Inwagen 1983, 62)

Enter David Lewis, who is famous (well, *philosophy* famous at least) for explaining that the situation is not as cut and dried as van Inwagen represents it to be. The article in which Lewis (1981) responded to the consequence argument is something of a classic; van Inwagen himself describes Lewis's article as "the finest essay that has ever been written in defense of compatibilism—possibly the finest essay that has ever been written about any aspect of the free-will problem" (van Inwagen 2008, 330).

In order to get a handle on Lewis's argument, let's look at a simplified regimentation of the consequence argument. The argument refers to "doing otherwise" in general, but let's have a specific example of doing otherwise to refer to. (We'll use an example very similar to the one that both van Inwagen and Lewis use.) Suppose you are in a context in which someone asks for a show of hands, and you decide to refrain from raising your hand. As long as this is a normal context, it seems that, even though you refrained from raising your hand in the actual circumstances, you were also able to raise your hand instead. In other words, there is an alternative situation in which, at the time in question, you raise your hand. So it would seem that even though you refrained from raising your hand you were also able to do otherwise (i.e., you were also able to raise your hand). Now we are ready to look at the argument:

(1) If determinism is true, then doing otherwise requires falsifying a law of nature.

(2) It's impossible to falsify a law of nature.
(3) Therefore, if determinism is true then it's impossible to do otherwise.

Lewis replies that the argument is unsound. The reason why it's unsound, he argues, is that the key notion of falsifying a law of nature is ambiguous between a *strong* reading and a *weak* reading. On the strong reading, to falsify a law of nature is to violate a law of nature directly; to bring about an event that is itself a law-breaking event, we might say. On the weak reading, to falsify a law of nature is to violate a law of nature *indirectly*; to bring about an event that would not itself be a law-breaking event, but that couldn't happen without some other law-breaking event happening first. In Lewis's parlance, this other law-breaking event is called a "divergence miracle."

> Had I raised my hand, a law would have been broken beforehand. The course of events would have diverged from the actual course of events a little while before I raised my hand, and, at the point of divergence there would have been a law-breaking event—a divergence miracle, as I have called it. But this divergence miracle would not have been caused by my raising my hand. If anything, the causation would have been the other way around. Nor would the divergence miracle have been my act of raising my hand. That act was altogether absent from the actual course of events, so it cannot get under way until there is already some divergence. Nor would it have been caused by any other act of mine, earlier or later. Nor would it have been any other act of mine. Nor is there any reason to say that if I had raised my hand there would have been some other law-breaking event besides the divergence miracle; still less, that some other law-breaking event would have been caused by, or would have been, my act of raising my hand. To accommodate my hypothetical raising of my hand while holding fixed all that can and should be held fixed, it is necessary to suppose one divergence miracle, gratuitous to suppose any further law-breaking.
>
> (Lewis 1981, 116–17)

Because of its reliance on the notion of divergence miracles, which are localized to particular actions, Lewis's view is sometimes referred to as "local miracle compatibilism."

Now let's apply this distinction (between the strong sense and the weak sense of "to falsify a law of nature") to the argument. Lewis's challenge is that this argument works only if there is an equivocation on the key notion of falsification; only if there is an illicit shift from one sense to the other as we move through the argument. If we use the strong sense consistently throughout the argument, then premise (2) is true but premise (1) is false. It is indeed impossible to do something that would falsify a law of nature directly, so (2) is true. But, according to Lewis, doing otherwise doesn't require falsifying a law of nature directly, even if determinism is true; it only requires falsifying a law indirectly. So (1) is false. On the other hand, if we use the weak sense consistently, then (1) is true but (2) is false. Doing otherwise (even if determinism is true) does indeed require falsifying a law of nature indirectly; but, claims Lewis, it's not impossible to falsify a law indirectly. On this interpretation, then, (1) is true but (2) is false.

So, to return to van Inwagen's spaceship example, Lewis would agree that the bureaucrat's demand is indeed incoherent, because he is demanding that the engineer build a spaceship that could directly violate a law of nature (by traveling faster than light). But Lewis would point out that doing otherwise, even given the truth of determinism, doesn't require directly violating a law of nature. Thus the spaceship example isn't relevant to a discussion of local miracle compatibilism.

Perhaps another, more mundane example will be helpful in illustrating Lewis's point. Suppose that you are using some simple graphic design software to edit the size of a square. Suppose further that the only way the software allows you to edit the size of the square is to click on one of the corners and drag it toward the center of the square (to make the square smaller) or away from the center of the square (to make the square larger). In this scenario, are you able to change the length of any of the sides of the square? Well, yes and no. You can't alter the length of any of the square's sides *directly*, but you can alter them *indirectly*—by dragging a corner. So, we might say, there's a weak sense of "changing the length of a side" in which you can change the length of the sides; but there's also a strong sense in which you can't.

If someone tried to put forward a "graphic design argument," claiming that nobody could change the size of the square because changing the size of the square would require changing the length of the sides (which is impossible), it would be pretty clear that the argument is unsound. What we should say in response is that we *can* change the size of the square, either because we don't have to change the length of the sides directly or because it is in fact possible to change the length of the sides (by dragging one of the corners). Lewis's response to the consequence argument is analogous to this response to the graphic design argument.

RESPONSES

Van Inwagen (2004) responds to Lewis's critique; Tognazzini (2016) argues that van Inwagen's response fails. Carl Ginet (1990, ch. 5) argues that Lewis's critique is flawed because it can't explain why we are sometimes unable to do otherwise; Pendergraft (2011) points out that other elements of the compatibilist view can fulfill that explanatory function. Beebee (2003) also criticizes Lewis; Oakley (2006) and Graham (2008) respond on behalf of Lewis. More recent discussions include Cutter (2017), Fischer (2021), and Looper (2021).

RECOMMENDED READING

Lewis, David. 1981. "Are We Free to Break the Laws?" *Theoria* 47: 113–21.
McKenna, Michael, and D. Justin Coates. 2021. "Compatibilism." In *The Stanford Encyclopedia of Philosophy*, edited by Edward N. Zalta, Fall 2021. https://plato.stanford.edu/archives/fall2021/entries/compatibilism.
van Inwagen, Peter. 2008. "How to Think About the Problem of Free Will." *Journal of Ethics* 12: 327–41.

WORKS CITED

Beebee, Helen. 2003. "Local Miracle Compatibilism." *Noûs* 37: 258–77.
Cutter, Brian. 2017. "What Is the Consequence Argument an Argument For?" *Analysis* 77: 278–87.
Einstein, Albert. 1907. "On the Relativity Principle and the Conclusions Drawn from It." *Jahrbuch Der Radioaktivität Und Elektronik* 4: 411–62.
Fischer, John Martin. 2021. "Local-Miracle Compatibilism: A Critique." In *Free Will: Historical and Analytic Perspectives*, edited by Marco Hausmann and Jörg Noller, 111–38. Basingstoke: Palgrave Macmillan.
Ginet, Carl. 1990. *On Action*. New York: Cambridge University Press.
Graham, Peter A. 2008. "A Defense of Local Miracle Compatibilism." *Philosophical Studies* 140: 65–82.
Looper, Brian. 2021. "What Freedom in a Deterministic World Must Be." *Mind* 130: 863–85.

Oakley, Shane. 2006. "Defending Lewis's Local Miracle Compatibilism." *Philosophical Studies* 130: 337–49.

Pendergraft, Garrett. 2011. "The Explanatory Power of Local Miracle Compatibilism." *Philosophical Studies* 156: 249–66.

Tognazzini, Neal A. 2016. "Free Will and Miracles." *Thought* 5: 236–38.

van Inwagen, Peter. 1983. *An Essay on Free Will.* Oxford: Clarendon Press.

van Inwagen, Peter. 2004. "Freedom to Break the Laws." *Midwest Studies in Philosophy* 28: 334–50.

CAN ELWOOD BUY AN EDSEL?

A THOUGHT EXPERIMENT INVOLVING DIFFERENT KINDS OF ABILITIES

In Chapter 14, we saw how David Lewis responded to the consequence argument, namely by putting forward a view that is sometimes called local miracle compatibilism. The distinctive feature of local miracle compatibilism is the claim that even though nobody can violate a law of nature, we are sometimes able to do things that would require a different set of laws. This is how we can have the ability to do otherwise even if determinism is true.

But of course there are two ingredients that, according to the consequence argument, work together to undermine our freedom if determinism is true. One ingredient is the laws of nature, but the other ingredient is the *past*. Recall from the chapter on determinism (Chapter 10) that we used L to represent the conjunction of all of the laws of nature and we used H to represent the entire past history of the world. If H and L together entail some action A, then (says the consequence argument) A is not free. So if there's one way of resisting the consequence argument that focuses on the laws, it stands to reason that there might be a way of resisting that focuses on the past. This view is sometimes called *backtracking compatibilism,* or *multiple pasts compatibilism.*

If you make a wrong turn, sometimes you have to backtrack: you have to retrace your steps until you find the place where you strayed

DOI: 10.4324/9781003126119-17

from the correct path. According to backtracking compatibilism, doing otherwise than we actually do requires some conceptual backtracking: if we were to do otherwise, then there would have been some point in the past at which we took a different path than we actually took. Figuring out where that point would be requires a hypothetical or conceptual retracing of our steps. When we engage in this type of backtracking, we are envisioning a different world—a world in which we do otherwise—and in that world we are asking what would need to change in the past in order for the alternative action to take place.

For an example of backtracking compatibilism, consider the view defended by John Perry (2004). He argues that it's not enough to simply identify the true propositions H and L and then point out that, because H and L are true, A must be true also. He argues that we need to look more closely at the relevant true propositions, and that we should start by distinguishing between a proposition *being* true and something *making* a proposition true. For example, consider the proposition, *I drank a cup of coffee this morning.* Various events, including some actions of mine, made that proposition true. Other propositions, including mathematical propositions (e.g., *The smallest prime number is even*) are true but not made true by any events. With that distinction in mind, Perry defines the notion of a proposition being *settled* as follows: A proposition is settled when (and only when) it is entailed by other propositions that have already been made true.

Now we are in a position to bring determinism into the picture and examine its effects on whether our actions can be free. If determinism is true, then H (i.e., the proposition about past, which is made true by all of the events that constitute it) and L (i.e., the proposition about the laws, which is made true by something other than events) entail everything about the future course of events, including our future actions. So any proposition about a future action of ours is already settled (if determinism is true).

Perry then distinguishes between a weak notion of ability and a strong notion of ability:

> Can one have the ability to perform or refrain from an action A at time *t*, even though the issue of whether one will perform A at *t* or refrain from doing so has been *settled* before *t*? A weak account of ability will allow us to answer *yes* to this question; a strong account will force us to answer *no*.
>
> (Perry 2004, 237)

In other words, if we adopt a strong account of ability, then someone being able to do otherwise than A entails that it not be settled ahead of time that they do A. On a weak account of ability, someone might be able to do otherwise than A even if it is settled ahead of time that they do A.

Your initial thought might be that the weak account of ability is wildly implausible. How on earth could anyone refrain from doing something if it's already settled that they'll do it? Perry supports the weak account with an analogy:

> It's 1956 and Elwood *doesn't* buy a new Edsel. He thinks they are ugly, ungainly, and overpriced. He doesn't want one. So he doesn't buy one. Now does it follow that he can't afford one? Of course not. He may have all the money he needs, and simply not want one. One question has to do with what he wants in a car and what he thinks about the Edsel. These facts, what he thinks about Edsels and what he wants in the way of a car, are pretty much located in Elwood's head. At any rate, they are not located down the street at the bank. But that's where the facts about how much money he has in his account, and how much credit the bankers will give him, reside. ... He may be loaded, so he can easily afford a fleet of Edsels. He can't buy the car without money or credit, but he can *not* buy the car even though he has plenty of money and plenty of credit.
>
> (Perry 2004, 241–42)

The idea here is that from this little vignette we can infer that Elwood *won't* buy an Edsel, but we can't infer that he *can't* buy an Edsel. (It may even be *settled* that he won't buy an Edsel, but it doesn't follow that he can't.) Facts about Elwood's financial abilities are very different from facts about Edsel's beliefs and desires, and those two sets of facts depend on very different things.

Perry then invites us to consider the possibility that facts about our abilities are different from facts about what we'll do. There's a lot of overlap between these sets of facts, to be sure (they are not quite *as* different as facts about what we can afford are different from facts about our beliefs and desires); but there are at least some differences. This means that these sets of facts could depend on different things as well. This, in turn, means that I might be able to do something even though it's settled that I won't do that thing.

Consider the simple account of ability proposed by Perry:

> A person has the ability to *bring it about that* R *in circumstance* K if (i) the person's repertoire of basic actions includes some movement M such that (ii) executing M in K will have the result that R.
>
> (Perry 2004, 245)

As Perry notes, someone can clearly satisfy conditions (i) and (ii) even if it's settled (by the past and the laws) that she won't make the relevant movement M. Even though it's settled that she *won't* execute M, it may still be true that she *can* execute M. This is because her abilities depend only on her repertoire of basic actions, whereas what she actually does also depends partly on the past and the laws.

RESPONSES

In addition to Perry (2004), Perry (2008) also offers a defense of backtracking compatibilism, along with a critique of John Martin Fischer's (2006) view. Fischer (2008) returns the favor with a critique of Perry's view. The essence of Fischer's critique is that Perry's view comes with "baggage." Even if, as Perry claims, we can sometimes still perform an action A despite its being settled that we won't perform A, this ability to do otherwise comes with a problematic implication. If it's settled that we won't perform A, then that means that our not doing A is entailed by something that's already been made true. Thus, if we are able to do A, then we are able to do something that would require the falsity of something that's already been made true. And Fischer argues that this is a fatal flaw: we should never endorse a view according to which we can do things that require the falsity of something that's already made true.

See Holliday (2012) for an extension of Fischer's critique of backtracking compatibilism; see also Cyr and Law (2020) for a helpful recent discussion.

RECOMMENDED READING

Cyr, Taylor, and Andrew Law. 2020. "Freedom, Foreknowledge, and Dependence." *American Philosophical Quarterly* 57: 145–54.

McKenna, Michael, and D. Justin Coates. 2021. "Compatibilism." In *The Stanford Encyclopedia of Philosophy*, edited by Edward N. Zalta, Fall 2021. https://plato.stanford.edu/archives/fall2021/entries/compatibilism.

Perry, John. 2004. "Compatibilist Options." In *Freedom and Determinism*, edited by Joseph K. Campbell, Michael O'Rourke, and David Shier, 231–54. Cambridge, MA: MIT Press.

WORKS CITED

Fischer, John Martin. 2006. *My Way: Essays on Moral Responsibility*. Oxford: Oxford University Press.

Fischer, John Martin. 2008. "My Way and Life's Highway: Replies to Steward, Smilansky, and Perry." *Journal of Ethics* 12: 167–89.

Holliday, Wesley H. 2012. "Freedom and the Fixity of the Past." *Philosophical Review* 121: 179–207.

Perry, John. 2008. "Can't We All Just Be Compatibilists?: A Critical Study of John Martin Fischer's *My Way*." *Journal of Ethics* 12: 157–66.

THE NEFARIOUS NEUROSURGEON

FRANKFURT'S COUNTEREXAMPLE TO THE PRINCIPLE OF ALTERNATIVE POSSIBILITIES

Suppose that you are captured by a hypnotist. He proceeds to hypnotize you, and under the influence of his hypnosis you rob a bank. Are you morally responsible for robbing the bank? It seems not: it seems that the hypnosis absolves you of responsibility. But what is it, exactly, about hypnosis that takes away someone's responsibility? One plausible answer is that you're not responsible for what you do under hypnosis because while you are hypnotized you *have no alternatives*; you *could not have done otherwise*. If we reflect on other types of situations in which we're not responsible—situations involving coercion, manipulation, and the like—it seems as though the lack of alternative possibilities is also what explains the lack of responsibility. (Although not everyone would agree that coercion and other forms of duress preclude responsibility; see for example Scanlon 1998, ch. 6.)

We can generalize these reflections by encapsulating them in a principle, which we will call *the principle of alternative possibilities.*

> **The principle of alternative possibilities:** Someone is morally responsible for performing an action only if they could have done otherwise.

DOI: 10.4324/9781003126119-18

Much of the twentieth-century discussion of moral responsibility simply presupposed that this principle, or something like it, was true. In 1969, however, Harry Frankfurt published a now-famous (or, for some, a now-infamous) article that challenged the principle of alternative possibilities. (The example Frankfurt develops is reminiscent of one that can be found in John Locke's *An Essay Concerning Human Understanding*, II.xxi.10. For discussion of Locke's view of freedom, see Rickless 2020.)

Frankfurt begins his challenge by distinguishing between two different types of factors that are relevant to the explanation of someone's behavior. First, there are the factors that produce the behavior; second, there are the factors that remove one or more alternatives. If we focus on cases in which someone doesn't have any alternatives, we can see that most of those cases are cases in which the factors that are producing the behavior are also the factors that are removing the alternatives. For example, in the little hypnosis story above, the hypnosis was the factor that was making you rob the bank and also the factor that prevented you from doing otherwise.

Frankfurt then points out that there are some cases, less likely but still possible, in which one set of factors produces the behavior while a *different* set removes the alternatives. He describes such a case, asking us to imagine a situation in which someone named Jones has been stripped of his alternative possibilities by a nefarious neurosurgeon named Dr. Black:

> Suppose someone—Black, let us say—wants Jones to perform a certain action. Black is prepared to go to considerable lengths to get his way, but he prefers to avoid showing his hand unnecessarily. So he waits until Jones is about to make up his mind what to do, and he does nothing unless it is clear to him (Black is an excellent judge of such things) that Jones is going to decide to do something other than what he wants him to do. If it does become clear that Jones is going to decide to do something else, Black takes effective steps to ensure that Jones decides to do, and that he does do, what he wants him to do. Whatever Jones's initial preferences and inclinations, then, Black will have his way.
>
> (Frankfurt 1969, 835)

In this case, due to the presence of Dr. Black and his machinations, there is a set of factors that removes all of Jones's alternatives. As it turns out, however, this set of factors is irrelevant to what Jones actually does. Even though Dr. Black is prepared to intervene and influence Jones's behavior, such intervention is not necessary:

> Now suppose that Black never has to show his hand because Jones, for reasons of his own, decides to perform and does perform the very action Black wants him to perform. In that case, it seems clear, Jones will bear precisely the same moral responsibility for what he does as he would have borne if Black had not been ready to take steps to ensure that he do it. It would be quite unreasonable to excuse Jones for his action, or to withhold the praise to which it would normally entitle him, on the basis of the fact that he could not have done otherwise. This fact played no role at all in leading him to act as he did. He would have acted the same even if it had not been a fact. Indeed, everything happened just as it would have happened without Black's presence in the situation and without his readiness to intrude into it.
>
> (Frankfurt 1969, 836)

In Frankfurt's case, the factors that produce Jones's action are different from the factors that remove Jones's alternatives. Dr. Black's presence and intentions render Jones unable to do otherwise, but they do not play any role in bringing about Jones's action. (Recall that since Jones does what Black wants, Black never actually exerts any causal influence over Jones's behavior.) Instead, it is Jones himself, "for reasons of his own," who brings about his action. And since Jones did what he did on his own, without influence or intervention from Black or anyone else, it seems that he remains responsible for his action.

It would appear, then, that we have a counterexample to the principle of alternative possibilities. The principle says that having alternatives is necessary for being responsible, but in Frankfurt's case it seems that Jones is morally responsible for what he did even though he has no alternatives.

Frankfurt's case is interesting in its own right, but it also has broader implications. If it is indeed a genuine counterexample to the principle of alternative possibilities, then it would seem that causal determinism is not the serious threat to moral responsibility that it's often made out to be. We would also have reason to question the (relatively) standard way of conceiving the relationship between moral responsibility, free will, and alternative possibilities. On the standard way of thinking, alternative possibilities are essential for free will and free will is essential for moral responsibility. On this way of thinking, if determinism rules out alternative possibilities then that fact would rule out free will, which would in turn rule out moral responsibility. In other words, it seems that if determinism precludes responsibility, it does so by removing alternative possibilities. But if moral responsibility is compatible with a lack of alternative possibilities, then there is a mistake in the standard picture. Either alternative possibilities aren't connected to free will in the way we thought they were, or free will isn't connected to moral responsibility in the way we thought it was.

RESPONSES

As you might imagine, not everyone has agreed that Frankfurt's case is a genuine counterexample to the principle of alternative possibilities. Perhaps the most influential objection is one that focuses on the details that allow Dr. Black to control Frankfurt's behavior. The response can be framed as a dilemma for Frankfurt: The process that leads up to Jones's action is either deterministic or indeterministic. If it's deterministic, then the case can't be used to help support the compatibility of moral responsibility and determinism. (If we are trying to argue that moral responsibility is compatible with determinism, we can't simply describe a deterministic case in which we stipulate that the person is responsible!) If, on the other hand, the case is indeterministic, then Jones has alternatives after all, since there's no way for Black to guarantee that Jones does what Black wants him to do. (Even if Jones shows a sign that he's going to do what Black wants him to do, Jones could always change his mind and do something else instead.) Either way, then, it seems that the case can't be used as a counterexample to the principle of alternative possibilities. In response to this objection, various modifications to the original example have been proposed, which have in turn prompted further objections.

Nelkin (2011, ch. 3) represents a different sort of critique of the Frankfurt cases. This type of critique argues that if we analyze the relevant concepts (e.g., the concept of "ability") correctly, then it will become clear that the Frankfurt cases do not undermine the importance of the ability to do otherwise. Nevertheless, alternatives are not required for moral responsibility in general; they are only required for *blameworthiness*. Nelkin supports this asymmetry (2011, ch. 5) by appealing to the principle that *ought implies can*: If someone ought to do (or refrain from doing) something, then they have to be able to do (or refrain from doing) that thing.

Others (e.g., Leon and Tognazzini 2010) have argued that the Frankfurt cases can teach us something important about the concept of moral responsibility even if they are not airtight counterexamples to the principle of alternative possibilities.

RECOMMENDED READING

Fischer, John Martin. 2010. "The Frankfurt Cases: The Moral of the Stories." *The Philosophical Review* 119: 315–36.

Leon, Felipe, and Neal A. Tognazzini. 2010. "Why Frankfurt-Examples Don't Need to Succeed to Succeed." *Philosophy and Phenomenological Research* 80: 551–65.

McKenna, Michael, and David Widerker. 2003. "Introduction." In *Moral Responsibility and Alternative Possibilities: Essays on the Importance of Alternative Possibilities*, edited by David Widerker and Michael McKenna. New York: Routledge.

Robb, David. 2020. "Moral Responsibility and the Principle of Alternative Possibilities." In *The Stanford Encyclopedia of Philosophy*, edited by Edward N. Zalta, Fall 2020. https://plato.stanford.edu/archives/fall2020/entries/alternative-possibilities.

WORKS CITED

Frankfurt, Harry G. 1969. "Alternate Possibilities and Moral Responsibility." *The Journal of Philosophy* 66: 829–39.

Nelkin, Dana Kay. 2011. *Making Sense of Freedom and Responsibility*. Oxford: Oxford University Press.

Rickless, Samuel. 2020. "Locke on Freedom." In *The Stanford Encyclopedia of Philosophy*, edited by Edward N. Zalta, Spring 2020. https://plato.stanford.edu/archives/spr2020/entries/locke-freedom.

Scanlon, T. M. 1998. *What We Owe to Each Other*. Cambridge, MA: Harvard University Press.

THE AVALANCHE

BETTY'S SECRET MISSION

In the movie *The Wizard of Oz*, a tornado damages Dorothy's family's farm. Presumably nobody was morally responsible for this: neither for the occurrence of the tornado, nor for the fact that tornadoes cause damage to the area(s) where they touch down, nor for the damage itself. This observation might just seem like common sense, and thus barely worthy of mention. But if we look for a general explanation of our non-responsibility judgment in this case, we encounter a type of principle that shows up in various challenges to free will.

In Chapter 8, for example, we saw that an important ingredient in the argument for theological fatalism is a *transfer of necessity* principle: if something is necessary, and if the one thing necessarily leads to another, then the other thing is necessary too. In this chapter we'll look a little more closely at a related principle about the (alleged) transfer of *non-responsibility*. Fischer and Ravizza (1998, ch. 6) call this principle "Transfer-NR," and they express it in three parts:

(1) If P obtains and no one is even partly morally responsible for P; and

(2) if P obtains then Q obtains, and no one is even partly morally responsible for the fact that if P obtains then Q obtains; then

(3) Q obtains, and no one is even partly morally responsible for Q.

DOI: 10.4324/9781003126119-19

According to Transfer-NR, once we substitute propositions for P and Q, then we can say the following: If (1) and (2) are true, then (3) is also true. This principle supports and explains our intuitions about lots of ordinary cases, including the tornado case above.

If Transfer-NR is valid, then it seems that we can easily construct an argument that determinism is incompatible with moral responsibility. Remember that, if determinism is true, a complete description of the world (including its past history and its laws of nature) at any time will entail what happens next. Now just plug in this complete description of the world for P, and plug in any action for Q. It seems that nobody is even partly responsible for the complete description of the world (especially if we are describing it a time in the distant past), and that nobody is even partly responsible for that description entailing what happens next. (Indeed, how could anyone be responsible for such an entailment relationship?) Thus, nobody is even partly responsible for Q, where Q covers any possible action.

Fischer and Ravizza (1998, 155–58) propose a counterexample to Transfer NR, which they call "Erosion." The Erosion case is a case of *preemptive overdetermination* (which we'll talk more about below). To set up Erosion, they first describe a preliminary case called "Avalanche":

> Betty is a double-agent who has been instructed to start an avalanche that will destroy an enemy base at the foot of a large, snow-capped mountain. To accomplish her mission, Betty places dynamite in the cracks and crevices of a glacier near the top of the mountain. At t_1 she pushes the plunger detonating the explosives and starting an avalanche. The avalanche rumbles down the hill, gaining ever greater force, until some time later, say t_3, it crushes the enemy outpost. Assume that the success of the mission depends upon the base being destroyed at exactly t_3. Given that Betty acts freely in setting the explosives and in starting the avalanche, it seems that she is responsible for her action and for the consequence to which it leads: *that the enemy base is crushed by an avalanche at t_3.* Unbeknownst to Betty, however, another soldier from her army, Ralph, is hiding slightly below her on the mountain. Betty's commanding officers had reason to doubt her loyalty, and to test it they assigned her the task of destroying the enemy camp. But to ensure that the mission succeeded, they secretly sent Ralph along with instructions to start the avalanche himself (if Betty did not) by using explosives placed a few feet below Betty's. In this way, if Betty had not detonated the explosives at t_1, Ralph still would have had time to detonate his own explosives at t_2,

> thereby ensuring the consequence *that the enemy base is crushed by an avalanche at t3.*

Avalanche is almost a counterexample to Transfer-NR, but not quite (as Fischer and Ravizza themselves acknowledge). To see why, let's get clear on what the P and Q represent:

P   *Ralph detonates his explosives at t2.*
Q   *The enemy base is crushed by an avalanche at t3.*

We can now substitute those statements in place of P and Q in (1)–(3) above. In order for Avalanche to be a counterexample to Transfer-NR, (1) and (2) need to be true and (3) needs to be false. But in Avalanche, (1) is false: it's false that no one is even partly morally responsible for Ralph detonating his explosives. He's responsible, or his commanding officer is responsible, or perhaps they share responsibility, but either way (1) is false.

But now consider Erosion, which is built on Avalanche in a way that does seem to produce a counterexample to Transfer-NR:

> Call the following case, "Erosion." It is exactly like "Avalanche" except that in this instance the counterfactual intervener, Ralph, is to be replaced by *natural forces* that have no conscious design and bear no responsibility. As before, imagine that Betty plants her explosives in the crevices of the glacier and detonates the charge at *t1*, causing an avalanche that crushes the enemy fortress at *t3.* Unbeknownst to Betty and her commanding officers, however, the glacier is gradually melting, shifting, and eroding. Had Betty not placed the dynamite in the crevices, some ice and rocks would have broken free at *t2*, starting a natural avalanche that would have crushed the enemy camp at *t3.* ... As in "Avalanche," Betty acts freely, and she is responsible for the consequences of her action. This is true even though conditions were present, for which no one was even partly responsible, that were sufficient to bring about the consequence *that the enemy camp is destroyed by an avalanche at t3.* Thus, "Erosion" is a counterexample to Transfer NR ...
> (Fischer and Ravizza 1998, 157)

In this case, Q represents the same thing but P represents something different:

P   *Natural forces start an avalanche at t2.*
Q   *The enemy base is crushed by an avalanche at t3.*

Here it would seem that (1) and (2) are true: nobody is responsible for the erosion, and nobody is responsible for the fact that the erosion would create an avalanche that destroys the enemy base. And yet it seems that (3) is false: Betty is indeed responsible for the destruction of the enemy base, since she's the one who detonated the explosives that caused the avalanche!

Above I referred to Erosion as a *preemptive overdetermination* case. It's an overdetermination case because the destruction of the base is overdetermined: Betty's actions will lead to its destruction, but even if she weren't around then the erosion would still lead to its destruction. Betty's actions and the erosion are two independent sets of events, each of which by itself would lead to the destruction. And it's a case of preemption because the erosion never gets the chance to cause the avalanche that it would have caused if Betty hadn't been around. Betty's actions preempt the effects of the erosion.

RESPONSES

McKenna (2001) offers some criticism of Fischer's Erosion case; Fischer (2004) responds, and McKenna (2008) provides additional discussion. Arguments that rely on a principle like Transfer-NR are often called *direct arguments* for incompatibilism about moral responsibility and determinism. Some arguments (such as the consequence argument; see Chapter 13) argue *indirectly* for the incompatibility of moral responsibility and determinism. These arguments are indirect because they first argue that something (such as the ability to do otherwise) is required for moral responsibility, and then that determinism rules out that thing that's necessary for moral responsibility.

Incompatibilists who rely on the direct argument are often called *source incompatibilists* because they think the truth of determinism would make something else, rather than us ourselves, the source of our actions. According to source incompatibilists, determinism precludes free will, but not because it takes away our alternative possibilities; instead, determinism precludes free will in virtue of taking away our sourcehood. For further discussion of source incompatibilism, see McKenna (2001), Pereboom (2003), Timpe (2007), Shabo (2010), and Tognazzini (2011).

RECOMMENDED READING

Fischer, John Martin, and Mark Ravizza. 1998. *Responsibility and Control: A Theory of Moral* Responsibility. Cambridge: Cambridge University Press.

Levy, Neil, and Michael McKenna. 2009. "Recent Work on Free Will and Moral Responsibility." *Philosophy Compass* 4: 96–133.

WORKS CITED

Fischer, John Martin. 2004. "The Transfer of Nonresponsibility." In *Freedom and Determinism*, edited by Joseph K. Campbell, Michael O'Rourke, and David Shier, 189–209. Cambridge, MA: MIT Press.

McKenna, Michael. 2001. "Source Incompatibilism, Ultimacy, and the Transfer of Non-Responsibility." *American Philosophical Quarterly* 38: 37–51.

McKenna, Michael. 2008. "Saying Good-Bye to the Direct Argument the Right Way." *Philosophical Review* 117: 349–83.

Pereboom, Derk. 2003. "Source Incompatibilism and Alternative Possibilities." In *Moral Responsibility and Alternative Possibilities*, edited by David Widerker and Michael McKenna, 185–200. New York: Routledge.

Shabo, Seth. 2010. "Uncompromising Source Incompatibilism." *Philosophy and Phenomenological Research* 80: 349–83.

Timpe, Kevin. 2007. "Source Incompatibilism and Its Alternatives." *American Philosophical Quarterly* 44: 143–55.

Tognazzini, Neal A. 2011. "Understanding Source Incompatibilism." *The Modern Schoolman* 88: 73–88.

THE BROKEN STEERING WHEEL

WHAT TYPE OF CONTROL IS REQUIRED FOR MORAL RESPONSIBILITY?

Free will, as we have seen (e.g., in the introduction to Part II), is often conceptualized as the thing that makes us eligible for moral responsibility; we might say that it is the *control condition* on moral responsibility. It is also generally agreed that there is a second condition on moral responsibility, namely an *epistemic condition* having to do with knowledge or awareness. (Articulation of these two conditions traces back to Aristotle's *Nicomachean Ethics*, III.1.) So even if someone has the right kind of control in performing an action, they might not be responsible for its consequences if they are not aware of those consequences (or perhaps not aware of the moral features of those consequences). For example, suppose that a terrorist has connected a bomb to my office light switch so that when I turn on my light it detonates the bomb, blowing up a building downtown. Even if I turn the light on as an exercise of the right kind of control, I am not morally responsible for the explosion and its consequences. I didn't know about the bomb, and it's not plausible to say that I *should have* known about it. So my action of turning on the light would fail to satisfy the epistemic condition, and this is why I wouldn't be responsible for the explosion.

Let's return our focus to the control condition. What kind of control are we talking about? An initial response, as we have also seen, is that this type of control that makes us eligible for moral responsibility

DOI: 10.4324/9781003126119-20

is the ability to do otherwise. If I raise my coffee cup to my mouth so that I can take a sip, having the ability to do otherwise would mean that I can also refrain from raising the cup. And many people have thought that the ability to do otherwise is incompatible with determinism, which would seem to mean that moral responsibility is also incompatible with determinism.

John Martin Fischer, however, has argued that this incompatibilist view is unwarranted because it fails to distinguish between different types of control that we might have over our actions. To help introduce this distinction, Fischer presents the following thought experiment:

> Let's say you are driving your car and it is functioning normally. You want to go to the coffee house, so you guide the car to the right (into the parking lot for the coffee house). Your choice to go to the coffee house is based on your own reasons in the normal way, and the car's steering apparatus functions normally. Here you have a certain distinctive kind of control of the car's movements—you have "guidance control" of the car's going to the right. This is more than mere causation or even causal determination; you might have causally determined the car's going to the right by sneezing (and thus jerking the steering wheel to the right) or having an epileptic seizure (and thus slumping over the wheel and causing it to turn to the right) without having exercised this specific and distinctive sort of *control*. Supposing that there are no "special" factors at work—that is, no special psychological impairments, brain lesions, neurological disorders, causal determination, and so forth—and imagining (as above) that the car's steering apparatus is not broken, you had it in your power (just prior to your actual decision to turn to the right) to continue going straight ahead, or to turn the car to the left, and so forth. That is, although you exercise guidance control in turning the car to the right, you presumably (and apart from special assumptions) possessed freedom to choose and do otherwise: you had "regulative control" over the car's movements. In the normal case, we assume that agents have both guidance and regulative control—a signature sort of control of the car's movements, as well as a characteristic kind of control *over* the car's movements.
>
> Whereas these two sorts of control are typically presumed to go together, they can be prized apart. Suppose that everything is as above, but that the steering apparatus of your car is broken in such a way that, if you had tried to guide the car in any direction other than the one in which you actually guide it, it would have gone to the right anyway—in just the trajectory it actually traveled. The defect in the steering apparatus plays

no role in the actual sequence of events, but it would have played a role in the alternative scenario (or range of such scenarios). Given this sort of preemptive overdetermination, although you exhibit guidance control of the car's going to the right, you do *not* have regulative control over the car's movements: it would have gone in precisely the same way, no matter what you were to choose or try.

(Fischer 2007, 56–57)

Perhaps you recognized, as you were reading that passage, that the situation in which you turn right on your own but couldn't have turned left bears some resemblance to Frankfurt's counterexample to the principle of alternative possibilities (see Chapter 16). In fact, we could think of Frankfurt cases as examples in which this intuitively plausible driving scenario is modified so that *all* of the different alternative possibilities are removed: trying to turn left, hitting the brakes, attempting to jump out of the car while it's moving, and so on. Even when all of those possibilities are removed, someone could (arguably) still be responsible for turning right if they do so on the basis of their own reasons in a normal way.

Fischer's thought experiment above also plays a crucial role in the development of his overall theory of moral responsibility. Fischer's claim is that guidance control, rather than regulative control, is the strongest type of control required for moral responsibility; guidance control is what makes us eligible for moral responsibility.

The next step, of course, is to provide an analysis of guidance control, to help us understand what it is and how it can serve as the control condition for moral responsibility. Fischer and Ravizza (1998) develop a comprehensive account of guidance control, and Fischer has continued to refine it over the years. For our purposes, however, a rough and intuitive characterization should be sufficient.

On Fischer's view, whether an agent exercises guidance control depends on whether the internal source of the agent's action—the "mechanism" from which the action flows—exhibits certain characteristics. These characteristics include *reasons-responsiveness* and *ownership*. To take ownership of one's action (or the mechanism of one's action) is simply to endorse it, or to be disposed to endorse it, upon reflection. It is to accept it as part of oneself or at least intimately associated with oneself. The notion of reasons-responsiveness is a little bit more complicated, but it refers to a phenomenon that we're all

familiar with. Suppose that you are at the coffee shop, deciding between the large and the medium. You opt for the medium, because
you had a good night of sleep last night. But if you had slept less,
then you would have opted for the large. Your choice of the medium
coffee is reasons-responsive, because if you had had a *reason* to make a
different choice (e.g., less sleep the night before) then you would have
made that different choice. Your mechanism of action is responsive to
reasons to do otherwise.

According to Fischer, then, the mechanism of action must be
suitably reasons-responsive, and it must belong to the agent in the
right way (the agent has to have taken ownership of it). Suitable
reasons-responsiveness is what Fischer calls "moderate" reasons-
responsiveness: an agent operating with a moderately responsive
mechanism would recognize and respond to reasons to do otherwise
in a variety of alternative circumstances—where at least some of those
reasons are moral reasons and the set of reasons that produce the responses exemplify some rational pattern. (For more detail, see Fischer
and Ravizza 1998.) The resulting theory is a sophisticated version
of compatibilism known as *semicompatibilism*. (It's *semi*compatibilism
because one can endorse Fischer's view whether or not one believes
that determinism rules out the ability to do otherwise.)

RESPONSES

Fischer's theory of moral responsibility is one of the most well-
respected and widely discussed views in the philosophical literature
on free will. It is a paradigm case of an *actual-sequence* view of moral
responsibility, so called because whether or not someone is morally
responsible for an action depends primarily on features of the actual
sequence that led up to the action, rather than on what happens in
alternative sequences. (For example, if you are exhibiting the right
kind of control over the steering wheel in the actual sequence, then it
doesn't matter what would happen in the alternative sequences.) For
a notably different way of developing an actual-sequence view, see
Sartorio (2016).

For a detailed discussion of Fischer and Ravizza (1998), see Fischer
and Ravizza (2000a, 2000b), Mele (2000), Bratman (2000), and Stump
(2000).

RECOMMENDED READING

Fischer, John Martin. 2007. "Compatibilism." In *Four Views on Free Will*, by John Martin Fischer, Robert Kane, Derk Pereboom, and Manuel Vargas, 44–84. Malden, MA: Blackwell.

Fischer, John Martin, and Mark Ravizza. 2000a. "Précis of Responsibility and Control: A Theory of Moral Responsibility." *Philosophy and Phenomenological Research* 61: 441–45.

WORKS CITED

Aristotle. *Nicomachean Ethics.*

Bratman, Michael E. 2000. "Fischer and Ravizza on Moral Responsibility and History." *Philosophy and Phenomenological Research* 61: 453–58.

Fischer, John Martin, and Mark Ravizza. 1998. *Responsibility and Control: A Theory of Moral Responsibility*. Cambridge: Cambridge University Press.

Fischer, John Martin, and Mark Ravizza. 2000b. "Replies." *Philosophy and Phenomenological Research* 61: 467–80.

Mele, Alfred R. 2000. "Reactive Attitudes, Reactivity, and Omissions." *Philosophy and Phenomenological Research* 61: 447–52.

Sartorio, Carolina. 2016. *Causation and Free Will*. Oxford: Oxford University Press.

Stump, Eleonore. 2000. "The Direct Argument for Incompatibilism." *Philosophy and Phenomenological Research* 61: 459–66.

SHARK-INFESTED WATERS

A PUZZLE ABOUT RESPONSIBILITY FOR OMISSIONS

We are (sometimes) morally responsible for our actions, and (sometimes) for the consequences of those actions. But what about our *failures* to act, i.e., our *omissions*? Some of the difficulties that arise when we try to answer responsibility questions about omissions can be seen by considering two related examples from John Martin Fischer and Mark Ravizza:

> In "Sloth," John is walking along a beach, and he sees a child struggling in the water. John believes that he could save the child with very little effort, but he is disinclined to expend any energy to help anyone else. He decides not to try to save the child, and he continues to walk along the beach.
>
> Is John morally responsible for failing to save the child? Unbeknownst to John, the child was about to drown when John glimpsed him, and the child drowned one second after John decided not to jump in the water. The facts of the case exert pressure to say that John is not morally responsible for failing to save the child: after all, the child would have drowned, even if John had tried to save it. John may well be morally responsible for deciding not to try to save the child and even for not trying to save the child, but he is *not* morally responsible for not saving the child.
>
> (Fischer and Ravizza 1998, 125)

DOI: 10.4324/9781003126119-21

We should note a couple of important features of this thought experiment before we look at the next one. First, it highlights the distinction between actions, omissions, and the consequences of those actions or omissions. Even if someone isn't responsible for an outcome, they could still be responsible for trying to bring about (or prevent) that outcome, or for *failing* to try to bring about (or prevent) that outcome.

Fischer and Ravizza claim that the details of the case "exert pressure" toward a verdict of "not morally responsible for failing to save the child." And this seems plausible: even if John had tried to save the child, his actions wouldn't have made a difference; thus it seems we should say that John is not responsible for not saving the child.

Now consider a variation on the Sloth case. In this one, it's not *impossible* for John to save the child (as it was in Sloth), but there is an essentially insurmountable obstacle in place:

> "Sloth" is no different in this respect [i.e., with respect to John's responsibility] from a case ("Sharks") exactly like it, except that the child would not have drowned immediately; rather, a patrol of sharks that (unbeknownst to John) infested the water between the beach and the struggling child would have eaten John, had he jumped in.
>
> (Fischer and Ravizza 1998, 125)

In Sharks, it's not impossible for John to save the child because there's a chance that the sharks wouldn't notice him, or that he could fend them off, or perhaps that they would get distracted by some other prey. But it still seems that John is not morally responsible for failing to save the child. Is he still responsible for failing to *try* to save the child? This is a difficult question. Fischer and Ravizza seem to think that our responsibility verdicts should be the same in Sharks as they are in Sloth. And that seems true when we focus on the failure to save the child, but it's not so clear what to say about the failure to *try* to save the child. If John in the Sloth case hadn't realized that it was too late to save the child, then it seems plausible to think that he at least should have tried to save the child. On the other hand, it seems less plausible to say that John in the Sharks case should have tried to save the child, since he would have died (and not just failed) trying to save the child. It would seem a little unfair to blame him for not doing something that would have gotten him killed. Of course, he doesn't know about the Sharks, so in some sense it was a matter of luck that there was some obstacle that rendered him blameless for his laziness. (For more on moral luck, see Chapter 44.)

Fischer and Ravizza (1998, 126–27) also consider an example of refraining from doing something bad ("Flat Tire"). In this case, someone refrains from robbing a wealthy motorist who is stranded with a flat tire. Unbeknownst to them, the stranded car is being watched, and they would have been prevented from completing the robbery. So in this case there is also an obstacle, one that seems to result in a verdict of "not responsible" for failing to rob the motorist.

Taken together, these cases suggest that we are not responsible for refraining from an action if we can't perform that action (Fischer and Ravizza 1998, 127). If this is right, then there seems to be a puzzling asymmetry between actions and omissions. As we have seen in an earlier chapter (Chapter 16), someone can (arguably) be morally responsible for an action even though they couldn't have done otherwise; in other words, responsibility for actions might not require alternative possibilities. But the lesson of Sloth, Sharks, and similar cases seems to be that responsibility for omissions *does* require alternative possibilities. As Fischer and Ravizza put it, there is an asymmetry between positive agency and negative agency, at least when we are assigning moral responsibility.

RESPONSES

As Fischer (2017) acknowledges, various criticisms of the asymmetry claim convinced him to abandon it in favor of a view according to which both actions and omissions require mere guidance control, rather than regulative control. (For more on guidance control, see Chapter 18.) Criticisms of Fischer's more recent view can be found in Byrd (2007), Clarke (2014), Swenson (2015, 2016), and Sartorio (2016). Swenson (2015), for example, argues that reflection on omissions cases like Sloth and Sharks should cause us to doubt whether the Frankfurt-style cases (see Chapter 16) can serve as genuine counterexamples to the principle of alternative possibilities; and Swenson (2016) rejects some attempts to assuage those doubts. For a more general treatment of the metaphysics of omissions, see Bernstein (2015).

RECOMMENDED READING

Clarke, Randolph. 2014. *Omissions: Agency, Metaphysics, and Responsibility*, chapter 5. New York: Oxford University Press.
Fischer, John Martin, and Mark Ravizza. 1998. *Responsibility and Control: A Theory of Moral Responsibility*, chapter 5. Cambridge: Cambridge University Press.
Sartorio, Carolina. 2016. *Causation and Free Will*, chapter 2. New York: Oxford University Press.
Swenson, Philip. 2016. "The Frankfurt Cases and Responsibility for Omissions." *Philosophical Quarterly* 66: 579–95.

WORKS CITED

Bernstein, Sara. 2015. "The Metaphysics of Omissions." *Philosophy Compass* 10: 208–18.
Byrd, Jeremy. 2007. "Moral Responsibility and Omissions." *Philosophical Quarterly* 57: 56–67.
Fischer, John Martin. 2017. "Responsibility and Omissions." In *The Ethics and Law of Omissions*, edited by Dana Kay Nelkin and Samuel C. Rickless, 148–62. New York: Oxford University Press.
Swenson, Philip. 2015. "A Challenge for Frankfurt-Style Compatibilists." *Philosophical Studies* 172: 1279–85.

PROFESSOR PLUM'S UNFORTUNATE UPBRINGING

A MURDER MYSTERY

Imagine an extremely lifelike humanoid—so lifelike that nobody can tell the difference between him and an ordinary human. Let's call him "Professor Plum." Professor Plum was created by a team of neuroscientists and engineers who can control his every move. They have a rather dim view of human nature, so in trying to make him as human as possible they programmed Plum (and control him) so that he makes decisions on the basis of what will be best for him; in other words, he is an *egoist*.

Professor Plum (who we will hear more about below) is the protagonist of Derk Pereboom's four-case manipulation argument for incompatibilism. Although Pereboom wasn't the first to present such an argument, his version of the argument (which can be found in ch. 4 of Pereboom 2001) has probably become the most influential. Let's start with a simplified version of the argument:

(1) If an agent is manipulated into performing some action, then that agent is neither free nor responsible for the action (even if the action satisfies compatibilist conditions for acting freely).
(2) There is no freedom-relevant difference between manipulated agents and causally determined agents.

DOI: 10.4324/9781003126119-22

(3) Therefore, if an agent is causally determined to perform some action, then that agent is neither free nor responsible for that action (even if the action satisfies compatibilist conditions for acting freely).

In other words, Pereboom argues that compatibilists are in trouble because they are forced to say that some agents are still free in spite of being manipulated (which seems to be a ridiculous thing to have to say).

Let's take a closer look at the argument. Premise (1) seems hard to deny; manipulation, as noted above, is simply one of those things that obviously undermines free will. Of course, there are lots of difficult questions about *how much* and *what kinds* of manipulation are fatal to freedom, but for now we can just imagine a significant degree of manipulation that is well above the threshold for what undermines freedom. (We'll look at some different types of manipulation below.)

Premise (2) is where most of the action is. Why should we think that someone who's manipulated is in the same position (with respect to freedom) as someone who is causally determined? This is where Pereboom introduces four different cases, which center around someone (our very own Professor Plum) killing someone else (named White). Each of the cases differs slightly from the previous case, and together they represent something of a continuum from complete manipulation to causal determinism. In response to each case, the reader is invited to assent to the judgment that the agent in the case is neither free nor morally responsible for the action in question.

Here is a condensed version of each of the four cases, taken from McKenna and Pereboom (2016, 165–66):

> **Case 1**: Professor Plum was created by a team of neuroscientists, who can manipulate him directly through radio-like technology, but he is as much like an ordinary human being as is possible, given his history. The scientists "locally" manipulate him to undertake a process of reasoning, directly producing his every state moment by moment, which leads to the killing of White for egoistic reasons.
>
> **Case 2**: Plum is like an ordinary human being, except he was created by a team of neuroscientists who, although they cannot control him directly, have programmed him from the outset to weigh reasons for action so that he is often but not exclusively egoistic, with the result that in the circumstances he is causally determined to undertake the process that results in his killing White.

Case 3: Plum is an ordinary human being, except that he was determined by the rigorous training practices of his home and community so that he is often but not exclusively rationally egoistic (exactly as egoistic as in Cases 1 and 2). His training took place at too early an age for him to have had the ability to prevent or alter the practices that determined his character. In his current circumstances, Plum is thereby caused to undertake the process that results in his killing White.

Case 4: Physicalist determinism is true, and Plum is an ordinary human being, generated and raised under normal circumstances, who is often but not exclusively rationally egoistic (exactly as egoistic as in Cases 1–3). Plum's killing of White comes about as a result of his undertaking the relevant process.

With these cases in mind, we can construct a sub-argument in favor of (2):

(4) Plum is neither free nor responsible in Case 1.
(5) Case 2 is similar enough to Case 1 that we should say the same thing about Plum's freedom in Case 2 as we say about it in Case 1. (And the same holds for Cases 2 and 3, and Cases 3 and 4.)
(6) Therefore, Plum is neither free nor responsible in Case 4.

If (4) and (6) are both true, then we ought to make the same freedom judgment whether the agent is subject to manipulation or causal determinism. In other words, we now have support for

(2) There is no freedom-relevant difference between manipulated agents and causally determined agents.

Pereboom's argument, then, starts from a relatively uncontroversial claim about manipulation undermining freedom and gradually moves us to the incompatibilist conclusion that causal determinism also undermines freedom.

RESPONSES

Pereboom's argument has been widely discussed. (He presents an updated version of the four-case argument in Pereboom 2014, ch. 4.) There are basically two options for the compatibilist who wants to resist Pereboom's conclusion. First, she can claim that there *is* actually a relevant difference between Case 1 and Case 2, Case 2 and Case 3, or Case 3 and Case 4. In other words, she can deny (5) above. (And then of course she will need to explain what the relevant difference is, and which cases it affects). This is often called a *soft-line* reply. For example, someone might point out that there's an important difference between Case 2 and Case 3—namely that Case 3 involves a human whereas Case 2 does not—and then argue that that difference in turn makes a difference to what we say about free will in those cases.

Al Mele's (2006, 138–44) response to Pereboom's argument can be classified as a soft-line reply, although Mele appeals to more than just differences between pairs of cases. Mele points out that what Pereboom needs, in order for his argument to work, is for determinism to be the relevant factor in all the cases. And Pereboom would seem to agree: "The best explanation for the intuition that Plum is not morally responsible in the first three cases is that his action results from a deterministic causal process that traces back to factors beyond his control" (2001, 116). But if the presence of determinism is not essential to our reaction to the cases, then it's hard to see why determinism would be the best explanation of our intuition that Plum isn't responsible. And, as it turns out, determinism is not in fact essential to the cases. Mele asks us to imagine variations on cases 1–3 in which the relevant processes operate exactly as described in Pereboom's original cases, except that those processes are indeterministic. The vast majority of the time, they operate as advertised; but in rare circumstances, the processes instead render Plum incapacitated. And again, whether or not the processes operate as usual or incapacitate Plum is undetermined. Now suppose that, in each of the modified cases, the processes operate as advertised. We still have the intuition that Plum is not responsible, but the case isn't deterministic so it can't be determinism that's driving the intuition. Mele's proposal is that it's simply the manipulation that Plum undergoes, and not anything about determinism, that explains our intuitions. And since that manipulation isn't present in Case 4, there's a relevant difference between Cases 3 and 4. Hence a soft-line reply. (For another soft-line reply, see Demetriou 2010.)

The second option is a *hard-line* reply, which essentially involves biting the bullet and arguing that, contrary to initial appearances, Plum is in fact responsible for freely murdering White. (The use of "hard-line" and "soft-line" to characterize replies to Pereboom traces back to Haji and Cuypers 2006.)

Perhaps the most influential version of the hard-line reply can be found in McKenna (2008). (For another hard-line reply, see Jeppsson 2020.) McKenna points out that the compatibilist can simply take the argument in (4)–(6) and run it in reverse:

(7) Plum is free and responsible in Case 4.
(8) Case 3 is similar enough to Case 4 that we should say the same thing about Plum's freedom in Case 3 as we say about it in Case 4. (And the same holds for Cases 2 and 3, and Cases 1 and 2.)
(9) Therefore, Plum is free and responsible in Case 1.

The incompatibilist is going to endorse (4), and therefore (6); but the compatibilist is going to endorse (7), and therefore (9). It would seem, then, that we have reached a stalemate.

RECOMMENDED READING

McKenna, Michael. 2008. "A Hard-Line Reply to Pereboom's Four-Case Manipulation Argument." *Philosophy and Phenomenological Research* 77: 142–59.

McKenna, Michael, and Derk Pereboom. 2016. *Free Will: A Contemporary Introduction*, chapter 7. New York: Routledge.

Mele, Alfred R. 2006. *Free Will and Luck*, chapter 6. New York: Oxford University Press.

WORKS CITED

Demetriou, Kristin. 2010. "The Soft-Line Solution to Pereboom's Four-Case Argument." *Australasian Journal of Philosophy* 88: 595–617.

Haji, Ishtiyaque, and Stefaan E. Cuypers. (2006). Hard- and soft-line responses to Pereboom's four-case manipulation argument. *Acta Analytica* 21: 19–35.

Jeppsson, Sofia. 2020. "The Agential Perspective: A Hard-Line Reply to the Four-Case Manipulation Argument." *Philosophical Studies* 177: 1935–51.

Pereboom, Derk. 2001. *Living Without Free Will*. Cambridge: Cambridge University Press.

Pereboom, Derk. 2014. *Free Will, Agency, and Meaning in Life*. New York: Oxford University Press.

ROLLING BACK AND REPLAYING THE UNIVERSE

WALKING HOME AFTER THE LECTURE

Imagine a world in which reality is like a video that gets rolled back and replayed over and over again. The interesting thing about this simple thought experiment is that it has been used to argue for very different positions in the free will debate. William James, in "The dilemma of determinism," uses it as a sort of defense of libertarianism:

> What is meant by saying that my choice of which way to walk home after the lecture is ambiguous and [a] matter of chance as far as the present moment is concerned? It means that both Divinity Avenue and Oxford Street are called; but that only one, and that ... *either* one, shall be chosen. Now, I ask you seriously to suppose that this ambiguity of my choice is real; and then to make the impossible hypothesis that the choice is made twice over, and each time falls on a different street. In other words, imagine that I first walk through Divinity Avenue, and then imagine that the powers governing the universe annihilate ten minutes of time with all that it contained, and set me back at the door of this hall just as I was before the choice was made. Imagine then that, everything else being the same, I now make a different choice and traverse Oxford Street. You, as passive spectators, look on and see the two alternative universes—one of them with me walking through Divinity Avenue in it, the other with the same me walking through Oxford Street. Now, if you are determinists, you believe one of these universes to have been from eternity impossible:

DOI: 10.4324/9781003126119-23

> you believe it to have been impossible because of the intrinsic irrationality or accidentality somewhere involved in it. But looking outwardly at these universes, can you say which is the impossible and accidental one, and which the rational and necessary one?
>
> (James 1956 [1884], 155–56)

How is this a defense of libertarianism? Well, James is responding to the determinist's complaint that, if indeterminism were true, then events (including our actions) would be subject to a sort of randomness that would undermine our freedom (cf. Chapter 11). He uses this example to argue that we have no reason to believe that indeterminism would be anything like freedom-undermining randomness.

Suppose that the Divinity Avenue universe is the one that's determined to take place. If that's true, and if indeterminism is a problem, then it would seem that any other course of events (e.g., one including the Oxford Street route) would be random—chaotic—in a freedom-undermining way. And if a course of events is chaotic in a freedom-undermining way, then we should be able to observe at least some of the chaos. But, says James, there's nothing we can observe about the alternative course of events that gives us any indication of a threat to freedom: "In other words, either universe *after the fact* … would, to our means of observation and understanding, appear just as rational as the other" (James 1956 [1884], 156). Thus, the complaint about indeterminism is not justified.

James invites us to imagine a situation in which a hypothetical choice is "made twice over"; I described it as a situation in which reality gets rolled back and replayed. Let's call any argument that appeals to this type of rolling back and replaying as a "rollback argument." Thus, James uses a rollback argument in support of libertarianism—or, more precisely, in support of the claim that there's no reason to be concerned about the indeterminism that would have to be true if libertarianism is true.

Without taking a stand on the ultimate prospects of James's argument, we can note the puzzling fact that rollback arguments have also been used to argue *against* libertarianism. Suppose that we rolled back and replayed the universe 1 million (or more) times, each time observing the route that James chooses on his way home. If indeterminism is true, then there's no way to reliably predict how many times James would choose Divinity Avenue and how many times he would choose Oxford Street. Even if we held fixed *every single detail* about James and his surroundings leading up to his choice, we still wouldn't be able to predict it. Roderick Chisholm, himself a libertarian, endorses this way of talking about free choices in general:

> No set of statements about a man's desires, beliefs, and stimulus situation at any time implies any statement telling us what the man will try, set out, or undertake to do at that time. ... For at times the agent, if he chooses, may rise above his desires and do something else instead.
> (Chisholm 2003 [1964], 12)

This way of thinking about choices, according to the rollback argument against libertarianism, makes it hard to see how they can be free.

Why is that? Well, the desires and beliefs that Chisholm refers to (together perhaps with other psychological states, including the psychological states that make up someone's character) are supposed to be what *explain* someone's free choices. My choice to drink a cup of coffee (for example) can't be free unless it is the result of my beliefs, desires, and other mental states in the right kind of way. (Perhaps more is required for freedom, but this much at least is required for freedom.) If you can't point to any beliefs and desires that made a difference to my choice to drink the coffee, then you should doubt whether it was actually free. But that seems to be precisely our predicament with respect to James's route choices (and choices in general, on the libertarian view). Since identical sets of beliefs and desires produce different choices (depending on which replay we're looking at), there doesn't seem to be anything among those beliefs and desires that makes the difference between, say, choosing Divinity Avenue and choosing Oxford Street.

This argument is one member of a broader family of *luck arguments against libertarianism*. Luck arguments start with the assumption that luck is incompatible with free will, and then argue that the indeterminism that's required for libertarianism infuses our choices with luck.

RESPONSES

One initial response to the luck argument might be to say that free choices in an indeterministic world are not in fact fundamentally unpredictable, because if we were to replay them over and over again, they would gradually converge toward a set of objective probabilities. For example, if we replayed James's choice enough times, perhaps it turns out that he chooses Divinity Avenue 78% of the time and Oxford Street 22% of the time. His choice might seem random in any given replay, but the probabilities will eventually converge toward 0.78 and 0.22. (Similarly, the result of any given coin toss might seem random, but given enough tosses the ratio of heads to tails will approach 50/50.)

At this point it seems that the libertarian faces a dilemma: if we were to roll back and replay the universe over and over again, it's either impossible to predict what an agent will do, or there is an objective probability that can be assigned to each possible choice. But fundamental unpredictability doesn't seem to be consistent with free will (for the reasons mentioned above), and our choices being governed by objective probabilities doesn't seem to be consistent with free will either.

Mele (2006) provides a comprehensive treatment of the luck problem for libertarians (see especially his chapters 3 and 5). The basic idea behind Mele's proposed solution is that an agent can exercise partial control over the objective probabilities that govern her actions, in virtue of making prior free choices. This, of course, leaves open the question of how she can be in control of the first choice for which she is morally responsible. Mele answers that whenever that first responsible choice occurs (probably at some point in young childhood), the standards for moral responsibility are going to be lower than they are for fully formed adult choices. Thus, there will be early choices for which there is just enough control to launch the child onto a trajectory of making responsible choices and influencing the probabilities that in turn govern subsequent choices.

Franklin's (2011) response to the luck problem for libertarians includes the claim that we can provide a satisfactory explanation of undetermined actions even if we can't provide a *contrastive* explanation. (A contrastive explanation of why someone performed action A rather than action B would explain why she performed A rather than—in contrast to—B.) In particular, he argues that what gives someone the right kind of control over an action (and thus makes it free) may not enable a contrastive explanation; so perhaps there will be some free actions for which no contrastive explanation is available.

Nelkin (2011, ch. 6) also includes a helpful discussion of contrastive action explanation.

Lara Buchak (2012), in her discussion of the rollback argument, points out that part of what supports the argument is the claim that there is an objective probability that the action in question will occur. (This is the second horn of the dilemma considered above.) Buchak argues, however, that this assumption is unwarranted when applied to actions. There may not be any convergence toward an objective probability for a particular action, no matter how many times we replay the universe. She then suggests two ways in which the libertarian can adopt her response without being pushed back toward the first horn of the dilemma.

For additional discussion, see Almeida and Bernstein (2011) and Tognazzini (2015).

RECOMMENDED READING

Buchak, Lara. 2013. "Free Acts and Chance: Why the Rollback Argument Fails." *The Philosophical Quarterly* 63 (250): 20–28.

Chisholm, Roderick M. 2003 [1964]. "Human Freedom and the Self." In *Free Will*, 2nd edition, edited by Gary Watson, 26–37. Oxford: Oxford University Press.

Franklin, Christopher Evan. 2011. "Farewell to the Luck (and Mind) Argument." *Philosophical Studies* 156: 199–230.

James, William. 1956 [1884]. "The Dilemma of Determinism." In *The Will to Believe and Other Essays in Popular Philosophy*, 145–83. New York: Dover.

WORKS CITED

Almeida, Michael, and Mark Bernstein. 2011. "Rollbacks, Endorsements, and Indeterminism." In *The Oxford Handbook of Free Will*, 2nd edition, edited by Robert Kane, 484–95. New York: Oxford University Press.

Mele, Alfred R. 2006. *Free Will and Luck*. New York: Oxford University Press.

Nelkin, Dana Kay. 2011. *Making Sense of Freedom and Responsibility*. New York: Oxford University Press.

Tognazzini, Neal A. 2015. "Grounding the Luck Objection." *Australasian Journal of Philosophy* 93: 127–38.

SURVEYING THE FOLK

THE IMPORTANCE OF FOLK INTUITIONS

An important methodological question in philosophy is whether and to what extent our theorizing should be guided by everyday, commonsense beliefs and judgments. (These beliefs and judgments are sometimes collectively referred to as "folk intuitions.") However we end up answering this methodological question, folk intuitions will constitute an important data set that needs to be explained by our philosophical theories. Perhaps our theory agrees with folk intuitions, in which case it will shed some light on the relevant concepts at issue, explaining why we use those concepts in the way that we do and providing some additional analytical clarity to our folk understanding. Or perhaps our theory disagrees with folk intuitions, in which case we'll need to explain how our commonsense beliefs and judgments have been led astray. (This latter explanation is sometimes called an "error theory," i.e., an explanation of how and why certain beliefs and judgments are in error.) Thus, folk intuitions are an important data set for the free will debate as well. If folk intuition strongly favors either compatibilism or incompatibilism, then that's something that needs to be taken into account in our theorizing.

Until recently, there has been very little systematic examination of folk intuitions about free will, and in particular whether or not the folk tend to think that free will is compatible with determinism. Philosophers who speak to large audiences, whether inside or outside of

DOI: 10.4324/9781003126119-24

the classroom, will have a sense of what their audience thinks about the compatibility question, but these observations may not generalize very well. Part of the reason for this failure to generalize is that the way the free will debate is presented could affect the judgments that these audiences express. To get a more accurate sense of folk intuitions, we would need to provide a thought experiment (or a set of thought experiments) that has at least two important features. First, each thought experiment needs to be one in which someone performs an action in a deterministic world. Second, the situation needs to be described in a way that doesn't prejudice the respondent toward either answer to the compatibility question.

This is precisely the approach taken by Eddy Nahmias and his co-authors in their 2006 paper. They point out that numerous philosophers have claimed that incompatibilism is the default position of the folk—that is, that folk intuitions tend to line up with the claims of incompatibilists (Nahmias et al. 2006, 29). Thus, Nahmias et al. frame their research as an answer to the question of whether incompatibilism is in fact intuitive. They take the claim that it *is* intuitive to be equivalent to the following prediction:

Prediction: When presented with a deterministic scenario, most people will judge that agents in such a scenario do not act of their own free will and are not morally responsible for their actions.

(Nahmias et al. 2006, 36)

Observations that align with this prediction confirm the claim that incompatibilism is intuitive, whereas observations that conflict with this prediction disconfirm the claim.

By way of testing this prediction, Nahmias and his coauthors came up with three different deterministic situations. In each of these situations, however, determinism is described in a different way. In the first, determinism is described in terms of perfectly accurate prediction; in the second, it's described in terms of restarting and replaying the universe; in the third, it's described in terms of complete causation. Here's the thought experiment involving accurate prediction:

Imagine that in the next century we discover all the laws of nature, and we build a supercomputer which can deduce from these laws of nature and from the current state of everything in the world exactly what will be happening in the world at any future time. It can look at everything about the way the world is and predict everything about how it will be with 100% accuracy. Suppose that such a supercomputer existed, and it looks at the state of the universe at a certain time on March 25, 2150 A.D., twenty years before Jeremy Hall is born. The computer then deduces from this information and the laws of nature that Jeremy will definitely rob Fidelity Bank at 6:00 p.m. on January 26, 2195. As always, the super-computer's prediction is correct; Jeremy robs Fidelity Bank at 6:00 pm on January 26, 2195.

(Nahmias et al. 2006, 87)

Participants were presented with this thought experiment and then asked whether Jeremy acted of his own free will when he robbed the bank. Recognizing that the depiction of a wrong action might influence the results, Nahmias et al. also presented two variations to different sets of participants: one involving a positive action (saving a child) and one involving a neutral action (going jogging). In each case, whether the action was morally negative, positive, or neutral, a significant majority of participants judged that Jeremy acted of his own free will, or was morally responsible for his action (Nahmias et al. 2006, 87). In both of the alternative scenarios (the replay scenario and the complete causation scenario), judgments about free will and moral responsibility were roughly the same: a significant majority of the participants agreed that the subjects in the scenarios acted freely and/or were morally responsible for their actions.

Based on these findings, it would seem that the prediction above is incorrect, and that compatibilism is actually the intuitive view.

RESPONSES

The results described above were disputed in Nichols and Knobe (2007), who argue that folk intuitions are neither compatibilist nor incompatibilist in general. Rather, people's intuitive responsibility judgments tend to incline toward compatibilism or incompatibilism depending on how the relevant cases are described. If they are de-scribed abstractly, then people tend to give incompatibilist responses; but if they are described more concretely, then people tend to give compatibilist responses (so they would join Nahmias et al. in rejecting the prediction above, but for different reasons). Vargas (2006) suspects that we might also see variation in answers between different groups (e.g., between members of different religious traditions).

The next project, then, would be to try and figure out what psychological mechanisms are producing these differences, and whether the details of these mechanisms give us insight into the correctness or centrality of either set of intuitions. (Nichols and Knobe argue that responses to abstract cases are more indicative of the folk *theory* of moral responsibility, which would mean the incompatibilist intuitions are more central to the folk conception of free will.) Murray and Nahmias (2014) respond by reporting on some further studies in which it appears that the folk are more worried about *bypassing* than about determinism. When people are presented with cases in which the deterministic causes of action somehow bypass an agent's mental states, then they respond with incompatibilist judgments; but when people are presented with cases in which deterministic causes pass through the agent's own mental states, they respond with compatibilist judgments.

It appears that we are left with the unsatisfying conclusion that it's not yet clear what consensus, if any, can be drawn from folk judgments about free will. (See Vargas 2013, ch. 1 and Björnsson and Pereboom 2016 for confirmation of this observation; see Sommers 2010 for a "sympathetic critique" of the studies mentioned in this chapter.)

RECOMMENDED READING

Björnsson, Gunnar, and Derk Pereboom. 2016. "Traditional and Experimental Approaches to Free Will and Moral Responsibility." In *Companion to Experimental Philosophy*, edited by Justin Sytsma and Wesley Buckwalter, 142–57. Malden, MA: Wiley-Blackwell.

Sommers, Tamler. 2010. "Experimental Philosophy and Free Will." *Philosophy Compass* 5: 199–212.

Vargas, Manuel. 2013. *Building Better Beings: A Theory of Moral Responsibility*, chapter 1. Oxford: Oxford University Press.

WORKS CITED

Murray, Dylan, and Eddy Nahmias. 2014. "Explaining Away Incompatibilist Intuitions." *Philosophy and Phenomenological Research* 88: 434–67.

Nahmias, Eddy, Stephen G. Morris, Thomas Nadelhoffer, and Jason Turner. 2006. "Is Incompatibilism Intuitive?" *Philosophy and Phenomenological Research* 73: 28–53.

Nichols, Shaun, and Joshua Knobe. 2007. "Moral Responsibility and Determinism: The Cognitive Science of Folk Intuitions." *Noûs* 41: 663–85.

Vargas, Manuel. 2006. "Philosophy and the Folk: On Some Implications of Experimental Work for Philosophical Debates on Free Will." *Journal of Cognition and Culture* 6: 239–54.

METAPHYSICAL FLIP-FLOPPING

A STARTLING HEADLINE

Suppose that you wake up tomorrow and, as you're checking the news, you read a startling headline: DETERMINISM IS TRUE. As you read the article, it turns out that two different groups of physicists, working independently, have made the same discovery, and that discovery makes it clear that determinism is true. (This example is based on a similar story told by Fischer 1994, 191.)

Since libertarians about free will believe that free will exists but also that it's incompatible with determinism, they would be forced to make a choice. They would either have to give up on their belief in free will (and thus become hard determinists), or they would have to give up on their belief in incompatibilism (and thus become compatibilists). Compatibilists, on the other hand, could accept the news without changing their views at all. (More on this difference below.)

Peter van Inwagen is an example of an incompatibilist who has said that he would choose the second option, retaining his belief in free will but giving up on incompatibilism (1983, 219). John Martin Fischer and Mark Ravizza (who discuss this dilemma in the context of moral responsibility rather than free will) have described the second option as an objectionable type of "metaphysical flip-flopping":

> So, for example, Peter van Inwagen has argued forcefully that causal determinism is incompatible with moral responsibility. Since he is very confident that we are indeed morally responsible, he concludes that

DOI: 10.4324/9781003126119-25

causal determinism must be false. But he says that, in the unlikely event he were convinced that causal determinism were true, he would probably reconsider his position that causal determinism is incompatible with moral responsibility!

(Fischer and Ravizza 1998, 253–54)

The reason why Fischer finds this objectionable is that it seems to make a metaphysical view depend on an apparently independent empirical thesis. The compatibility question is a question about whether there's a possible world in which both determinism is true and free will exists. Why should a fact about the physical structure of the actual world make a difference to a claim that there is or is not a different world in which both determinism and freedom exist?

We can generalize these considerations to make a methodological point about philosophical theories. Consider, for example, Descartes' account of human personhood as found in his *Treatise of Man*. He is aiming to give an account of the body and its operations, and he thought that the pineal gland was involved in several important bodily operations—including sensation, imagination, and memory.

Let's focus on the phenomenon of sensation. Any theory of sensation is going to need to explain the data, which include our experiences of sensation and our widely held commonsense beliefs about sensation. (This doesn't mean that a theory of sensation needs to *endorse* all of our commonsense beliefs; but if it's going to reject a commonsense belief, then its explanation of the data needs to include a hypothesis about why and how common sense went wrong.) A theory of sensation is also going to have to make reference to the faculties that are at work in instances of sensation, and perhaps to some physical attributes that enable those faculties.

Now consider Descartes' theory of sensation, which relied upon some very specific claims about the pineal gland. If these claims turned out to be wrong (as they did), then his theory would be undermined. An alternative theory of sensation that didn't depend on any claims about the pineal gland would be more *resilient* than Descartes' theory. (This is assuming that both theories do a roughly equally good job of explaining the data.) It's not that it would be more resilient in the sense that people would have a harder time giving up on the belief; it would be more resilient in the sense that it could encounter more empirical opposition without crumbling. This alternative theory doesn't care, so to speak, whether or not brain science learns new things about the pineal gland because none of its details involve the pineal gland.

Perhaps another way to think about this is in terms of theoretical *demandingness*. Descartes' theory of sensation made various demands upon the world, including the demand that the pineal gland operate in a certain way. A rival theory of sensation that doesn't make any demands of the pineal gland is going to have a better chance of being true in virtue of being less demanding. Descartes' theory is dependent upon other claims about the pineal gland, whereas the rival theory is not subject to these dependencies.

It seems then, that theoretical resilience (like resilience in general) is a good thing. If two competitor theories are roughly equally good at explaining the data, but one of the theories is significantly more resilient—or significantly less demanding—than the other, then we have a reason to think that the resilient theory is more likely to be true. (So resilience resembles the theoretical virtue of simplicity: simpler theories are more likely to be true (other things being equal), and the same can be said for resilient theories.)

The claim here is not that Descartes should have known better about the pineal gland. (Although Gert-Jan Lokhorst 2021 has argued that, in fact, Descartes should have known better.) Instead, the claim is that Descartes' theory would have been stronger if it hadn't been so tightly wedded to empirical claims about specific bodily organs. (And although we are making the point with the benefit of hindsight, it's a point that also could have been made by a contemporary of Descartes.) Sensation probably requires some sort of connection to the body, so a good theory of sensation will reflect that; but too much detail about the specific mechanisms of sensation will render the theory especially vulnerable to empirical refutation.

For similar reasons, Fischer (2012a, 2012b) has argued that one of our criteria for evaluating different accounts of responsibility should involve theoretical resilience: in particular, an adequate theory of moral responsibility should be resilient with respect to empirical discoveries about determinism or indeterminism. If our theory of moral responsibility—and thus our view of humans as morally responsible agents who are appropriate subjects of praise, blame, and other reactive attitudes—would be undermined by the empirical discovery that the world is fundamentally deterministic (or indeterministic), then there's an important sense in which moral responsibility "hangs on a thread." And, argues Fischer, moral responsibility shouldn't hang on a thread.

RESPONSES

As Timpe (2013, 143–44) has pointed out, the resilience criterion cuts against some compatibilist views as well. For example, soft determinism—the view that free will is not only compatible with determinism but *requires* determinism—suffers from a lack of resilience just as much as libertarianism does. Both views require that causation operate in a certain way; they just differ about what that way is.

Bailey and Seymour (2021) offer a sustained defense of the flip-flopping libertarian. On their view, a disposition to flip-flop is simply an implicit acknowledgment that the evidence for free will is stronger than the evidence for incompatibilism. If we get new evidence telling us that determinism is true, then the rational thing to do is give up on incompatibilism. And as long as the evidence for free will is *independent* of the evidence for incompatibilism, then we don't need to take the hypothetical discovery of (the truth of) determinism into account as we evaluate different theories of free will.

We noted above that theoretical resilience is analogous to theoretical simplicity: both are theoretical virtues in the sense that, other things being equal, a theory that possesses the virtue is more likely to be true. Thus we may be able to glean insights from discussions of theoretical simplicity and apply them to questions about theoretical resilience. For a comprehensive recent treatment of theoretical simplicity, see Sober (2015).

RECOMMENDED READING

Bailey, Andrew M., and Amy Seymour. 2021. "In Defense of Flip-Flopping." *Synthese*.
Fischer, John Martin. 1994. *The Metaphysics of Free Will: An Essay on Control*. Oxford: Blackwell.

WORKS CITED

Descartes, René. 1972 [1664]. *Treatise of Man*. Translated by Thomas S. Hall. Cambridge, MA: Harvard University Press.

Fischer, John Martin. 2012a. "Deep Control: The Middle Way." In *Deep Control: Essays on Free Will and Value*, 3–29. New York: Oxford University Press.

Fischer, John Martin. 2012b. "Indeterminism and Control: An Approach to the Problem of Luck." In *Deep Control: Essays on Free Will and Value*, 85–105. New York: Oxford University Press.

Fischer, John Martin, and Mark Ravizza. 1998. *Responsibility and Control: A Theory of Moral Responsibility*. Cambridge: Cambridge University Press.

Lokhorst, Gert-Jan. 2021. "Descartes and the Pineal Gland." In *The Stanford Encyclopedia of Philosophy*, edited by Edward N. Zalta, Winter 2021. https://plato.stanford.edu/archives/win2021/entries/pineal-gland.

Sober, Elliott. 2015. *Ockham's Razors: A User's Manual*. Cambridge: Cambridge University Press.

Timpe, Kevin. 2013. *Free Will: Sourcehood and Its Alternatives*, 2nd edition. London: Bloomsbury.

van Inwagen, Peter. 1983. *An Essay on Free Will*. Oxford: Clarendon Press.

THE FUNDAMENTAL FREE WILL PUZZLE?

A TENSION BETWEEN SUBJECTIVE AND OBJECTIVE PERSPECTIVES

Many of the puzzles that we have been looking at depend on specific details of the situation described: what kinds of causes are at work, how an agent's psychology is structured, whether an action is predictable, and so on. In this chapter we will step back and take a broader look at the free will problem as a more general puzzle, independently of any of the details of a specific thought experiment. In so doing, we will borrow from Thomas Nagel, who is one of the most insightful big-picture thinkers in recent history.

In chapter 14 of his *Mortal Questions*, Nagel attempts to characterize a common structure or pattern that can be found in various perennial philosophical debates. He describes this common thread as a tension between a *subjective* point of view and an *objective* point of view:

> There is a tendency to seek an objective account of everything before admitting its reality. But often what appears to a more subjective point of view cannot be accounted for in this way. So either the objective conception of the world is incomplete, or the subjective involves illusions that should be rejected.
>
> (Nagel 1979, 196)

DOI: 10.4324/9781003126119-26

As Nagel acknowledges, to describe *the* subjective and *the* objective point of view is misleading. Instead there is a continuum ranging from radically narrow subjectivity on one end to completely detached objectivity on the other end. Any two perspectives can be compared with respect to their relative subjectivity or objectivity. The tension arises when two perspectives that are located at different points on the continuum wrestle, so to speak, for priority: "The opposition between subjective and objective can arise at any place on the spectrum where one point of view claims dominance over another, more subjective one, and that claim is resisted" (1979, 206).

One of the areas in which this pattern arises is the problem of free will. Nagel describes what happens to our attempts to theorize about free will as we shift from the subjective to the objective perspective:

> But the problem is not that the idea of agency clashes with this or that particular conception of what happens in action, viewed externally as a type of event. It is not predictability that creates the problem, for I make many choices and do many things that are completely predictable. It is just that when I pick the shiny apple instead of the rotten one, it is *my doing*—and there is no room for this in an external account of the event, deterministic or not. The real problem stems from a clash between the view of action from inside and *any* view of it from outside. Any external view of an act as something that happens, with or without causal antecedents, seems to omit the doing of it.
>
> Even if an action is described in terms of motives, reasons, abilities, absence of impediments or coercion, this does not capture the agent's own idea of himself as its source. His actions appear to him different from other things that happen in the world, but not merely a different kind of happening, with different causes or none at all. They seem in some indescribable way not to *happen* at all (unless they are quite out of his control), though things happen when he does them. And if he sees others as agents too, their actions will seem to have the same quality. The tendency to express this conception of agency in terms of freedom from antecedent causes is a mistake, but an understandable one. When the act is viewed under the aspect of determination by antecedents, its status as an event becomes prominent. But as appears upon further investigation, no account of it as an event is satisfactory from the internal viewpoint of the agent doing it.
>
> (Nagel 1979, 198–99)

Here we see the general pattern of opposition mentioned above: An abstract, external perspective on actions treats them as events, whether determined or not. And if someone tries to assert the dominance of that external perspective, proponents of the more concrete subjective perspective resist that assertion, because it is inconsistent with our view of actions as our doings, having their source in us.

In addition to the free will problem, Nagel identifies four other examples that illustrate the tension between objectivity and subjectivity: the meaning of life, personal identity, the mind-body problem, and consequentialist (as opposed to agent-centered) views of right and wrong. The problem of free will, however, is unique, because both facts and values are lost in the abstraction process:

> The trouble occurs when the objective view encounters something, revealed subjectively, that it cannot accommodate. Its claims to comprehensiveness will then be threatened. The indigestible lump may be either a fact or a value. The problems of personal identity and mind-body arise because certain subjectively apparent facts about the self seem to vanish as one ascends to a more objective standpoint. The problems about consequentialism and the meaning of life arise from a corresponding disappearance of certain personal values with the ascent to a more and more detached and impersonal point of view. The problem of free will combines both effects.
>
> (Nagel 1979, 210)

Nagel doesn't explicitly characterize the fact(s) and value(s) that are lost in the process of taking a more objective perspective on free will. But we can infer from what's quoted above that the relevant "facts about the self" have to do with our selves as the *source* of our actions, which is what makes them belong to us. And a brief earlier mention of moral responsibility sheds light on which personal values are lost in the abstraction process:

> The connection of this problem with moral responsibility is that when we view actions, our own or others', merely as part of the general course of events, it seems impossible to attribute them to individuals in a way that makes sense of the attitudes we take toward someone we regard as the source of an action. Certain attitudes toward the agent, rather than just about him, lose their footing.
>
> (Nagel 1979, 199)

The relevant values, then, are the values that are bound up in a certain set of attitudes (often called the *reactive attitudes*) and the expectations that give rise to those reactive attitudes. For example, it is our expectation of good will that, when violated, tends to give rise to resentment. (For more on the reactive attitudes, see Chapter 38.)

RESPONSES

Nagel offers some additional reflections on this fundamental puzzle in chapter 7 of *The View from Nowhere*, in which he strikes an even more pessimistic tone:

> I change my mind about the problem of free will every time I think about it, and therefore cannot offer any view with even moderate confidence; but my present opinion is that nothing that might be a solution has yet been described. This is not a case where there are several possible candidate solutions and we don't know which is correct. It is a case where nothing believable has (to my knowledge) been proposed by anyone in the extensive public discussion of the subject.
>
> (Nagel 1986, 112)

The problem, argues Nagel, is that we can't shake the threat of the external perspective (compatibilist accounts of freedom are implausible) but we also can't articulate the internal perspective in a coherent way ("it is impossible to give a coherent account of the internal view of action which is under threat") (Nagel 1986, 113). As McKenna and Pereboom (2016, 56) point out, Nagel seems to be saying that free will is incompatible with *both* determinism *and* indeterminism. Although a few philosophers (e.g., Pereboom 2001) have arrived at similar conclusions, most prefer to argue either that a compatibilist account is plausible, or that a libertarian account can be made coherent.

Peter van Inwagen (2008) concurs, broadly speaking, with Nagel's way of characterizing the fundamental free will puzzle. On his view, we are faced with an apparently sound argument that free will is incompatible with determinism, but also an apparently sound argument that free will is incompatible with *in*determinism. Although he doesn't put the point in terms of Incompatibilist Mountain (see Chapter 13), we could say that both the ascent problem and the descent problem seem unsolvable. But if free will is incompatible with both determinism and indeterminism, then free will is impossible; and if free will is impossible, then nobody is ever at fault for anything.

> These are the three arguments that create the problem of free will. Each of them is *prima facie* correct, but at least one of them must contain some error. But which? And where does the error (or where do the errors) lie? That is the problem of free will.

(van Inwagen 2008, 340)

RECOMMENDED READING

Nagel, Thomas. 1979. "Subjective and Objective." In *Mortal Questions*, 207–22. Cambridge: Cambridge University Press.

O'Connor, Timothy, and Christopher Franklin. 2021. "Free Will." In *The Stanford Encyclopedia of Philosophy*, edited by Edward N. Zalta, Spring 2021. https://plato.stanford.edu/archives/spr2021/entries/freewill.

van Inwagen, Peter. 2008. "How to Think About the Problem of Free Will." *Journal of Ethics* 12: 327–41.

WORKS CITED

McKenna, Michael, and Derk Pereboom. 2016. *Free Will: A Contemporary Introduction*. New York: Routledge.

Nagel, Thomas. 1986. *The View from Nowhere*. Oxford: Oxford University Press.

Pereboom, Derk. 2001. *Living Without Free Will*. Cambridge: Cambridge University Press.

PART III

PRACTICAL REASON

This part of the book represents a slight shift in focus. Rather than focusing on threats to free will—phenomena that give us reason to doubt the existence of free will—we're going to focus on more general questions about *practical reason*. (Although a few threats will arise as well.) Practical reason(ing) is simply reasoning about what to *do*. (It stands in contrast to theoretical reasoning, which is reasoning about what to *believe*.) Thus, the chapters in this section ask questions about the extent of our free choices, the value of our free choices, and the explanation of our free choices. (For the most part we will simply take for granted that we sometimes choose freely, and then explore puzzles that arise in light of this assumption.)

We'll begin in Chapter 25, "Freedom to Choose the Good," with a question about what makes free will valuable. Is it the ability to do otherwise? This is perhaps the default view. But as we will see, there is some psychological research that prompts us to look for alternative accounts of what we value in a free choice. Asking these questions about value prompts us to reflect (and introspect) on our own experience of acting freely, and of our agency more broadly. Of course, there's no guarantee that our perception of our own agency is accurate; so in Chapter 26 ("Is Conscious Choice an Illusion?") we will briefly look at some lab experiments that appear to undermine these

DOI: 10.4324/9781003126119-27

perceptions. The good news (at least for those of us who believe in free will) is that the current state of scientific research doesn't appear to give us a compelling reason to doubt the existence of free will.

In the next chapter ("The Daily Wavester") we will point out some surprising implications of the way we talk about our abilities. In certain situations, we are inclined to endorse the truth of certain subjunctive conditionals involving what we can and cannot do; but some of these conditionals conflict with our intuitions about the fixity of the past. But even if we ignore the type of counterfactual reasoning that brings out these tensions, we can still get into trouble just by examining the way that we tend to use *can*-claims (i.e., statements using the word "can"). We'll go looking for this trouble in Chapter 28 ("Reading *Emma*").

These puzzles about ability statements arise no matter what type of choice we are talking about, whether momentous or mundane. But we also might wonder whether there are specific features of a choice situation that make the choice more or less relevant to our freedom. Are the choices that we're torn about more relevant to our free will because they force us to wrestle with "competing sets of reasons" (Chapter 29)? Or are the choices that flow smoothly more relevant because they are more reflective of our character?

Sometimes we are torn over what choice to make because we are deliberating under duress. Chapter 30 ("The Captain in the Storm") considers choices made under various types of duress and asks about the effect of that duress on the voluntariness of the choice. Chapter 31 ("One Thought too Many?") also examines a choice made under duress, but the focus there has to do with the moral dimensions of the choice. What can we infer about a person's character from the details of their moral deliberation?

Having looked briefly at voluntariness, we now turn our attention to *intention*—and in particular to the explanation of intentional action. Chapter 32 ("The Anxious Mountaineer") raises a puzzle about how to explain intentional action with reference to the reasons for that action, and Chapter 33 ("Acting against Better Judgment") asks whether (and how) it's possible to intentionally act against one's better judgment. Finally, Chapter 34 ("An Impossible Intention?") presents a case in which it seems that a very simple intention is actually impossible to form (at least if one is committed to keeping one's intentions rational).

FREEDOM TO CHOOSE THE GOOD

THE PARADOX OF CHOICE

As we've noted in earlier chapters, one of the reasons we care about free will is that having free will makes us eligible for moral responsibility. This way of defining freedom highlights its connection to something else that's important and perhaps even more fundamental than free will (namely, our moral responsibility practices). But we can also define freedom, as we have also noted in earlier chapters, as the ability to do otherwise. This definition (which is more about free will itself, rather than the role it plays in securing other things) evokes the "garden of forking paths" that we explored in Chapter 1.

If the essence of free will is having alternatives, then it would seem to follow that more alternatives would mean more free will. And this does seem to be true in certain circumstances. There is a clear sense in which someone who has been accepted to three different colleges has more freedom (at least with respect to where she attends college) than someone who has only been accepted to two. And someone who has been accepted to 20 colleges would have even more freedom. There is a complicating factor, however, which is sometimes called *the paradox of choice*. Psychological studies have shown that too many choices can actually have a negative impact on well-being. Here's how Barry

DOI: 10.4324/9781003126119-28

Schwartz puts the point in his comprehensive treatment of choice and its effects on human psychology:

> The "success" of modernity turns out to be bittersweet, and everywhere we look it appears that a significant contributing factor is the overabundance of choice. Having too many choices produces psychological distress, especially when combined with regret, concern about status, adaptation, social comparison, and perhaps most important, the desire to have the best of everything ... having the opportunity to choose is essential for well-being, but choice has negative features, and the negative features escalate as the number of choices increases.
>
> (Schwartz 2004, 221–22)

By itself, this fact about human psychology doesn't imply anything about the metaphysics of free will. But these findings do introduce some tension into our commonsense way of thinking about free will. If free will is one of the most valuable things we possess as humans—and if it essentially involves alternative possibilities—then it seems odd that an increase in alternatives can so easily lead to negative effects.

RESPONSES

So, assuming that these findings about human psychology are accurate, how *should* they inform our understanding of free will? We could say that adding alternatives makes us more free up to a certain point (which might vary from person to person), but beyond that point additional alternatives actually diminish our freedom. Or we could say instead that adding alternatives increases freedom indefinitely, but also that freedom becomes more difficult with additional alternatives (past a certain point). On this understanding, there would be degrees of freedom that aren't accessible to us, given our limitations as humans.

But perhaps these findings should prompt a more radical approach. What if the focus on alternatives, this picture of a garden of forking paths, is fundamentally mistaken?

Suppose that you are a piano player who has been invited to play at Carnegie Hall. You spend months working up the piece you'll be playing, endlessly practicing so that your performance will be as close to perfect as possible. Now imagine, on the eve of your performance, that God appears to you and gives you a choice: Would you rather retain your current abilities with respect to the piano piece you'll be playing, or would you rather be slightly transformed so that you can't help but play it perfectly? Playing the piano wouldn't feel any different (for example, you would still feel fully aware and in control of your actions)—it's just that you wouldn't be able to make a mistake. Your only option would be perfection. Would you accept this offer? How difficult would it be to decide?

There's a lot of value in musical performance, but there are other types of human performance that are even more valuable. Arguably the most valuable type of performance is *moral* performance: engaging in the types of activities and ways of being that are characteristic of moral excellence. So now consider an even more striking divine offer: you can retain your current moral abilities and propensities, or you can be transformed so that you invariably make the morally superior choice. Your only option would be moral perfection. Would you accept this offer? How difficult would it be to decide?

If you feel any pull toward accepting the offer of moral perfection, then that provides at least some evidence that alternative possibilities are not the only thing that we value about free will. Perhaps alternatives are not even the *main* thing we value about free will.

One person who would presumably accept the offer of moral perfection is Saint Augustine (although perhaps "not yet"). In certain places at least, Augustine describes the pinnacle of freedom not as the ability to do otherwise, but as the ability to *choose the good*. For example, Jesse Couenhoven cites a passage from Augustine in which he's discussing divine freedom:

> If only that one is free which is able to will two things, that is, good and evil, God is not free, since he cannot will evil ... are you going to praise God in such a way that you take away his freedom? Or should you not rather understand that there is a certain blessed necessity by which God cannot be unjust?
> (*Unfinished Work Against Julian*, as cited in Couenhoven 2012, 401)

According to this passage, God is free even when he doesn't have alternatives; thus alternatives cannot be the essence of divine freedom. And presumably Augustine would say that divine freedom is the ideal freedom, to which humans should aspire. Couenhoven refers to this conception of freedom as *normative* freedom.

There is definitely something attractive about the ability to choose the good, but many would see normative freedom as having two strikes against it: first because it is heavily dependent on at least some of the tenets of Christian theism, and second because it implies compatibilism.

In response to the second challenge, Timpe (2017) has argued for a normative conception of freedom that is consistent with libertarianism. On this view, someone can be morally responsible for choosing the good despite not being able to choose otherwise, but only if the choice in question ultimately traces back to a character-forming action that wasn't determined. (Timpe here is building on the "virtue libertarianism" of Dean Zimmerman 2012.)

In response to the first challenge, note that the core idea of normative freedom—the claim that the essence of freedom is an ability to choose the good—need not depend on any theistic claims. For example, Susan Wolf (1990) has developed a normative theory of freedom that doesn't make use of any theistic starting points. She understands free will as an ability that renders us eligible for moral responsibility, and she argues that the relevant ability is "the ability to act in accordance with Reason," which is "the ability to act in accordance with, and on the basis of, the True and the Good" (Wolf 1990, 71).

It would seem, then, that we are faced with competing visions of free will at its finest. According to the alternative possibilities vision, the essence and ideal of free choice is the ability to choose between alternatives. To be the most free is to have the best (not necessarily the most!) access to alternatives. Because some alternatives are worse than others, this conception of free will entails imperfection. The competitor view is the normative vision. According to the normative vision, the essence and ideal of free choice is the ability to choose the good. To be the most free is to invariably choose the good.

RECOMMENDED READING

Couenhoven, Jesse. 2012. "The Necessities of Perfect Freedom." *International Journal of Systematic Theology* 14: 396–419.
Wolf, Susan. 1990. *Freedom within Reason.* Oxford: Oxford University Press.

WORKS CITED

Schwartz, Barry. 2004. *The Paradox of Choice*. London: HarperCollins.

Timpe, Kevin. 2017. "The Best Thing in Life Is Free: The Compatibility of Divine Freedom and God's Essential Moral Perfection." In *Free Will and Classical Theism: The Significance of Freedom in Perfect Being Theology*, edited by Hugh J. McCann, 133–51. Oxford: Oxford University Press.

Zimmerman, Dean. 2012. "An Anti-Molinist Replies." In *Molinism: The Contemporary Debate*, edited by Ken Perszyk, 163–86. Oxford: Oxford University Press.

IS CONSCIOUS CHOICE AN ILLUSION?

LIBET'S (ACTUAL) EXPERIMENT(S)

This book focuses on thought experiments, which take place primarily in the imagination rather than in a lab. This reliance on imagination, however, doesn't mean that thought experiments can't be rigorous or valuable; see Williamson (2016) on some ways in which imagination leads to knowledge. (Williamson (2010) also offers a short defense of the value of imagination, intended for a popular audience.) But the experiments that are the subject of this chapter are in fact lab experiments, which purport to have some troubling implications for free will. The most famous of these experiments were conducted by a neuroscientist named Benjamin Libet (1985, 2004).

Alfred Mele provides a helpful summary of Libet's experiments:

> Libet's main innovation ... was a method for timing conscious experiences that could then be correlated with measurable brain events. He was particularly interested in experiences of urges, intentions, or decisions. Participants in the experiments were instructed to flex a wrist whenever they felt like it and then report a bit later on when they first became conscious of their intention or urge to do the flexing. ... Readings of electrical conductivity were taken from the scalp, using EEG (electroencephalogram) technology. Brain activity involves measurable

DOI: 10.4324/9781003126119-29

electricity—more in some places, depending on what parts of the brain are most active.

(Mele 2014, 8–9)

Other studies using EEG measurements have shown that brain activity increases in the moments leading up to an intentional bodily movement. In other words, agents exhibit what has been called *readiness potential* prior to intentional movement. So Libet wanted to measure the presence of readiness potential and then compare that to agential awareness of deliberation and decision, as reported by the agents themselves. These experiments delivered some surprising observations: the relevant brain activity increased *prior* to the agent's indication of decision awareness. Libet (and others since Libet) have taken this to mean that we don't have free will, because our conscious choices seem to lag behind our brain activity. (This conclusion has made quite a splash in the popular press. See, for example, Overbye (2007) and Cave (2016); but see Nahmias (2011) and Gholipour (2019) for rebuttals.)

Libet's experiments appear to show, in other words, that our brain is making our choices prior to our conscious awareness of them. What the subjects identify as the initiator of their choice appears to come after some prior factor, which would seem to make *that* factor the initiator of our choice instead. And if we don't initiate our own choices then it seems that those choices aren't as free as we think they are.

RESPONSES

By themselves, these experiments don't have any implications for free will. Thus, in order to understand how to respond to the challenge they represent, we need to look at more of the argument. The way to show how these experiments (or any other scientific experiments) might have implications for free will is to connect them with a bridge principle, or a set of bridge principles, specifying what a particular empirical finding has to do with the metaphysics of free will. For example, a principle that says something like, "If an experiment has such-and-such results, then so-and-so is true about free will." Putting together the reported results of Libet's experiments with this type of bridge principle, we can articulate Libet's challenge in the form of the following simple argument:

(1) Libet's experiments show that our choices are made unconsciously, before we're aware of them.
(2) If our choices are made unconsciously, before we're aware of them, then free will is an illusion.
(3) Therefore, free will is an illusion.

Unfortunately for this argument, there are significant problems with both premises.

As Mele points out (2014, 12–15), there are at least two problems with (1). First, the presence of readiness potential prior to conscious awareness of a choice doesn't show that our choices are made unconsciously. It's possible, for example, that readiness potential shows up in lots of situations, but only some of those situations culminate in choices. On this picture—which is a plausible and natural picture (readiness, after all, doesn't always lead to action)—we are getting ready to make decisions all the time, but we don't always convert that readiness potential into action. Until this possibility is ruled out, we have reason to doubt the truth of (1).

Another problem with (1) is that the type of choice measured in the experiments (flexing one's wrist at an arbitrary time) isn't really representative of a choice that involves a deliberative weighing of reasons. In order to accept (1), we would also need some reasons to think that the choices observed in the experiments are representative of all of our apparently free choices.

Let's now examine (2). It would seem that it's relatively easy to devise a counterexample to this premise (cf. Mele 2014, 15–17). Suppose that we deliberate rationally and consciously, and that those deliberations generate a free choice. As it happens, our brain architecture is set up so that the decision is actually made before we're aware of it, but it's still the result of a rational deliberation process that, when unfettered, generates a free choice. In this situation, we make unconscious choices but free will is not an illusion.

So it would appear that Libet's ambitious conclusion is not supported by his experiments. (For a different way of resisting the argument, see Herdova 2016.) This doesn't, of course, mean that the experiments should be ignored, or even that they don't represent a challenge to free will. Like any good input in the free will debate, they should prompt us to think longer and harder about free will and its relationship to the persons who (appear to) exercise it. For a comprehensive recent engagement with these types of questions (in light of Libet's work), see Sinnott-Armstrong and Nadel (2011).

RECOMMENDED READING (OR LISTENING)

Cyr, Taylor, and Matthew Flummer. 2013. "The Free Will Show: Episode 22: The Libet Experiment with Tim Bayne." https://podcasts.apple.com/us/podcast/episode-22-the-libet-experiment-with-tim-bayne/id1525456786?i=1000532793073.

Mele, Alfred R. 2014. *Free: Why Science Hasn't Disproved Free Will*. New York: Oxford University Press.

Shepherd, Joshua. 2017. "Neuroscientific Threats to Free Will." In *The Routledge Companion to Free Will*, edited by Kevin Timpe, Meghan Griffith, and Neil Levy, 423–33. New York: Routledge.

WORKS CITED

Cave, Stephen. 2016. "There's No Such Thing as Free Will." *The Atlantic*, May 17. www.theatlantic.com/magazine/archive/2016/06/theres-no-such-thing-as-free-will/480750.

Gholipour, Bahar. 2019. "A Famous Argument Against Free Will Has Been Debunked." *The Atlantic*, September 10. www.theatlantic.com/health/archive/2019/09/free-will-bereitschaftspotential/597736/.

Herdova, Marcela. 2016. "Are Intentions in Tension with Timing Experiments?" *Philosophical Studies* 173: 573–87.

Libet, Benjamin. 1985. "Unconscious Cerebral Initiative and the Role of Conscious Will in Voluntary Action." *Behavioral and Brain Sciences* 8: 529–39.

Libet, Benjamin. 2004. *Mind Time: The Temporal Factor in Consciousness*. Cambridge, MA: Harvard University Press.

Nahmias, Eddy. 2011. "Is Neuroscience the Death of Free Will?" *Opinionator* (blog). November 13. https://opinionator.blogs.nytimes.com/2011/11/13/is-neuroscience-the-death-of-free-will.

Overbye, Dennis. 2007. "Free Will: Now You Have It, Now You Don't." *The New York Times*, January 2. www.nytimes.com/2007/01/02/science/02free.html.

Sinnott-Armstrong, Walter, and Lynn Nadel, eds. 2011. *Conscious Will and Responsibility: A Tribute to Benjamin Libet*. Oxford: Oxford University Press.

Williamson, Timothy. 2010. "Reclaiming the Imagination." *New York Times*, August 15. https://opinionator.blogs.nytimes.com/2010/08/15/reclaiming-the-imagination.

Williamson, Timothy. 2016. "Knowing by Imagining." In *Knowledge through Imagination*, edited by Amy Kind and Peter Kung, 113–23. Oxford: Oxford University Press.

27

THE DAILY WAVESTER

A WORLD RECORD SURFER

Dale Webster, aka the "Daily Wavester," owns the world record for the most consecutive days of surfing: 14,641 days—more than 40 years—from September 3, 1975 to October 4, 2015. He caught at least three waves every day, no matter the weather and no matter what was going on in his personal life: neither births nor deaths nor medical emergencies could keep him out of the water (Douglas 2015).

Numerous lessons could be drawn from Webster's example (both positive and negative): lessons about perseverance, commitment, and meaning in life, to name just a few. But let's focus on a relatively obscure facet of the case: let's ask about the truth or falsity of certain *subjunctive conditionals* pertaining to Dale's situation.

A subjunctive conditional is a statement about what would be true if certain other things were true. For example, "If I were to try to catch that 20-foot wave, I would injure myself" is a subjunctive conditional. The way we evaluate a subjunctive conditional is by considering our actual situation (the actual world) and then adjusting the details in our imagination so that the adjusted situation fits the antecedent conditions stated in the subjunctive conditional. (If we're using a subjunctive conditional to describe a world that we know to be different from the actual world, then the subjunctive conditional is called a *counterfactual*, because it is describing a situation that runs counter to fact.)

So let's evaluate "If I were to try to catch that 20-foot wave, I would injure myself." (The antecedent conditions involve me trying to catch

DOI: 10.4324/9781003126119-30

the wave, and the predicted outcome is the injury.) We begin the evaluation process by imagining a situation in which I try to catch the 20-foot wave in question. It's important, when imagining the adjusted situation, to change as few details as possible so that the imagined situation matches the actual situation as closely as possible. If we imagine the situation in which I try to catch the wave as part of another possible world, then we might say that we are trying to imagine the nearest possible world in which I try to catch that wave. (So one thing we would need to hold fixed is my meager surfing ability.) Finally, we use our rational capacities—our logical abilities, our knowledge of empirical or moral facts, and our rational intuition—to determine whether the outcome predicted by the conditional is in fact part of the possible world we are imagining. If it is, then the subjunctive conditional is true; if it's not, then the subjunctive conditional is false. In this case, then, the nearest possible world is one in which the wave is huge and my surfing abilities are meager; so it's plausible to think that the nearest world in which I try to catch a 20-foot wave is indeed a world in which I sustain some sort of injury. In other words, our sample counterfactual appears to be true.

The reason why we are interested in exploring some of the counterfactuals that are relevant to Dale Webster's situation is that they call into question certain intuitive principles about our relationship to—and our degree of control over—the past. (The Webster case, and the treatment of it below, is reminiscent of John Martin Fischer's discussion of "the salty old seadog" in Fischer 1994, 80–81.)

It seems to be a commonsense truism that the degree of control we have over the past is *zero* control; the past is fixed. If your doing something means that some detail about the past would have to have been different, then you can't do that thing. We can summarize this insight as a principle of the fixity of the past:

> **The fixity of the past:** If performing an action A would require a different past, then nobody can perform A.

(See Chapter 8 for more on the fixity (or necessity) of the past.) Perhaps you've never thought about the fixity of the past in these terms, but the basic idea is plausible, widely accepted, and encapsulated in cliches such as "There's no use crying over spilled milk."

But now consider the morning of February 29, 2004: Dale Webster is about to break the previous world record for most consecutive days of surfing (10,407). Other than the significance of the date, it's a regular morning. Suppose that he's getting ready to head to the beach for his surf session. At this moment, *can he refrain from surfing*? I think most of us would be inclined to answer in the affirmative: of course he can refrain from surfing!

But think about what would probably have to be true if he were to refrain from surfing. Given what we know about Webster and his dedication to surfing, something truly devastating would have to happen, *prior to his decision*, in order to make it so that he refrains from surfing. In other words, the nearest possible world in which he refrains from surfing on the date in question is a world in which something happened, prior to his decision, that made it prohibitively difficult for him to go surfing. But this is just another way of saying that *Webster's refraining would require a different past*.

If we were to combine this point about Webster's refraining with our principle about the fixity of the past, then we would get the following argument:

(1) If doing something requires a different past, then nobody can do that thing.
(2) Webster's refraining from surfing implies a different past.
(3) Therefore, Webster can't refrain from surfing.

Unfortunately, the conclusion in (3) contradicts what we said earlier, namely that Webster *can* refrain from surfing. (Indeed, it seems obvious that he can refrain from surfing.) The argument in (1)–(3) is valid, though, so if the conclusion is false then (1) or (2) must be false. But both (1) and (2) seem plausible: (1) is our principle about the fixity of the past; and (2) seems true in virtue of what we know about Webster and his deeply ingrained habits (and the values and commitments implied by those habits). It appears, then, that we face a dilemma: we either have to accept an implausible conclusion or we have to deny (at least) one of two plausible premises.

RESPONSES

Is there a way out of this dilemma? Fischer (1994, 82) points out that we might be justified in rejecting (2). Perhaps what would be true if Webster were to refrain is not that something in the past would have been different, but instead that he would have been acting out of character. Or perhaps his choice to refrain from surfing would simply be inexplicable. In order to provide a genuine way out of the dilemma, these alternative counterfactuals would have to involve spontaneous events that have the same causal history as Webster's actual decision to go surfing. (If one of these alternatives required a different causal history, then the alternative would give us no reason to reject (2).) Such spontaneous events do seem possible, but on the other hand they also seem less likely than incapacitating events (e.g., injuries) that involve slight changes in causal history. The most natural story (i.e., the nearest possible world) in which Webster refrains appears to be one in which something happens prior to the decision (and the decision remains explicable) rather than the decision being inexplicable. (For further recent discussion of this type of case, see Mackie 2017 and Cyr and Law 2020.)

The upshot is that we appear to be forced to choose only one of two plausible claims: the fixity of the past and the claim that Webster can refrain from surfing. This is unfortunate, but perhaps even more unfortunate is that there's no consensus about which choice is the correct one, and no clear path forward for those wishing to persuade the other side. This type of situation has been characterized by Fischer (1994, 83–85) as a *dialectical stalemate.* I have described this particular stalemate as unfortunate, but Fischer (drawing from Nozick 1981) points out that perhaps it's not so unfortunate after all. Despite an understandable desire for coercive arguments, philosophy at its best can only invite, rather than force, acceptance.

RECOMMENDED READING

Fischer, John Martin. 1994. *The Metaphysics of Free Will: An Essay on Control*, chapter 4. Oxford: Blackwell.
Mackie, Penelope. 2017. "Fischer and the Fixity of the Past." *European Journal for Philosophy of Religion* 9.

WORKS CITED

Cyr, Taylor, and Andrew Law. 2020. "Freedom, Foreknowledge, and Dependence." *American Philosophical Quarterly* 57: 145–54.
Douglas, Ashtyn. 2015. "Everyday Dale Ends His Streak." *Surfer Magazine*, October 6. www.surfer.com/features/everyday-dale-ends-his-streak.
Nozick, Robert. 1981. *Philosophical Explanations*. Cambridge, MA: Harvard University Press.

28

READING *EMMA*

PUZZLING OVER THE WORD "CAN"

In Chapter 27 we looked at some puzzles that arise when we ask whether Dale Webster can refrain from surfing. In this chapter we're going to look at some related, but distinct, questions involving our use of one small but troublesome word.

Suppose that you are a fan of Jane Austen, and that you're trying to introduce your friend to her work, so you've lent him your only copy of *Emma*. Now let's ask: Can you read *Emma*? On one understanding of this question, the answer is obviously *yes*: you have read it in the past, you have read lots of things similar to it, and you have retained the requisite skills and abilities, as demonstrated by the fact that you are currently reading the words on this page. But there is another equally legitimate understanding of the question according to which the answer is obviously *no*: your friend has your only copy, so of course you can't read it right now. The trouble, or at least part of the trouble, here is with the English word *can*. It's a familiar word, and one that all competent English speakers are capable of using and understanding; but if we try to analyze what exactly it means, we run into trouble. As van Inwagen (1989, 401) says, "the word 'can' is one of the trickiest of all the little philosophically interesting Anglo-Saxon words. It is not only ambiguous; it is ambiguous in a rather complicated way."

J. L. Austin discusses the "reading *Emma*" example (which traces back to P. H. Nowell-Smith) in his classic article, "Ifs and Cans" (1961

DOI: 10.4324/9781003126119-31

[1956]: 169ff.). As Austin points out, there are two important facets of a can-claim (or a can-question). The person making the claim (or asking the question) might be interested in someone's *ability* to do something, or they might be interested in someone's *opportunity* to do something. In the example above, you retain the ability to read *Emma* even when you lack the opportunity (due to your copy of the book being on loan). In similar fashion, abilities to walk or swim or engage in other sorts of physical activity don't go away when sleep or other forms of incapacitation deprive one of the opportunity to exercise those abilities.

Unfortunately, wrestling with the meaning of can-claims and can-questions doesn't end with disambiguating between ability and opportunity. Austin provides an example from the game of golf:

> Consider the case where I miss a very short putt and kick myself because I could have holed it. It is not that I should have holed it if I had tried: I did try, and missed. It is not that I should have holed it if conditions had been different: that might of course be so, but I am talking about conditions as they precisely were, and asserting that I could have holed it. There is the rub. Nor does "I can hole it this time" mean that I shall hole it this time if I try or if anything else: for I may try and miss, and yet not be convinced that I could not have done it; indeed, further experiments may confirm my belief that I could have done it that time although I did not.
>
> But if I tried my hardest, say, and missed, surely there *must* have been *something* that caused me to fail, that made me unable to succeed? So that I *could not* have holed it. Well, a modern belief in science, in there being an explanation of everything, may make us assent to this argument. But such a belief is not in line with the traditional beliefs enshrined in the word *can*: according to *them*, a human ability or power or capacity is inherently liable not to produce success, on occasion, and that for no reason (or are bad luck and bad form sometimes reasons?).
>
> (Austin 1961 [1956], 166n1)

Can I make a three-foot putt? Yes, and I will (almost) always make a putt of that distance when I try. (We could ask analogous questions about other games of skill, such as darts; replace "make the putt" with "hit the dartboard.") Can I make a six-foot putt? Yes, but I'll only make one of those about half the time. What about a *sixty*-foot putt? Well, given enough attempts I'll eventually hole one, so it's tempting to say that I can do this as well. But clearly there's a different sense of "can" at work as we shift our focus from three-foot putts to sixty-foot putts. The shift, however, is not a shift from focusing on abilities to focusing on opportunities (or vice versa). Instead, the issue has to do with likelihood of success. To say that I can do something is of course to say that there would be a good chance of success if I tried; but one lesson from Austin's putting example is that the truth of a can-claim does not *guarantee* success. (Conversely, failure does not guarantee the falsity of a can-claim.) And as we move up the continuum of likelihood, from a guarantee of failure toward a guarantee of success, it's not clear where we'll find the threshold at which can-claims become true. The presence of these borderline cases means that "can" is not just ambiguous (between ability and opportunity) but also vague.

RESPONSES

A. M. Honoré (1964) responds to Austin, focusing on the distinction between a general sense of "can" and a particular sense of "can," rather than focusing on the distinction between ability and opportunity. He offers an alternative (and in some ways more optimistic) analysis of the issues raised by Austin's discussion. Peter van Inwagen (1983, 13) also distinguishes between the general sense and the particular sense of the term, simply stipulating that the particular sense is the one that's relevant to free will.

So stipulation is an option here, but we could also follow van Inwagen's later (2008) recommendation and simply avoid the term altogether. He notes the problems caused by the ambiguity of the past-tense "could have done otherwise" and on that basis recommends substituting *ability* in place of that and other terms:

> All the phrases that have been used in definitions of "free will" (and in statements of the free-will thesis) can be defined in terms of, or dispensed with in favor of, "able." For example, the much-used phrase "within one's power" can be defined like this: "It is within x's power to" means "x is able to."
>
> (van Inwagen 2008, 333)

(For a helpful discussion of the general category of "practical abilities," see Mele 2003.)

Perhaps the best approach, then, is to set aside "can" (and related terms) in favor of "is able to" (and related terms). Unfortunately, as is evident in some of the more recent work on this topic (e.g., Schwarz 2020; Carter 2021; Boylan forthcoming), there are some difficulties with the term "ability" as well. Substituting ability-talk for can-talk might represent progress, but there is still much theoretical work to be done.

RECOMMENDED READING

Mele, Alfred R. 2003. "Agents' Abilities." *Noûs* 37: 447–70.
van Inwagen, Peter. 2008. "How to Think About the Problem of Free Will." *Journal of Ethics* 12: 327–41.

WORKS CITED

Austin, J. L. 1961 [1956]. "Ifs and Cans." In *Philosophical Papers*, edited by J. O. Urmson and G. J. Warnock, 151–80. Oxford: Clarendon Press.
Boylan, David. Forthcoming. "Does Success Entail Ability?" *Noûs*.
Carter, J. Adam. 2021. "Exercising Abilities." *Synthese* 198: 2495–2509.
Honoré, A. M. 1964. "Can and Can't." *Mind* 73: 463–79.
Schwarz, Wolfgang. 2020. "Ability and Possibility." *Philosophers' Imprint* 20: 21.
van Inwagen, Peter. 1983. *An Essay on Free Will*. Oxford: Clarendon Press.
van Inwagen, Peter. 1989. "When Is the Will Free?" *Philosophical Perspectives* 3: 399–422.

29

COMPETING SETS OF REASONS

TORN DECISIONS, SELF-FORMING ACTIONS, AND TRANSFORMATIVE CHOICES

Think about a time when you were torn between two options. Maybe the decision was relatively mundane, like what to order for dinner, or maybe it was much more significant—like where to go to college, or which job offer to accept. For these significant decisions, there's often a deep conflict between two (or more) things that you value deeply or desire strongly. You have reasons in favor of both, and you can't figure out which set of reasons is stronger.

Mark Balaguer provides a vivid example of a torn decision:

> Ralph, a lifelong resident of Mayberry, North Carolina, is trying to decide whether or not to move to New York City. He has safety-and-stability-based reasons for wanting to stay in Mayberry (he's been offered a position as assistant day-shift manager at the local Der Wienerschnitzel and is clearly being groomed for the manager position, and his sweetheart, Robbi Anna, has offered him her hand in marriage); and he has fame-and-fortune-based reasons for wanting to move to New York (he longs to be the first person to start at middle linebacker for the Giants while simultaneously starring on Broadway in a musical production of Sartre's *Nausea*). He deliberates for several days, considering all of his reasons for choosing, but he is unable to come to a view as to which set of reasons is stronger. He feels genuinely torn.
>
> (Balaguer 2010, 72)

DOI: 10.4324/9781003126119-32

Balaguer defines torn decisions in terms of the opposing reasons mentioned above, also adding the requirement that the person who feels torn has to simply make the decision without resolving the conflict. (We'll be more interested in the conflict itself, rather than the way it gets resolved.)

Robert Kane (1996, 126) also provides a vivid example of a torn decision, in which a businesswoman witnesses a mugging while she's on her way to an important meeting. She is moved by compassion for the victim, but she recognizes that stopping to help will make her late for the meeting (which could have disastrous effects on her career). Thus, she is torn between stopping to help the victim and continuing on to her meeting. As Kane construes it, the struggle here is a moral one: will she do the thing that her conscience tells her is right, or will she give in to self-interest? This is a choice that Kane (2005, ch. 11) describes as "self-forming": the choice she makes will form her character in such a way that her sets of reasons will be different (even if only slightly) the next time she faces a similar conflict. Over time, she may get to a point where the decision is no longer a torn decision: her self-interested reasons will either clearly outweigh, or clearly be outweighed by, the moral reasons generated by her conscience.

So some torn decisions will also be self-forming. (It's an open question whether Ralph's decision above will contribute to the formation of his character, but it's plausible to think that it will. For an example of a torn decision that doesn't involve self-formation, consider a choice between two of your favorite desserts.) But there is a subset of self-forming choices in which the formation is more radical—radical enough that it warrants the label of *trans*formation. A transformative choice, at least as it's been discussed in recent philosophical literature, is one that fundamentally transforms one's perspective, one's character, or some other fundamental facet of who a person is. This transformation might occur via the experiences that result from the choice (Paul 2014) or it might occur via the process of the choice itself (Chang 2015). Either way, one key element of a transformative choice is that the only way to know what it's like to make the choice (or to experience its consequences) is to go ahead and make the choice. Our usual strategy of making choices by imagining the possibilities and then examining the reasons for or against actualizing those possibilities won't work—because we're incapable of genuinely imagining the possibilities. We can look at external descriptions of those possibilities, but we have no access to the subjective perspective of being in them.

Some have described drug usage, at least in its early stages, as a type of transformative behavior (although not in those terms; see Watson 1999, 598). People tend to underestimate what it will be like to crave the drug, and as a result they overestimate their future ability to resist those cravings. A more optimistic example of a transformative choice is having a child (cf. Paul 2015): there's just no way to capture what it's like to have a child without actually having the child.

RESPONSES

A natural question to ask, when confronted with self-forming and self-transforming choices (many of which will be torn choices), is whether these types of choices are more closely connected with free will and moral responsibility than other types of choices. At an intuitive level at least, it would seem that the decisions that are the most free are the ones that will have the most impact on our character, which are presumably the self-forming choices. And it might further seem that these crucial character-forming choices have to be choices in which the agent is torn between two or more options. (If the choice is obvious, then it would seem that the relevant character states have already been pretty much formed.) According to this idea, the only way a choice can genuinely form an agent's character is if their beliefs, desires, and other psychological states are balanced on a knife's edge. In this type of situation, a decision is an endorsement of one set of values over another that will push the agent, so to speak, into one character trajectory or another.

This all seems natural enough (although see Herdova 2020 for a consideration of transformative experiences that gives rise to some concerns about our ability to form our characters). This natural line of reasoning leads, however, to the surprising conclusion that a relatively small number of choices are actually free choices. Our self-forming choices are a relatively small subset of our overall choices, and an even smaller number of those self-forming decisions are torn decisions. At its most extreme, this view would imply that an overwhelming majority of your actions are free only in a derivative sense, because they are determined by your character (which was formed via the handful of crucial free choices that you made over the course of your development as a free agent). This wouldn't mean that *moral responsibility* is rare, because we could be responsible for our choices in virtue of forming our character to be the way that it is. But free will itself would be extremely rare.

This view is often called *restrictivism* about free will. Balaguer (2010) is a type of restrictivist, since he limits free will to torn decisions. But van Inwagen pushes the view even further:

> If this is correct, then there are at most two sorts of occasion on which the incompatibilist can admit that we exercise free will: cases of an actual struggle between perceived moral duty or long-term self-interest, on the one hand, and immediate desire, on the other; and cases of a conflict of incommensurable values. Both of these sorts of occasion together must account for a fairly small percentage of the things we do. And, I must repeat, my conclusion is that this is the largest class of actions with respect to which the incompatibilist can say we are free. The argument I have given shows that the incompatibilist ought to deny that we have free will on any occasions other than these.
>
> (van Inwagen 1989, 417–18)

Our natural line of reasoning seems to have led us to a pretty implausible place: it feels as though we exercise free will all the time, but according to restrictivism this feeling is usually illusory. Perhaps the solution is simply to relax the restrictions a little bit. A more dramatic solution, however, would be to reject the starting point. We have been treating a certain sort of torn decision as paradigmatic of agency, but what if the opposite is true? What if the choice that represents your agency best is one in which the choice is so closely aligned with your character that it is practically impossible for you to do otherwise? It doesn't seem right to call these choices the most free, but they do seem to be the ones that express our fundamental selves most clearly. Anybody can wrestle with a choice, and two very different people could have the same sets of conflicting reasons. It seems that we learn more about a person from decisions that flow most strongly from their character, and that suggests that perhaps torn decisions are not as important as they initially seemed to be. (See Chapter 25 for a related discussion.)

RECOMMENDED READING

Kane, Robert. 2005. *A Contemporary Introduction to Free Will*, chapter 11. Oxford: Oxford University Press.

Paul, L. A. 2015. "What You Can't Expect When You're Expecting." *Res Philosophica* 92: 149–70.

WORKS CITED

Balaguer, Mark. 2010. *Free Will as an Open Scientific Problem*. Cambridge, MA: MIT Press.

Chang, Ruth. 2015. "Transformative Choices." *Res Philosophica* 92: 237–82.

Herdova, Marcela. 2020. "Barking Up the Wrong Tree: On Control, Transformative Experiences, and Turning Over a New Leaf." *The Monist* 103: 278–93.

Kane, Robert. 1996. *The Significance of Free Will*. New York: Oxford University Press.

Paul, L. A. 2014. *Transformative Experience*. Oxford: Oxford University Press.

van Inwagen, Peter. 1989. "When Is the Will Free?" *Philosophical Perspectives* 3: 399–422.

Watson, Gary. 1999. "Excusing Addiction." *Law and Philosophy* 18: 589–619.

THE CAPTAIN IN THE STORM

SOME PUZZLES INVOLVING VOLUNTARINESS

Most of the early chapters of this book focus on threats to free will and moral responsibility that are global and absolute, like fatalism or determinism. There are other phenomena, however, that threaten free will in a more localized way: manipulation, coercion, and other forms of duress. There's no question about whether these phenomena exist; it's just a question of whether and to what extent they diminish our freedom.

This is also a good place to stop and note that, even though we have been focusing on the concepts of free will and moral responsibility as capturing the most valuable features of human agency, there are other important concepts in the neighborhood, such as *autonomy* and *voluntariness*. Take voluntariness, for example. Sometimes "voluntary" is just treated as a synonym for "free," which would imply that all voluntary acts are free (and vice versa). But someone might want to treat voluntary actions as a subset of free actions. They might want to define voluntariness as merely being able to do what one wants, and then claim that acting freely requires more than merely being able to do what one wants. They could then describe the debate over classical compatibilism (see Chapter 12) as the debate over whether freedom is more than just voluntariness.

Let's set aside the global threats for a moment and focus on some of the more localized threats mentioned above. Let's focus in particular

DOI: 10.4324/9781003126119-33

on choices made under duress. One paradigm example of a choice made under duress is a choice made in response to a *threat*. (Here we are shifting our discussion of "threats" to consider threats to specific agents (which may or may not undermine their freedom), rather than threats to free will in general.) Another example of a choice made under duress, although less commonly referred to that way, is a choice made in response to *temptation*. Both types of choices are puzzling because there seems to be a sense in which they are voluntary but also a sense in which they are involuntary.

Consider first a choice made in response to a threat, which could also be described as a choice made in the presence of fear. A helpful example comes from Aquinas (*Summa Theologica*, IaIIae Q6 a6), who is building on an example discussed by Aristotle (*Nicomachean Ethics*, 1110a9–19). Thus Aquinas:

> When *fear* is the motive of an act, the act remains a human act, and is voluntary. But, since such an act would not be done were it not for the stress of fear, there is something involuntary about it. The captain of a vessel who throws valuable cargo overboard to lighten ship in a storm does what he chooses to do; his act is, *in itself* or *simply*, a voluntary act. But the same act is *in a way* an involuntary act inasmuch as it would not be done were it not for fear of disaster; there is in the act an element of involuntariness. Hence we say that an act done out of fear (not merely done *in* fear or *with* fear) is *simply* voluntary, and, *in some respects*, involuntary.

This type of case is structurally similar to a type of case that we encounter all too often. Most of us have never had to throw valuable cargo overboard to avoid capsizing a boat in a storm; but many of us have had to abandon something valuable for the sake of something even more valuable. For example, many people have had to evacuate their homes so as to avoid a wildfire, leaving behind many valuable things for the sake of preserving their lives and a few of the things they care about most. (Although no one should have to do this, being forced to do it does help clarify what really matters in a way that no amount of careful theorizing will quite be able to simulate.)

But what does it mean for an act to be partly voluntary but also partly involuntary—or as Aquinas puts it, "*simply* voluntary" and yet "*in some respects* involuntary"? Before we answer this question, let's look at the related puzzle having to do with choices made in response to temptations. Aquinas says in one place that temptation (i.e., an appeal to desires or passions, which Aquinas groups under the term "concupiscence") can *increase* voluntariness:

> *Concupiscence* is strong tendency or desire in the sensitive appetites. When the will permits the influence of concupiscence to rise out of the sentient order into the intellective order, this influence can strongly affect the will and its acts. Inasmuch as concupiscence makes the will [and its acts] more intense, it is said to increase voluntariness; inasmuch as it hurries and hampers free and deliberate choice, concupiscence lessens voluntariness.
>
> (*Summa Theologica*, IaIIae Q6 a7)

In apparent conflict with this claim, Aquinas acknowledges in another place that the passions can *reduce* voluntariness:

> Accordingly if we take passion as preceding the sinful act, it must diminish the sin: because the act is a sin insofar as it is voluntary and exists in us. Now a thing is called in us through reason and will: and therefore the more reason and will do anything of their own accord, and not through the impulse of passion, the more it is voluntary and exists in us. In this respect passion diminishes sin, in so far as it diminishes its voluntariness.
>
> (*Summa Theologica*, IaIIae Q77 a6)

The bottom line, as Aquinas notes, is that we experience some ambivalence when we encounter these kinds of cases. When we consider the captain throwing cargo overboard in the storm (or someone giving in to temptation), there is a certain sense in which their actions are voluntary; after all, they resemble other clearly voluntary actions in lots of ways. They are (or at least can be) performed in response to reasons, and in a way that demonstrates a significant amount of control. (See Chapter 18 for a brief discussion of reasons-responsiveness.) But they are also accurately described as actions taken against one's will, or against one's better judgment.

So we have (at least) two puzzles. First, we have to make sense of what it means for an action to be both partly voluntary and partly involuntary. Second, we have to sort out the different ways that voluntariness is affected by temptations, in contrast to threats.

RESPONSES

Paul Hoffman (2005) offers an insightful presentation and discussion of these puzzles. First, he offers a helpful gloss on the way in which a choice made out of fear is simply voluntary but in some respects involuntary. The "simply" modifier restricts our consideration to the actual circumstances, whereas "in some respects" indicates that we can consider hypothetical situations that differ from the actual situation. So to say that the act of throwing cargo overboard is *simply voluntary* is to say that it is voluntary in the actual circumstances. In the actual circumstances (which include a storm threatening to capsize the ship), the captain is responsive to reasons and exhibiting sufficient control to render the action voluntary. But if we were to ask the captain whether he would prefer those circumstances to other hypothetical circumstances not involving the storm, he would say no: he would clearly prefer the alternative situations in which there's no storm (or at least not such a severe storm). So the actual choice, given the actual circumstances, is voluntary; but the captain's being in those circumstances is in an important respect against his will. He would prefer to be in a different situation in which the act of throwing cargo overboard was not choice-worthy.

One benefit of this analysis is that it allows us to affirm the rationality (and even praiseworthiness) of certain choices made under duress, while still acknowledging the element of involuntariness introduced by the circumstances of duress. But this analysis can't be the whole story about *temptations*, because we want to say that there can be something blameworthy about giving in to temptation, even when the agent (i) exercises various kinds of reasons-responsive control but (ii) would prefer to be in a different situation without the temptation.

Hoffman (2005) again provides helpful insight. He highlights Aquinas' distinction between *reason* and *will*. We can endorse the rationality of a person making a difficult choice under duress, even though the situation in which she has to make it obtains against her will. She would prefer not to be under threat, but given that she is, the right thing to do is often something that wouldn't be the right thing to do in other circumstances. A person succumbing to temptation, however, cannot say the same thing. He might prefer not to be facing temptation, but given that he is, the right thing to do is still to resist temptation. Perhaps he is letting his desires cloud his judgment in some way (perhaps they are producing a kind of moral ignorance), or perhaps he is temporarily suffering from some other defect of rationality. Either way, we cannot endorse the rationality of his choice; he is not making a choice in accord with reason.

For more detail on Aquinas' approach to the passions, see King (1999). For a comprehensive treatment of his approach to wrongdoing, see McCluskey (2017). Also, thinking about the phenomenon of giving in to temptation quickly brings to mind *weakness of will*. For discussion of this issue, as it pertains to Aquinas and as it pertains to moral responsibility in general, see Kent (2007) and Chapter 33, respectively.

RECOMMENDED READING

Hoffman, Paul. 2005. "Aquinas on Threats and Temptations." *Pacific Philosophical Quarterly* 86: 225–42.

O'Keefe, Tim. 2021. "Ancient Theories of Freedom and Determinism," §2 ("Voluntary Action, Moral Responsibility, and What Is 'Up to Us'"). In *The Stanford Encyclopedia of Philosophy*, edited by Edward N. Zalta, Spring 2021. https://plato.stanford.edu/archives/spr2021/entries/freedom-ancient/.

WORKS CITED

Aristotle. *Nicomachean Ethics*.

Aquinas, Thomas. 1947 [ca. 1265–73]. *Summa Theologica*. Translated by Fathers of the English Dominican Province. www.ccel.org/ccel/aquinas/summa.

Kent, Bonnie. 2007. "Aquinas and Weakness of Will." *Philosophy and Phenomenological Research* 75: 70–91.

King, Peter. 1999. Aquinas on the Passions. In *Aquinas's Moral Theory: Essays in Honor of Norman Kretzmann*, edited by Scott MacDonald and Eleonore Stump, pp. 101–32. Ithaca, NY: Cornell University Press.

McCluskey, Colleen. 2017. *Thomas Aquinas on Moral Wrongdoing*. Cambridge: Cambridge University Press.

31

ONE THOUGHT TOO MANY?

WHEN LOVED ONES ARE IN DANGER

The "one thought too many" objection most often arises in discussions of normative ethical theory, but it's also relevant to agency and practical reason. The objection is attributed to Bernard Williams, who was opposed to any kind of systematization of morality, and especially a systematization that emphasized impartiality or abstract generality. Thus, he was opposed to both consequentialism and Kantianism, but especially consequentialism (Chappell and Smyth 2018).

Williams describes a situation in which someone can only rescue one of two people in danger, and chooses the one who is his wife. This type of case raises lots of interesting questions, but the relevant point for our purposes is the following: If the rescuer decided to rescue his wife by appealing to some general moral principle that allows us to prioritize those who are close to us, then that would be *one thought too many*. The better thing, morally speaking, would simply be to rescue his wife because she's his wife (Williams 1981 [1976], 18–19).

Because this objection touches upon moral deliberation and reasons for action, it's also relevant to discussions of practical reason and agency more broadly. One general type of question that runs through all these discussions has to do with evaluations of agents and their characters: Upon reflection, is the person who deliberates less in this case (i.e., has fewer thoughts) more praiseworthy than the person who coldly (albeit rationally) formulates and evaluates arguments in favor of the

DOI: 10.4324/9781003126119-34

different possible courses of action? (And if so, does that fact about our intuitions undermine some (or all) attempts to systematize morality?)

We have talked about deliberation, and in particular the question of whether deliberation is even possible if we already know the outcome (see Chapter 6). This case from Williams highlights a different type or dimension of deliberation, namely *moral* deliberation. There won't always be a bright line between moral deliberation and other kinds of deliberation (and a single deliberative process can engage in numerous different types of deliberation), but it does seem safe to say that moral deliberation is distinct insofar as it invites a moral evaluation of the deliberator. Deliberating about whom to save in a life-or-death crisis is clearly an instance of moral deliberation; deliberating about which pair of identical socks to wear is not (absent some unusual special circumstances). Deliberating about whether to exercise might be an example of a borderline case. (We seem to have quite a bit of moral freedom regarding our physical activity, but on the other hand exercise has an impact on our own well-being, and thus by extension the well-being of those who care about us. Also, see W. D. Ross's (2002 [1930]) version of ethical intuitionism, which includes self-improvement as one of our *prima facie* moral duties.)

One way in which discussion of Williams's thought experiment connects up with considerations that are more squarely within the metaphysics and ethics of free will and moral responsibility has to do with its implicit reliance on counterfactual reasoning. As Susan Wolf (2012) points out, the standard view about the thought experiment seems to be that a moral exemplar wouldn't stop in the moment to deliberate about whether they were permitted by morality to rescue their spouse; but they *would* reflect afterward on whether what they did was morally permissible. In fact, they probably would have *already* reflected on what to do in such a situation (at least if they are also a rational exemplar), among other counterfactual situations that they might find themselves in. They have imagined possible worlds in which such things happen to them, and they have consulted morality to see what they are permitted or perhaps even obligated to do in such situations.

RESPONSES

Discussion of Williams's case, and his comments on it, have been voluminous. For a recent defense of consequentialism against Williams's criticisms, see Mason (1999). For a recent discussion of Williams's critique of Kantianism, see Smyth (2018).

One of the more interesting responses to the case is the one from Wolf (2012) herself, in which she claims that Williams is gesturing toward a view that is more radical than most have recognized. On the standard view, as noted above, the moral exemplar would not engage in moral deliberation during the moment of crisis (they would simply do the right thing without thinking about it), but they *would* engage in a type of counterfactual moral deliberation. Wolf puts forward a competing ideal in which the exemplar does not necessarily possess an unconditional commitment to morality. According to this competing ideal, someone who is always subjecting deliberation to a moral system suffers from an overly restrictive evaluative framework:

> As I understand Williams, and as I am inclined to say myself, there is nothing wrong, strictly speaking, with the hypothetical deliberator. But there is nothing especially right about him, either—his response to the invitation to morally deliberate is not part of a universally plausible and attractive ideal.
>
> ... I have offered glimpses of an alternative ideal—or at least glimpses of a psychological profile that could be filled out so as to constitute an ideal. The profile includes categorical desires for concrete individuals, such as a life partner, that play an important enough role in a person's life as to forbid an unconditional commitment to morality per se or to constraining one's actions absolutely to those that would be permissible from an impartial point of view. Due to this feature of the profile, the subject is not likely to engage in moral deliberations, even hypothetically, about whom to save when one's wife and a stranger are in equal peril. Nor is he likely to see this as a failing in himself. But the profile also includes a substantial commitment to morality and takes judgments that issue from an impartial perspective seriously in many contexts. ... These features of the profile explain why, although the subject may run the risk of offending against the moral or the impartial point of view, he will hope to be able to avoid that risk. ...
>
> As long as [this] is a legitimate ideal, however, one that it is reasonable and decent for a person to have, the Standard View is wrong.
>
> (Wolf 2012, 91–92)

According to Wolf, then, reflection on Williams's simple thought experiment leads us to ponder a surprising ideal in which the person who has reached the pinnacle of moral excellence might nevertheless, in extreme circumstances, set aside the constraints of morality.

RECOMMENDED READING

Williams, Bernard. 1981 [1976]. "Persons, Character, and Morality." In *Moral Luck: Philosophical Papers 1973–1980*, 1–19. Cambridge: Cambridge University Press.

Wolf, Susan. 2012. "Love, Morality, and the Ordering of Commitment." In *Luck, Value, and Commitment: Themes from the Ethics of Bernard Williams*, 71–92. Oxford: Oxford University Press.

WORKS CITED

Chappell, Sophie-Grace, and Nicholas Smyth. 2018. "Bernard Williams." In *The Stanford Encyclopedia of Philosophy*, edited by Edward N. Zalta, Fall 2018. https://plato.stanford.edu/archives/fall2018/entries/williams-bernard.

Mason, Elinor. 1999. "Do Consequentialists Have One Thought Too Many?" *Ethical Theory and Moral Practice* 2: 243–61.

Ross, W. D. 2002 [1930]. *The Right and the Good*. Oxford: Clarendon Press.

Smyth, Nicholas. 2018. "Integration and Authority: Rescuing the 'One Thought Too Many' Problem." *Canadian Journal of Philosophy* 48: 812–30.

32

THE ANXIOUS MOUNTAINEER

A PUZZLE ABOUT EXPLAINING INTENTIONAL ACTIONS

The value that we place on our freedom is one of the reasons why we turn to questions about the conditions for free will, and about whether the truth of determinism (for example) would imply that we fail to meet those conditions. A set of closely related questions—which overlap significantly but not completely with free will questions—involve whether, when, and to what extent our actions are *intentional*. We're all familiar with the distinction between an intentional action and an unintentional action, at least on an intuitive level, but it turns out to be surprisingly difficult to come up with a set of necessary and sufficient conditions that will tell us exactly what makes an action intentional (or prevents an action from being intentional).

Donald Davidson was one of the philosophers who wrestled with these questions about intentional action, and also questions involving the *explanation* of actions. Typically when we explain an agent's action, we do so by providing reasons that the agent performed the action. (When we provide the reasons for an action, we can say that we *rationalize* the action.) One of Davidson's many important contributions to these discussions was his defense of the view that reasons cannot explain an action unless they also *cause* the action (Malpas 2021).

If Davidson's view is correct, then when we are trying to explain intentional action, we need to identify reasons (usually in the form of

DOI: 10.4324/9781003126119-35

beliefs, desires, or other attitudes) that caused the action. The problem that Davidson recognizes is that it's possible for the relevant attitudes to cause an action in the wrong way. Thus we need to be able to discern whether and when the relevant attitudes have caused an action in the right way. Davidson, unfortunately, is pretty pessimistic about the possibility of such discernment, and he provides an example to support his pessimism:

> What I despair of spelling out is the way in which attitudes must cause actions if they are to rationalize the action.
>
> Let a single example serve. A climber might want to rid himself of the weight and danger of holding another man on a rope, and he might know that by loosening his hold on the rope he could rid himself of the weight and danger. This belief and want might so unnerve him as to cause him to loosen his hold, and yet it might be the case that he never chose to loosen his hold, nor did he do it intentionally.
>
> (Davidson 2001 [1973], 73)

In this example we have an action (the climber loosening his hold on the rope) and the following relevant attitudes: the climber's desire to rid himself of the weight (and thus make himself safer) and the climber's belief that loosening his hold on the rope would accomplish that desire. Those attitudes cause the action, but in this case they *don't* fully explain the action. (The proper explanation has to also cite the fact that the climber became unnerved as he pondered the desire(s) and the belief.) One way to describe this situation is to say that there is a *deviant causal chain* from attitudes to action. The attitudes do cause the action, and they would rationalize the action in normal circumstances, but not in special circumstances such as that of Davidson's climber. So even if we can identify a set of attitudes that caused an action (and would make it rational in normal circumstances), there's still no guarantee that the action was intentional (Davidson 2001 [1973], 73).

This may not be a problem for our ordinary judgments of intentionality, which we can render with relative ease. But for those who are interested in providing a comprehensive metaphysical analysis of rational, intentional action, cases like this present quite a problem. Intentional action, despite our first-person familiarity with it and our ability to recognize it in the wild, is exceedingly difficult to analyze.

(For a discussion of how deviant causal chains can wreak havoc in the context of moral and criminal responsibility, see Chapter 50.)

RESPONSES

Since Davidson's theory of action is a causal theory, one response to this problem of deviant causal chains is to advocate for a *non-causal* theory of action. (See Pink 2011 for an overview of non-causal theories.) Unfortunately, non-causal theories have their own difficulties in explaining intentional action (Clarke 2003, 21–24).

One recent attempt to solve the problem of causal deviance can be found in Schlosser (2007). According to Schlosser, the solution lies in an appeal to the *content* of the mental states that cause the action. To explain an action, we don't merely cite its cause, and we don't merely provide the reason(s) for which it was performed; we have to cite both the cause and its content. As Schlosser puts it, "Being caused and causally explained in virtue of content, an action is not merely a response to a cause, but … a response to the content of the mental state in the light of which its performance appears as intelligible" (2007, 192).

Mawson (2016) connects up Davidson's mountaineer case with the debate over classical compatibilism (see Chapter 12) by deploying it as a counterexample to Hume's conception of freedom:

> According to Hume, as long as one does what one wants to do as a causal result of one's most wanting to do that thing, and as long as the want from which one acts is a characteristic one, that is sufficient for one to be doing what one does freely. Humean freedom then is quite compatible with determinism. It is easy to show that Humean freedom isn't what the majority of us think of as freedom by what might thus be called "counterexamples" to it, that is to say situations in which a given person seems to satisfy Hume's conditions for freedom yet the man on the Clapham omnibus [i.e., an ordinary person on the street] would say of that person that he/she is not free. Davidson's nervy mountaineer might be one such.
>
> (Mawson 2016, 145–46)

Bayne and Levy (2006) consider a different element of Davidson's thought experiment, namely the *phenomenology* of the action: the experience of the mountaineer as he lets go of the rope. It seems plausible to say that an experience of agency involves an experience of one's beliefs and desires causing one's actions. But the nervous mountaineer presumably experiences his beliefs and desires causing him to let go of the rope, without experiencing the letting go as an intentional action. So we need an account of what it takes for an experience of one's mental states causing one's actions to generate an experience of agency. (Bayne and Levy also connect up their discussion with some recent work in the cognitive sciences; see Chapter 26 for a related discussion.)

RECOMMENDED READING

Clarke, Randolph. 2003. *Libertarian Accounts of Free Will*, chapter 2. Oxford: Oxford University Press.

Wilson, George, and Samuel Shpall. 2016. "Action." In *The Stanford Encyclopedia of Philosophy*, edited by Edward N. Zalta, Winter 2016. https://plato.stanford.edu/archives/win2016/entries/action.

WORKS CITED

Bayne, Tim, and Neil Levy. 2006. "The Feeling of Doing: Deconstructing the Phenomenology of Agency." In *Disorders of Volition*, edited by Wolfgang Prinz and Natalie Sebanz, 49–68. Cambridge, MA: MIT Press.

Davidson, Donald. 2001 [1973]. "Freedom to Act." In *Essays on Actions and Events*, 59–74. Oxford: Oxford University Press.

Malpas, Jeff. 2021. "Donald Davidson." In *The Stanford Encyclopedia of Philosophy*, edited by Edward N. Zalta, Fall 2021. https://plato.stanford.edu/archives/fall2021/entries/davidson.

Mawson, T. J. 2016. "Classical Theism Has No Implications for the Debate between Libertarianism and Compatibilism." In *Free Will and Theism: Connections, Contingencies, and Concerns*, edited by Kevin Timpe and Daniel Speak, 142–57. Oxford: Oxford University Press.

Pink, Thomas. 2011. "Freedom and Action without Causation: Noncausal Theories of Freedom and Purposive Agency." In *The Oxford Handbook of Free Will*, edited by Robert Kane, 2nd ed., 349–65. Oxford: Oxford University Press.

Schlosser, Markus E. 2007. "Basic Deviance Reconsidered." *Analysis* 67: 186–94.

33

ACTING AGAINST BETTER JUDGMENT

A PUZZLE ABOUT WEAKNESS OF WILL

It's late, and you've got a big day tomorrow (you've got an important test, or perhaps a job interview), so you should probably get some rest. On the other hand, it would be nice to unwind a bit by watching an episode of that new show that you've been enjoying lately. You think about it for a bit, and you come to the conclusion that it really would be best if you went to bed. And yet … you end up watching an episode (or three) anyway.

This is a familiar phenomenon that most of us face on at least a semi-regular basis: we are tempted by something that we judge to be less than the best for us, and yet we still give in to temptation. This happens because we humans suffer from *weakness of will* (sometimes also called *akrasia*, or *incontinence*). We judge that a particular course of action would be best, but we can't get our will to follow that judgment, and we pursue some other course of action instead.

This is an intuitively plausible, commonsense way of looking at our unsuccessful encounters with temptation. Socrates, however, saw things differently; he actually thought that it was *impossible* to judge a course of action as best and then pursue some other course of action. (So we could say that Socrates was a skeptic about weakness of will.) On his view, giving in to temptation does not involve acting against our better judgment, but instead involves *revising* our judgment about

DOI: 10.4324/9781003126119-36

what's best; weakness of will is not actually a problem of the will, but instead a cognitive failure, or cognitive illusion. This type of failure occurs when an agent makes incorrect judgments about which action is most choice-worthy.

Socrates' view definitely has some plausibility as well. It does seem as though, in general, we make the choice that we think is best; and any choice that seems to be describable as acting against our better judgment could also be re-described as altering that judgment.

RESPONSES

Donald Davidson analyzes this puzzle by articulating some principles of practical reason that give rise to it. We can take these principles (in slightly modified form, and re-ordered; see Davidson 2001 [1969], 26–27) and use them to generate the conclusion that weakness of will doesn't exist:

(1) If someone judges that it would be better to do x than y, then they want to do x more than they want to do y.
(2) If someone wants to do x more than y, then they will do x (given that they do x or y).
(3) Therefore, if someone judges that it would be better to do x than y, then they will do x (given that they do x or y).

The problem, of course, is just what we already noted above: it seems like there are all kinds of cases in which someone judges that it would be better to do x than y (e.g., they judge that it would be better to go to bed rather than stay up to watch a TV show) and yet they do y anyway.

Davidson tries to sidestep the problem by arguing that the type of judgment that's relevant to weakness of will is different from the type of judgment that figures into (1)–(3) above. According to Davidson, when someone acts against their better judgment, they are acting in violation of an all-things-considered judgment, which Davidson refers to as a *conditional* judgment. Perhaps we might think of it this way: when considering x and y in the abstract as possible courses of action, the agent judges that x would be better than y. But the judgment in (1)–(3) is an *unconditional* judgment that leads directly to action. As Davidson says, "Reasoning that stops at conditional judgements … is practical only in its subject, not in its issue" (2001 [1969], 41). (For more on the distinction between these two types of judgment, see Davidson 2001 [1978].) A conditional judgment is a judgment about what it would be better to do, but it is not the kind of judgment that leads directly to action. And it is those judgments that lead directly to action that are relevant to (1)–(3).

The point here is reminiscent of a point made in Chapter 30. In that chapter, we noted that Aquinas used "simply" to refer to things that occurred in the actual circumstances; so an action that was "simply voluntary" was voluntary given the actual circumstances. We might think of the judgments in (1)–(3) along these lines: if someone "judges simply" that it would be better to do x than y, then they will want to do x and will do x. But when we say that someone acts against their better judgment, we're not talking about "simply judging" but rather a different type of judging that occurs in a hypothetical mode of reasoning.

That, at any rate, seems to be what Davidson wants to say. Does his solution work?

Gary Watson (1977) doesn't think so, but not because he disagrees with Davidson's attempt to reconcile (1)–(3) with the possibility of *akrasia*. Instead, he identifies a crucial ambiguity in the notion of wanting to do x more than y. The argument in (1)–(3) is invalid because it equivocates between these two different senses of wanting more. Thus, "socratism" about *akrasia* is false. Here's how Watson makes the case, which is built on a development in Platonic thought:

> He [i.e., the later Plato] came to realize that we are generally susceptible to motivation which is independent, in strength and origin, of our judgments concerning how it is best to act. Plato's distinction between the rational and nonrational parts of the soul may be taken as a distinction between sources of motivation. The rational part of the soul is the source of evaluations—judgments as to the value or worth of a particular course of action or state of affairs. The nonrational part of the soul is the source of such desires as arise from the appetites and emotions. These desires are blind in the sense that they do not depend fundamentally upon the agent's view of the good. Since these sources of motivation differ, they may conflict, and in certain cases, the desires of the nonrational soul may motivate the agent contrary to his or her "desires" for the good. In some such way, Plato tried to account for motivational conflict and for the possibility of both self-mastery and its opposite.

On the basis of this distinction, then, Plato rejected Socrates' (or his own earlier) view that a person's desires are always desires for the "good" and that what a person most desires is what is (thought) best. Elementary as these points are, they suffice to show the possibility of weakness of will. The desires of hunger and sex, the desires of anger and fear, do not depend upon one's assessment of the value of doing what one is thereby inclined to do. But if such desires exist, as they surely do, then it is possible that they are strong enough to motivate one contrary to one's judgment of what is best; it is possible that one's evaluations and desires diverge in certain cases in such a way that one is led to do things which one does not think worth doing, or as much worth doing as some available option. Hence socratism is false. There are no good theoretical grounds for denying *akrasia*.

(Watson 1977, 319–20)

(For additional discussion of this Platonic approach to moral psychology, see Chapter 36.)

If we take "someone wants to do x more than y" in the evaluational sense, then (1) is true (perhaps even trivially true) but (2) is false: Someone's valuing x more than y doesn't imply that they will be motivated to do x rather than y. If, alternatively, we take "someone wants to do x more than y" in the motivational sense, then (2) is true (perhaps by definition) but (1) is false: Unfortunately, thinking that something is better doesn't imply that we're more strongly motivated to pursue that thing.

RECOMMENDED READING

Sripada, Chandra. 2017. "Willpower, Freedom, and Responsibility." In *The Routledge Companion to Free Will*, edited by Kevin Timpe, Meghan Griffith, and Neil Levy, 444–53. New York: Routledge.

Stroud, Sarah, and Larisa Svirsky. 2021. "Weakness of Will." In *The Stanford Encyclopedia of Philosophy*, edited by Edward N. Zalta, Winter 2021. https://plato.stanford.edu/archives/win2021/entries/weakness-will.

Watson, Gary. 1977. "Skepticism about Weakness of Will." *The Philosophical Review* 86: 316–39.

WORKS CITED

Davidson, Donald. 2001 [1969]. "How Is Weakness of the Will Possible?" In *Essays on Actions and Events*, 25–35. New York: Oxford University Press.

Davidson, Donald. 2001 [1978]. "Intending." In *Essays on Actions and Events*, 75–90. New York: Oxford University Press.

34

AN IMPOSSIBLE INTENTION?

THE TOXIN PUZZLE

We have already encountered one puzzle about intentional action: if someone's beliefs, desires, and other attitudes are going to explain their intentional actions, then those mental states need to cause the action in the right way; but it's not at all clear how to specify what counts as the "right way" (see Chapter 32). Another puzzle about intentional action comes from Gregory Kavka (1983). In this case the puzzle is not about the causes of action, but about some surprising (apparent) constraints on forming rational intentions:

> You are feeling extremely lucky. You have just been approached by an eccentric billionaire who has offered you the following deal. He places before you a vial of toxin that, if you drink it, will make you painfully ill for a day, but will not threaten your life or have any lasting effects. (Your spouse, a crack biochemist, confirms the properties of the toxin.) The billionaire will pay you one million dollars tomorrow morning if, at midnight tonight, you *intend* to drink the toxin tomorrow afternoon. He emphasizes that you need not drink the toxin to receive the money; in fact, the money will already be in your bank account hours before the time for drinking it arrives, if you succeed. (This is confirmed by your daughter, a lawyer, after she examines the legal and financial documents that the billionaire has signed.) All you have to do is sign the agreement and then intend at midnight tonight to drink the stuff tomorrow afternoon. You are perfectly free to change your mind after receiving the money and not

DOI: 10.4324/9781003126119-37

drink the toxin. (The presence or absence of the intention is to be determined by the latest "mind-reading" brain scanner and computing device designed by the great Doctor X. As a cognitive scientist, materialist, and faithful former student of Doctor X, you have no doubt that the machine will correctly detect the presence or absence of the relevant intention.)

Confronted with this offer, you gleefully sign the contract, thinking "what an easy way to become a millionaire." Not long afterwards, however, you begin to worry ...

(Kavka 1983, 33–34)

Why does Kavka say that you, as the recipient of this offer, might "begin to worry" about whether becoming a millionaire is as easy as it seems? Why can't you just form the intention at midnight and then drop it later? (Once the money is in your bank account, there will be no reason to drink the toxin, and thus no reason to maintain the intention to drink the toxin.) No problem.

Upon further reflection, securing the money might not be so easy after all. The first thing to note is something that's only implicit in the description of the case above: this intention has to be a *rational* intention. In other words, the assumption is that it's not possible to intend to do something if you have no reason to do that thing. You might think that we can easily reject this assumption; for example, couldn't I intend to raise my arm right now, even though I have no reason to raise my arm? Well, I can definitely raise my arm, but in this case it seems that I *do* have a reason, which is the desire to demonstrate that I can do arbitrary things. So it seems that the apparent counterexamples to this assumption don't work. It's hard to imagine a case in which I intend to do something that I literally have no reason to do.

For an intention to be genuine, you have to actually plan on doing the thing intended, which typically means that the intention will persist from the time it's formed until the time of action. But in this case you know that there's not going to be any reason to do the thing when the time rolls around, so you can't actually form the intention *now* to do that thing. It's almost like your knowledge that there won't be any reason to drink the toxin tomorrow reaches back into the past and undermines your attempts to form the intention tonight.

What about a commitment device? Could you just drink the poison even though you don't need to, and thus secure the intention? Well, drinking the toxin would be just as irrational (if not more irrational) than merely forming the intention to do so. You have no reason to drink the toxin, because whether or not you drink the toxin makes no difference to whether you receive the money. You might have a reason to drink the toxin if you were expecting this type of offer to show up again, because drinking it now might demonstrate your commitment and thus make it more likely that you'll receive similar offers in the future. But as a one-time offer, which this is intended to be, there's just no reason to drink the toxin.

So this is not a traditional dilemma, in the sense that you have two choices but it appears that something bad will happen either way you choose. Instead, it's a puzzle because there's this desirable outcome, a million dollars, that seems to be easily within your grasp; but when you reach out to grab it, it appears to keep moving farther away.

To summarize: On the one hand, forming an intention to drink the toxin seems like a ridiculously easy thing to do: you form intentions all the time, and you form intentions to drink things (even if just implicitly) multiple times a day. In other words, the nearest possible world in which you find yourself in possession of a million dollars is tantalizingly close: just one small intention and you're there. On the other hand, claims Kavka, it turns out that this possibility of a million dollars is not after all accessible to you. The only way you can form a rational intention is if you have a reason to do something—and you will never have a reason to drink the toxin. (Again, this is because actually drinking it makes no difference to whether you'll get the million dollars.) Without that reason, it seems that there's nothing for the intention to work with, so to speak, and thus it can never be initiated.

RESPONSES

Alfred Mele nicely summarizes the implications of the toxin puzzle for philosophy of action:

> Can such reasons to intend [to do something while having no reason to do it] issue in appropriate intentions? If so, can these intentions issue in corresponding intentional actions—even though the agent has no reason to perform those actions? If these questions are properly given an affirmative answer, at least one popular thesis in the philosophy of action is false. One could not properly "define an intentional act as one which the agent does *for a reason*." A popular thesis about the *explanation* of

> intentional actions would be false as well—namely, that explaining an
> intentional action (qua intentional) requires reference to reasons for
> *action*.

(Mele 1992, 171)

Thus the toxin puzzle is primarily a problem for those who want to develop a theory of practical rationality. Most of these theorists want to define intentional actions as actions done for a reason, but given that definition they are forced to say that drinking the toxin cannot be an intentional action (since there's no reason to do it). If they want to allow that drinking the toxin can be intentional, then they will have to give up on defining intentional action as something done for a reason. Similarly, as Mele notes, most people who theorize about practical rationality want to *explain* intentional actions by appealing to the reasons for those actions. But here again, the explanation of the action of drinking the toxin cannot appeal to any reasons for drinking the toxin, since there are none.

Perhaps you're still skeptical that forming this intention to drink the toxin is actually impossible. If so, you would be in good company, since there are several philosophers who have criticized Kavka's view of this puzzle.

For example, Gauthier (1998) claims that when we are evaluating the rationality of an action, we ought to look at the overall situation, which includes the consequences of the available options. Since we would certainly have reason to want the money being offered, intending to drink (and even drinking) the toxin can be rational because it leads to an outcome that we have reason to prefer.

This solution is sometimes called the "rationalist solution" to the toxin puzzle because it tries to show that it can in fact be rational to intend to drink the toxin. For a criticism of the rationalist solution (including Gauthier's version of it), see Levy (2009).

RECOMMENDED READING

Kavka, Gregory S. 1983. "The Toxin Puzzle." *Analysis* 43: 33–36.
Mele, Alfred R. 1992. "Intentions, Reasons, and Beliefs: Morals of the Toxin Puzzle." *Philosophical Studies* 68: 171–94.

WORKS CITED

Gauthier, David. 1998. "Rethinking the Toxin Puzzle." In *Rational Commitment and Social Justice: Essays for Gregory Kavka*, edited by Jules L. Coleman and Christopher W. Morris, 47–58. Cambridge University Press.

Levy, Ken. 2009. "On the Rationalist Solution to Gregory Kavka's Toxin Puzzle." *Pacific Philosophical Quarterly* 90: 267–89.

PART IV

SOCIAL DIMENSIONS

For the most part, previous chapters have focused on relatively individualistic concerns: how individual decisions work, and what conditions have to be in place for those decisions to be the kind of decision for which we can be morally responsible. This part expands the circle a bit and examines some of the ways in which our actions, for better or worse, impinge upon other people. Our interest in free will isn't just metaphysical; it's personal, and it's also social.

The first few chapters in this part explore different models of the structure of our moral psychology. Is it better to think in terms of a hierarchy of desires (Chapter 35), or in terms of competing sources of motivation (Chapter 36)? The answer also has implications for how we think about addiction (Chapter 37).

The next three chapters examine general features of the moral community and our place in it. We examine the importance of the reactive attitudes (Chapter 38, "Escaping the Strains of Involvement"), and we home in on some puzzles involving one of the most central reactive attitudes: blame (Chapter 39). We then look at a troubling example (Chapter 40) of someone who seems to be operating at the margins of the moral community—a case that stretches our theorizing about blame to the breaking point. Part of the difficulty with extreme

DOI: 10.4324/9781003126119-38

cases like this is that we're not sure how to handle them from a moral *or* a legal perspective. Chapter 41 ("Problems with Pre-punishment") affords us a chance to look at some additional puzzles involving the legal perspective.

Speaking of evil and punishment, Chapter 42 ("The Unfortunate Fawn") introduces the problem of evil—the argument from evil against theism—and a response to the problem that appeals to free will.

Finally, Chapter 43 asks whether it makes sense to move beyond discussion of the social *dimensions* of agency and talk about social *agents* themselves.

35

A HIERARCHY OF DESIRES

HOW SHOULD WE THINK ABOUT INTERNAL CONFLICT?

Harry Frankfurt is famous for his (apparent) counterexample to the principle of alternative possibilities (see Chapter 16); but he is perhaps even more famous for the hierarchical model of human psychology that he introduces in his essay "Freedom of the Will and the Concept of a Person" (1971). One of Frankfurt's primary aims in this article is to use some observations about human psychology to help distinguish between persons and non-persons, and to do so in a way that helps explain why free will is so desirable. An essential element of his account is a hierarchical ordering of desires.

Consider an everyday desire, such as the desire for a cup of coffee. The object of the desire is the coffee, and the desire itself is a mental state that consists of some sort of positive attitude toward the object. Now note that there is an extremely wide range of things that can serve as the object of a desire: an object, a person, or a state of affairs (to mention just a few possibilities). Most relevant for our purposes is the fact that desires *themselves* can become the object of a desire. For example, I might find myself with a desire for a second cup of coffee, but then realize that it's only been an hour since I had my first cup. (It was a late night.) At that point I might want my desire for coffee to go away. In other words, I have a desire about a desire: I desire *that my desire for coffee subside*.

DOI: 10.4324/9781003126119-39

When we have desires about our desires, we are, figuratively speaking, moving up a level in our psychology; thus Frankfurt refers to desires about desires as second-order desires. (A third-order desire would be a desire about a desire about a desire, and so on.)

Two more definitions are needed before we can get Frankfurt's view on the table. Some of our desires move us to action, and others don't. Typically my desire for coffee will result in me drinking a cup, but sometimes it doesn't. When a desire does move us to action, we can describe that desire as our *will*. And we can take a desire that moves us to action and make it the object of a second-order desire: in other words, we can have a desire that one of our first-order desires be our will. I might have a desire to order both the steak and the fish, but I might also want the desire for fish to be my will—to be the one that moves me to action. Frankfurt describes this particular type of second-order desire as a second-order *volition*.

To be a person, on Frankfurt's view, is to have the capacity to form second-order volitions. This is a capacity to reflect on and then endorse or reject a first-order desire, making the judgment that we either want or don't want that first-order desire to move us to action.

Frankfurt provides some further support for his view by constructing a thought experiment involving a hypothetical creature that he calls a *wanton*. A wanton is at least minimally rational, and is capable of having desires, but *not* capable of forming second-order volitions:

> The essential characteristic of a wanton is that he does not care about his will. His desires move him to do certain things, without its being true of him either that he wants to be moved by those desires or that he prefers to be moved by other desires. The class of wantons includes all nonhuman animals that have desires and all very young children. Perhaps it also includes some adult human beings as well. In any case, adult humans may be more or less wanton; they may act wantonly, in response to first-order desires concerning which they have no volitions of the second order, more or less frequently.
>
> (Frankfurt 1971, 11)

To summarize: "When a person acts, the desire by which he is moved is either the will he wants or a will he wants to be without. When a *wanton* acts, it is neither" (1971, 14).

Of course, we are not just interested in personhood but also in free will. And as it turns out, Frankfurt thinks that second-order volitions are also essential for free will: "It is only because a person has volitions of the second order that he is capable both of enjoying and of lacking freedom of the will" (1971, 14). But Frankfurt's model also allows us to distinguish between two important types of freedom. We can recognize freedom of *action* as the freedom to do what we want to do. (For example, I typically have freedom of action with respect to my desires for coffee.) And then we can say that freedom of *will* goes beyond freedom of action. Freedom of will is the freedom to have the will that I want to have, which is to say the freedom to want what I want to want. And putting it that way, claims Frankfurt, helps us articulate the value of free will:

> A person who is free to do what he wants to do may yet not be in a position to have the will he wants. Suppose, however, that he enjoys both freedom of action and freedom of the will. Then he is not only free to do what he wants to do; he is also free to want what he wants to want. It seems to me that he has, in that case, all the freedom it is possible to desire or to conceive. There are other good things in life, and he may not possess some of them. But there is nothing in the way of freedom that he lacks.
>
> (Frankfurt 1971, 17)

According to Frankfurt, then, someone who is free to want what they want to want has in their possession everything that's valuable about free will.

RESPONSES

Frankfurt's view is worth examining for its own sake (although we will look at some criticism below), but it's even more important when placed in its historical context. As Heath White (2019) argues, Frankfurt shattered the prevailing assumption that obstacles to free will must come from outside the agent:

> Frankfurt [makes] the distinction between "persons" and "wantons" and defines it by saying that persons are those who are capable of second-order desires, while wantons are not. Only the former have the capacity for free will. Critically, however, what is gone in Frankfurt's account is the classical compatibilist idea that the only obstacles to free will are external to the agent. Since Frankfurt's article was published, discussion

of free will in analytic philosophy circles has been voluminous, but most participants concur on this basic point.

It is an oversimplification, but not wholly inaccurate, therefore, to say that "classical" compatibilism was a movement that began in 1651 with Hobbes's Leviathan and ended in [1971] with Frankfurt's "Freedom of the Will and the Concept of a Person." Or, put another way, analytic philosophers of the last generation have rediscovered a basic distinction in the philosophy of free will that was observed from Aristotle to the Enlightenment but lost (or rather, deliberately obscured) by the British empiricists.

(White 2019, 231)

(For more on classical compatibilism, see Chapter 12.)

Although most respondents have endorsed Frankfurt's insight about obstacles to the will, his hierarchical model hasn't been nearly as widely accepted. One representative critique of this model comes from Gary Watson (1975), who argues that Frankfurt has failed to identify the psychological distinction that is most relevant to free will and moral responsibility. On Watson's view, the relevant distinction is not the one between higher- and lower-order desires, but instead the (Platonic) distinction between desires and *values*. (For more on Watson's view, see Chapter 36.)

Watson points out that a second-order desire, despite occupying a higher level, is still just a desire. And if it's possible to be a wanton with respect to a first-order desire, then it's also possible to be a wanton with respect to a second-order desire (and a third-order desire, and so on). So it would seem that we could never settle the question of whether someone enjoys freedom of the will unless we could complete the impossible (or at least impractical) task of ruling out wantonness for an indefinite number of desire levels. As Watson notes, Frankfurt responds to this challenge by claiming that we can decisively identify with a first-order desire, and this decisive identification precludes the need for ruling out wantonness with respect to higher orders. As Frankfurt puts it, "this commitment 'resounds' throughout the potentially endless array of higher orders" (1971, 16).

One problem with this move is that it seems arbitrary (Watson 1975, 217–18). We wanted assurances that we wouldn't find any wantonness as we moved up the hierarchy of desires, and we're simply told that moving up isn't necessary in the case of decisive commitments.

And if Frankfurt tries to appeal to something else to explain why this move isn't arbitrary, then he is implicitly acknowledging that the hierarchy of desires isn't the fundamental feature of free agency; something else is more fundamental, because that other thing is required to avoid arbitrariness with respect to decisive commitments.

Another important critique, largely in agreement with Watson's, can be found in Scanlon (1998, 50–55). Scanlon takes issue with Frankfurt's focus on competing desires, because he thinks a framework that focuses on desires is too simplistic to adequately model our practical reasoning processes. Scanlon thinks that we should instead be talking about reasons themselves, and the complex ways in which they interact with each other in our practical thinking.

RECOMMENDED READING

Frankfurt, Harry G. 1971. "Freedom of the Will and the Concept of a Person." *Journal of Philosophy* 68: 5–20.
Watson, Gary. 1975. "Free Agency." *The Journal of Philosophy* 72: 205–20.

WORKS CITED

Scanlon, T. M. 1998. *What We Owe to Each Other*. Cambridge, MA: Harvard University Press.
White, Heath. 2019. *Fate and Free Will: A Defense of Theological Determinism*. Durham, NC: University of Notre Dame Press.

36

THE CONFLICT BETWEEN DESIRES AND VALUES

A PLATONIC APPROACH TO MORAL RESPONSIBILITY

As we saw in Chapter 35, Harry Frankfurt (1971) used a distinction between higher-order and lower-order desires to help distinguish between persons and non-persons. We also examined a powerful criticism from Gary Watson (1975). On Watson's view, the relevant distinction is not the one between higher- and lower-order desires, but instead the (Platonic) distinction between desires and *values*. In this chapter we're going to take a closer look at this latter distinction.

Watson characterizes the Platonic model in contrast to Hume's model. Hume, like Plato, acknowledges a divide between the rational part of the soul ("Reason") and the irrational part of the soul ("Appetite"), but he and Plato disagree about the role of the rational part. On Plato's view, the rational part of the soul serves as an alternative source of motivation through its role in producing values. Hume takes a different view:

> On Hume's account, Reason is not a source of motivation, but a faculty of determining what is true and what is false, a faculty concerned solely with "matters of fact" and "relations among ideas." It is completely dumb on the question of what to do. ... Its essential role would not be to supply motivation—Reason is not that kind of thing—but rather to calculate,

DOI: 10.4324/9781003126119-40

within a context of desires and ends, how to fulfill those desires and serve those ends. For Plato, however, the rational part of the soul is not some kind of inference mechanism. It is itself a source of motivation. In general form, the desires of Reason are desires for "the Good."

(Watson 1975, 207)

For Watson, then, the essential element of the Platonic view of human psychology is that values and desires generate two different sources of motivation:

Plato was calling attention to the fact that it is one thing to think a state of affairs good, worthwhile, or worthy of promotion, and another simply to desire or want that state of affairs to obtain. Since the notion of value is tied to (cannot be understood independently of) those of the good and worthy, it is one thing to value (think good) a state of affairs and another to desire that it obtain. However, to think a thing good is at the same time to desire it (or its promotion). Reason is thus an original spring of action. It is because valuing is essentially related to thinking or *judging* good that ... values provide reasons for action.

(Watson 1975, 208)

So values provide rational motivation for action, whereas desires provide irrational (perhaps a better word would be *non*rational) motivation for action. On Watson's view, our values express our view about the sort of life worth living; they "consist in those principles and ends" which, upon reflection, we would endorse "as definitive of the good, fulfilling, and defensible life" (1975, 215). And since motivation can come from different sources, that explains why we are sometimes pushed in different directions with respect to what to do.

This view contains a puzzling asymmetry. As noted above, if someone values something, then they will also desire it; but the reverse is not true. In other words, on this view it's possible to desire something that we do not value *at all*:

The cases in which one in no way values what one desires are perhaps rare, but surely they exist. Consider the case of a woman who has a sudden urge to drown her bawling child in the bath; or the case of a squash player who, while suffering an ignominious defeat, desires to smash his opponent in the face with the racquet. It is just false that the mother values her child's being drowned or that the player values the injury and suffering of his opponent. But they desire these things nonetheless. They desire them in spite of themselves. It is not that they assign to these actions an initial value which is then outweighed by other considerations. These activities are not even represented by a positive entry, however small, on the initial "desirability matrix."

(Watson 1975, 210)

Not everyone would agree with Watson that these rare cases involve a complete lack of valuing. But even if these cases do involve a minuscule positive entry on the desirability matrix, the broader point seems undeniable: there can be (and all too often *is*) a sharp divergence between what we desire and what we value.

This divergence between desire and value features prominently in Watson's account of what makes actions free or unfree: "The problem of free action arises because what one desires may not be what one values, and what one most values may not be what one is finally moved to get" (1975, 209). It's possible for us to be motivated to do things that we don't think are worth doing, and this possibility forms "the basis for the principal problem of free action: a person may be obstructed by his own will" (1975, 213). (So not everyone agrees with Nagel (and van Inwagen) that the main problem of free will has to do with its relationship to determinism; see Chapter 24.)

Recall that on Frankfurt's view, the main problem of freedom resides in a different conflict: a conflict between two different types of desire, namely lower-order desires and higher-order desires. If my desire to have that second cup of coffee moves me to action, but I don't *want* that desire to move me to action, then I don't have the will that I want and I am unfree in an important way.

Frankfurt and Watson, then, offer two importantly different accounts of freedom that rest on two different models of human psychology and thus describe failures of freedom in two different ways.

RESPONSES

In Chapter 30, we noted that there are some important agency-relevant descriptors that overlap significantly but not completely with our core descriptors ("free" and "morally responsible"). In that chapter we mentioned "autonomous" and "voluntary" but focused exclusively on the latter. Here it's worth noting that much of the discussion of Frankfurt's view, Watson's view, and related views has been in the context of theorizing about autonomous action, or personal autonomy more broadly.

Susan Wolf (2013 [1987]) groups both Frankfurt's view and Watson's view into the category of "deep-self" views, because they make it a requirement of moral responsibility that agents control not just their actions but their wills; and the locus of control of the will is supposed to come from a part of the self that runs even deeper than the will. (For Wolf's criticism of deep-self views, see Chapter 48.) For a different criticism of Watson's view, described as an "endorsement view," see Buss (2012). For a defense of Watson against Buss (and others), see Mitchell-Yellin (2014, 2015).

RECOMMENDED READING

Buss, Sarah, and Andrea Westlund. 2018. "Personal Autonomy." In *The Stanford Encyclopedia of Philosophy*, edited by Edward N. Zalta, Spring 2018. https://plato.stanford.edu/archives/spr2018/entries/personal-autonomy.

Dryden, Jane. n.d. "Autonomy." In *The Internet Encyclopedia of Philosophy*. https://iep.utm.edu/autonomy.

Mitchell-Yellin, Benjamin. 2015. "The Platonic Model: Statement, Clarification and Defense." *Philosophical Explorations* 18: 378–92.

WORKS CITED

Buss, Sarah. 2012. "Autonomous Action: Self-Determination in the Passive Mode." *Ethics* 122: 647–91.

Frankfurt, Harry G. 1971. "Freedom of the Will and the Concept of a Person." *Journal of Philosophy* 68: 5–20.

Mitchell-Yellin, Benjamin. 2014. "In Defense of the Platonic Model: A Reply to Buss." *Ethics* 124: 342–57.

Watson, Gary. 1975. "Free Agency." *The Journal of Philosophy* 72: 205–20.

Wolf, Susan. 2013 [1987]. "Sanity and the Metaphysics of Responsibility." In *Ethical Theory: An Anthology*, 2nd ed., 330–39. Chichester: Wiley-Blackwell.

CAN ADDICTION BE EXCUSED?

SOME DIFFICULTIES WITH THE WAY WE TREAT ADDICTION

Gary Watson (1999) explores a puzzle about addictions that affects responsibility judgments in both the legal and the moral realm. We can introduce the puzzle by considering the following argument, adapted from Watson (1999, 593). The argument has to do with criminal responsibility for drinking in public:

(1) If someone is a severe alcoholic, then he lacks control over his alcohol consumption.
(2) Is someone lacks control over a particular type of behavior, then he should not be punished for that behavior.
(3) Therefore, if someone is a severe alcoholic then he should not be punished for drinking in public.

This argument seems pretty compelling. As Watson points out, however, the courts have been reluctant to accept it because it threatens to license too much criminal behavior:

> Perhaps addictions are sources of volitional impairments, the courts seem to grant. Nevertheless, unless there is a way to "demarcate" the kind of impairment involved in addiction from the ways in which passions, prejudices, undue influenceability, weakness of will, etc. diminish

DOI: 10.4324/9781003126119-41

control (impairments that may well affect the "vast bulk of the population"), acknowledging this defense "threatens to tear the fabric of the criminal law as an instrument of social control." So it is not that claims of addiction do not draw upon powerful legally relevant principles; it is that the law cannot see a way of keeping this defense within predictable and reasonable bounds.

(Watson 1999, 596)

Thus, the challenge that Watson takes up has two parts. First, how are we to assess an agent's moral responsibility for addictive behavior? And second, how should the results of the first question influence our approach to criminal responsibility?

Gideon Yaffe (2001) provides a helpful framework for thinking about the first question. As he notes, we can group approaches to addictive behavior according to how they categorize that behavior. There are three basic categories, corresponding roughly to a success or failure of rationality or control: (i) rational behavior within the control of the agent; (ii) behavior that is irrational because it goes against the better judgment of the agent (e.g., weakness of will); and (iii) behavior that is not under the agent's control and is therefore not free. Some view addiction as eliminating freedom, some view addiction as merely producing irrational behavior, and some view addiction as just one of many influences on rational choice. On Yaffe's view, the best existing approaches will put addictive behavior in category (ii) or (iii)—but these approaches struggle to explain *which* of those two categories addictive behavior belongs in, and why.

We have looked at Frankfurt's (1971) view in some detail (see Chapter 35), but it's worth revisiting here because he has quite a bit to say about addictive behavior. First, recall that what Frankfurt claims to be distinctive about free agency is the ability to have and act on second-order desires (i.e., desires about what to desire). Now consider the unwilling addict (1971, 12–14). The unwilling addict has a desire for the drug, and also a desire to refrain from taking the drug. (Both of these desires are first-order desires.) He has a second-order desire that the desire to refrain be effective; he wants the desire to refrain to be his will. Unfortunately, the first-order desire to take the drug often wins out, so his actual will is different from what he wants it to be; this is the sense in which he is an unwilling addict.

Frankfurt's account seems to capture something important about many cases of addiction, but Yaffe's complaint seems apt. Is it more accurate to describe the unwilling addict as unfree (because he doesn't have the will that he wants to have), and therefore in category (iii)? Or is it more accurate to describe the unwilling addict as irrational (acting against his better judgment), and therefore in category (ii)? A case could be made for either answer.

It's also worth noting that Frankfurt describes a third sort of addict who might actually fall into category (i):

> In illustration, consider a third kind of addict. Suppose that his addiction has the same physiological basis and the same irresistible thrust as the addictions of the unwilling and wanton addicts, but that he is altogether delighted with his condition. He is a willing addict, who would not have things any other way. If the grip of his addiction should somehow weaken, he would do whatever he could to reinstate it; if his desire for the drug should begin to fade, he would take steps to renew its intensity.
>
> The willing addict's will is not free, for his desire to take the drug will be effective regardless of whether or not he wants this desire to constitute his will. But when he takes the drug, he takes it freely and of his own free will. I am inclined to understand his situation as involving the overdetermination of his first-order desire to take the drug. This desire is his effective desire because he is physiologically addicted. But it is his effective desire also because he wants it to be. His will is outside his control, but, by his second-order desire that his desire for the drug should be effective, he has made this will his own. Given that it is therefore not only because of his addiction that his desire for the drug is effective, he may be morally responsible for taking the drug.
>
> (Frankfurt 1971, 19–20)

If Frankfurt is right in his diagnosis of the willing addict—who might be responsible even though his will is not free—then addiction by itself does not automatically excuse someone from responsibility. What matters instead is whether he embraces or resists his desire to take the drug.

A significantly different approach to addiction (see Chapter 36) treats it as a result of competing sources of motivation, rather than conflicting sets of desires. The (unwilling) addict judges that it would be better not to engage in addictive behavior, but is overcome by his desire for the substance or activity to which he is addicted. Yaffe considers some representative examples of these views (including Watson's 1975 view) but argues that they also fail to give a clear answer to the question of whether addictive behavior should be placed in category (ii) or (iii). In particular, they have a hard time distinguishing between compulsive behavior (category (iii)) and weakness of will (category (ii)).

RESPONSES

One influential way of addressing this problem involves an appeal to *reasons-responsiveness*. (See Chapter 18 for a brief discussion of reasons-responsiveness.) For example, on Fischer and Ravizza's (1998) approach, we can distinguish between weakness and compulsion by looking at what the agent would do in a variety of counterfactual situations containing different reasons to refrain from the addictive behavior. If the agent's behavior would follow a recognizably rational pattern in these counterfactual situations (e.g., a pattern in which the addictive behavior starts to go away as the reasons to refrain become stronger and stronger), then we have reason to believe that the behavior is merely weak-willed rather than compulsive. Yaffe (2001, 214–15), however, suggests the "hydrophobic heroin addict" as a problem case for this analysis. A hydrophobic heroin addict would not take heroin if it somehow required swimming; but in other cases her decision to take or refrain from taking heroin follows a recognizable pattern of responsiveness to reasons. Does her behavior count as compulsive or merely weak-willed? It's not clear.

One potentially promising approach to these difficulties can be found in Levy (2006). Levy proposes that we gain deeper insight by considering "extended agency": the ability to shape one's values, and one's will more generally, over time. Perhaps we can ascertain the specific ways that addiction undermines responsibility by examining the ways in which it undermines our extended agency. Nevertheless, even this approach will no doubt face cases in which the verdict is unclear; Levy himself considers a few such cases.

Above we identified two parts to the challenge raised by Watson (1999). We have been focusing on the first question ("How are we to assess an agent's moral responsibility for addictive behavior?"), which is difficult enough, without even broaching the second question ("How should the results of the first question influence our approach to criminal responsibility?"). We won't be able to remedy that deficit in this chapter (although see Radoilska 2013 for an extended treatment of this and other related challenges of theorizing about addiction), but we can close with an insightful diagnosis from Watson:

> The law's resistance to addiction-based defenses runs counter to substantial evidence that addictive behavior can be less than fully responsible in legally pertinent ways. Nonetheless, the moral and practical reasons for resisting this defense are in the end probably decisive. Of course, this sort of conflict is not unusual; indeed it is inevitable. In order to do its job, the criminal law is severely limited in its capacity to respond to the merits of individual cases. We need legal institutions to be more or less heavy handed.
>
> (Watson 1999, 618)

Watson ends by proposing a speculative compromise solution that he borrows from Morse (2000). The compromise would involve introducing a new hybrid verdict of *guilty but only partially responsible*. The attractiveness of this proposal is that has the potential of allowing the legal system "to record the defendant's complicity in her own plight and, at the same time, to do at least some justice to the special difficulties under which she labors" (Watson 1999, 619).

RECOMMENDED READING

Duff, Antony. 2009. "Legal and Moral Responsibility." *Philosophy Compass* 4: 978–86.

Levy, Neil. 2006. "Autonomy and Addiction." *Canadian Journal of Philosophy* 36: 427–47.

Pickard, Hanna. 2017. "Addiction." In *The Routledge Companion to Free Will*, edited by Kevin Timpe, Meghan Griffith, and Neil Levy, 454–67. New York: Routledge.

Yaffe, Gideon. 2001. "Recent Work on Addiction and Responsible Agency." *Philosophy & Public Affairs* 30: 178–221.

WORKS CITED

Fischer, John Martin, and Mark Ravizza. 1998. *Responsibility and Control: A Theory of Moral Responsibility*. Cambridge: Cambridge University Press.

Frankfurt, Harry G. 1971. "Freedom of the Will and the Concept of a Person." *Journal of Philosophy* 68: 5–20.

Morse, Stephen J. 2000. "Hooked on Hype: Addiction and Responsibility." *Law and Philosophy* 19: 3–49.

Radoilska, Lubomira. 2013. *Addiction and Weakness of Will*. Oxford: Oxford University Press.

Watson, Gary. 1975. "Free Agency." *The Journal of Philosophy* 72: 205–20.

Watson, Gary. 1999. "Excusing Addiction." *Law and Philosophy* 18: 589–619.

ESCAPING THE STRAINS OF INVOLVEMENT

THE IMPORTANCE OF THE REACTIVE ATTITUDES

P. F. Strawson's famous article "Freedom and Resentment" (1962) has exerted (and continues to exert) a considerable amount of influence on contemporary discussions of free will and moral responsibility. It ranges over a wide variety of issues, but one important focus is on interpersonal relationships, and how certain facts about our interpersonal relationships neutralize the apparent threat that determinism poses to free will. Neal Tognazzini (2015) provides a particularly helpful summary of Strawson's article that artfully weaves together many of its main claims:

> One of the insights of P. F. Strawson's [article] is his provocative claim that the center of the moral responsibility universe is not freedom, or the ability to do otherwise, or the utility of punishment, but "our natural human commitment to ordinary inter-personal attitudes" (Strawson 1962, as reprinted in Watson 2003: 83). It is thus misguided, according to Strawson, to attempt to combat our anxiety about determinism either by trying to peer deeper into the metaphysical nature of persons (only to be frustrated that there "still seems to remain a gap" between the exercise of whatever capacity we locate and "its supposed moral consequences" (92)) or by appealing to how efficient our blaming practices are "in regulating behavior in socially desirable ways" (73). Instead,

DOI: 10.4324/9781003126119-42

Strawson suggests that we can regain our confidence simply by remembering, and acknowledging, that we are human—not any easy thing for a philosopher to do (especially one who does philosophy "in our cool, contemporary style" (77)), but a requirement for avoiding the varieties of skepticism that are a perennial hazard of the profession.

In this particular case, the relevant aspect of "our common humanity" (85) is "the general structure or web of human attitudes and feelings" (91) that makes possible, or perhaps even constitutes, ordinary interpersonal relationships. This structure includes attitudes that "rest on, and reflect, an expectation of, and demand for, the manifestation of a certain degree of goodwill or regard on the part of other human beings towards ourselves" (84), a demand that presupposes, or perhaps constitutes, the moral responsibility of those to whom it is addressed. Since this framework of attitudes is simply "given with the fact of human society" (91), being reminded that we are human should be enough to quell our anxiety about determinism—at least until we stop playing backgammon and head back into the philosophy classroom.

(Tognazzini 2015, 19–20)

Despite the importance of interpersonal relationships, Strawson recognizes that we may sometimes feel the need to temporarily withdraw from our interpersonal relationships. Instead of seeing ourselves as continuing participants in the system of mutual expectations of good will, sometimes we need to take a step back and look at things from a more detached, objective perspective:

We look with an objective eye on the compulsive behavior of the neurotic or the tiresome behavior of a very young child, thinking in terms of treatment or training. But we can sometimes look with something like the same eye on the behavior of the normal and the mature. We have this resource and can sometimes use it; as a refuge, say, from the strains of involvement; or as an aid to policy; or simply out of intellectual curiosity. Being human, we cannot, in the normal case, do this for long, or altogether. If the strains of involvement, say, continue to be too great, then we have to do something else—like severing a relationship.

(Strawson 2003 [1962], 80)

Most of us are probably at least somewhat familiar with this interpersonal tactic; but in this case looking at an extreme example will provide some additional illumination. The example comes from the graphic novel *Watchmen*, in which one of the characters, Jonathan Osterman (also known as Dr. Manhattan) is rendered superhuman by a lab accident. His body is disintegrated by a machine used for "intrinsic field experiments," but somehow he figures out how to put himself back together—and control physical matter in general. This ability to manipulate matter at the fundamental level renders him almost omnipotent. Unfortunately for Osterman, the accident also renders him almost emotionless. As you might imagine, these changes lead to some difficulties for his interpersonal relationships—culminating in an attempt to take refuge from the strains of involvement by transporting himself to Mars.

The kinds of emotions and attitudes that Dr. Manhattan is missing are important ones: praise, blame, gratitude, forgiveness, resentment, indignation, guilt, and a host of others. The collection of relevant attitudes is extremely diverse—so much so that it's hard to see what might unify them under a single category. One common thread, though, seems to be the presence (or at least the perception of the presence) of a certain *quality of will*. When someone shows (or seems to show) good will toward us, we are inclined toward gratitude; conversely, when someone shows (or seems to show) ill will toward us, we are inclined toward resentment. (Indignation typically arises when we perceive someone else to be displaying ill will toward another person; guilt typically arises when we perceive that we have displayed ill will toward someone else.) These attitudes—the *reactive attitudes*—are an essential feature of human life, and almost everyone agrees that they are intimately connected with moral responsibility. There is much controversy, however, over the exact relationship between the reactive attitudes and moral responsibility.

RESPONSES

Strawson's article has generated a prodigious amount of discussion, which continues apace. (It is interesting to note, as pointed out by Snowdon and Gomes (2021), that "Freedom and Resentment" is probably Strawson's most famous and widely discussed paper, even though it covers topics that he gave very little attention to, relative to his overall body of work.) For two recent snapshots of this discussion, see McKenna and Russell (2008) and Shoemaker and Tognazzini (2014).

Despite the controversy over whether and to what extent moral responsibility depends on the reactive attitudes, it's clear that a life (or a community) without the reactive attitudes would be an impoverished one indeed. In fact, a lack of capacity for the reactive attitudes is one way of characterizing the troubling (and puzzling) condition of *psychopathy*. One of the fundamental puzzles about psychopathy is that when we are asking whether the psychopath is responsible for his actions, we feel pulled in different directions. On the one hand, since the reactive attitudes are so important for moral responsibility, the inability to properly engage with the reactive attitudes suggests that psychopaths are not responsible for their actions. On the other hand, the types of behaviors characteristic of psychopathy incline us to believe that psychopaths are among the *most* blameworthy for their behavior. Given a plausible assumption that blameworthiness implies responsibility, it easy to see that we have reason to both accept and reject the claim that psychopaths are responsible for their bad behavior. (For additional discussion of psychopathy, see Chapter 40.)

Is Dr. Manhattan a psychopath? It seems unconventional to describe a superhero as a psychopath, but if an inability to experience and respond to the reactive attitudes is indeed distinctive of psychopathy, then we might be pushed toward classifying him that way. On the other hand, if his removal to Mars was prompted by interpersonal difficulties (as it appears to have been), then maybe he's not completely insensitive to the reactive attitudes after all.

RECOMMENDED READING

Russell, Paul. 2017. "Free Will and Moral Sentiments: Strawsonian Theories." In *The Routledge Companion to Free Will*, edited by Kevin Timpe, Meghan Griffith, and Neil Levy, 96–108. New York: Routledge.

Strawson, P. F. 1962. "Freedom and Resentment." *Proceedings of the British Academy* 48: 1–25. Reprinted in *Free Will*, 2nd ed., edited by Gary Watson, 72–93. Oxford: Oxford University Press, 2003.

Tognazzini, Neal A. 2015. "The Strains of Involvement." In *The Nature of Moral Responsibility: New Essays*, edited by Randolph Clarke, Michael McKenna, and Angela M. Smith, 19–44. Oxford: Oxford University Press.

WORKS CITED

McKenna, Michael, and Paul Russell, eds. 2008. *Free Will and Reactive Attitudes*. Burlington, VT: Ashgate.

Shoemaker, David, and Neal Tognazzini, eds. 2014. *Oxford Studies in Agency and Responsibility, Volume 2: "Freedom and Resentment" at 50*. Oxford: Oxford University Press.

Snowdon, Paul, and Anil Gomes. 2021. "Peter Frederick Strawson." In *The Stanford Encyclopedia of Philosophy*, edited by Edward N. Zalta, Summer 2021. https://plato.stanford.edu/archives/sum2021/entries/strawson.

HYPOCRITICAL BLAME

CASTING THE FIRST STONE

As we have seen in other chapters, one way to define free will is to say that it is an eligibility criterion for moral responsibility: to have free will is to exercise the type of control, whatever that may be, that makes someone eligible to be morally responsible for their actions. We could, in turn, then view moral responsibility as an eligibility criterion for praise and blame: to be morally responsible is to be eligible for the types of beliefs, emotions, and/or behaviors that are characteristic of praise and blame. But even if we are setting aside the questions and problems surrounding free will, and the questions and problems surrounding moral responsibility, there are still questions and problems surrounding praise and blame. In this chapter we'll focus on some of the puzzles that arise when we start thinking about the concept and practice of blame.

First, though, here's a quick justification for the focus on the negative (blame) rather than the positive (praise). There are various contexts in which blame seems appropriate (or at least natural) but praise does not. For example, private blame is a common phenomenon but private praise is not (Coates and Tognazzini 2013, 4–5). Also, the relative threshold for blame seems much lower than for praise: mildly bad behavior often seems to warrant some small amount of blame, but mildly good behavior does not seem to warrant any praise (Eshleman 2014). (See Talbert 2019 for more on the asymmetries

DOI: 10.4324/9781003126119-43

between praise and blame.) This suggests that blame is a richer (or at least more complicated) phenomenon, and worthy of special focus.

We saw in Chapter 38 that the negative reactive attitudes—chief among them resentment, indignation, and guilt—are a response to a demonstration of a lack of good will. These reactive attitudes are intimately tied up with blame, and perhaps even essential to blame. To blame someone is to treat them in a way that reflects a recognition of a lack of good will on their part. Thus, blame is inescapably inter-personal. Whereas we can imagine someone exercising free will in isolation, and even having or lacking moral responsibility in isolation, blame requires interaction with others (or at least observation of oth-ers). For this reason (among others), theorizing about blame is a messy business that uncovers numerous puzzles and apparent paradoxes.

One such puzzle has to do with the apparent inappropriateness of blame in certain circumstances. Blame is clearly inappropriate when the person being blamed isn't even blameworthy; and it can be inappropri-ate when it's disproportional to the offense. But let's focus on a different sort of inappropriateness, which has to do with the blamer's position, or *standing*. What exactly gives someone standing to blame, and what are some of the ways in which someone might forfeit their standing?

Consider the following exchange from *The Great Gatsby*, as high-lighted and discussed in Coates and Tognazzini (2013):

> "Wait a minute," snapped Tom, "I want to ask Mr. Gatsby one more question."
>
> "Go on," Gatsby said politely.
>
> "What kind of row are you trying to cause in my house anyhow?"
>
> They were out in the open at last and Gatsby was content.
>
> "He wasn't causing a row." Daisy looked desperately from one to the other. "You're causing a row. Please have a little self control."
>
> "Self control!" repeated Tom incredulously. "I suppose the latest thing is to sit back and let Mr. Nobody from Nowhere make love to your wife. Well, if that's the idea you can count me out ... Nowadays people begin by sneering at family life and family institutions and next they'll throw everything overboard."
>
> (Fitzgerald 1995 [1925], 136–37)

On the surface, this seems to be a relatively standard instance of a tragically common phenomenon: one spouse blaming another for unfaithfulness. (Here, of course, Tom is blaming not just his wife, Daisy, but also Gatsby, who is the other participant in the affair.) Someone encountering this case for the first time might feel themselves inclined toward sharing in Tom's resentment toward Gatsby and Daisy. As you may recall, however, the story is more complicated than that: Tom himself is already involved in an affair of his own.

Upon learning (or remembering) that Tom himself is engaged in the very type of behavior that he's blaming Daisy and Gatsby for, you are probably less inclined to share in Tom's resentment, and perhaps even inclined to turn some of it back toward Tom himself. Given this new information, there seems to be something inappropriate about Tom's blame. On the surface, the diagnosis is easy: because of his hypocrisy, he has forfeited his standing to blame. But how exactly does hypocrisy undermine blame? Is there a general account of when and how someone loses the standing to blame?

RESPONSES

A full answer to these questions would require developing and endorsing a theory of blame itself, which we obviously can't do here. But we can examine the different ways in which existing theories handle these questions and look for common themes. Coates and Tognazzini (2013) provide a helpful summary of how some prominent theories explain the impropriety of hypocritical blame.

According to T. M. Scanlon (2008), blame is a way of highlighting that someone has demonstrated a lack of good will in a way that impairs their relationship with the blamer. When someone impairs a relationship, it's appropriate to point that out, and pointing it out also serves as a signal that the blamer will be adjusting their interactions with the wrongdoer in light of the impairment. On Scanlon's view, then, Tom's hypocritical blame is inappropriate because the impairment has already occurred, and he was the one that brought it about. On the other hand, it would seem that Daisy's unfaithfulness has impaired the relationship even more, so it's not as though there's nothing for Tom to bring attention to. Perhaps Scanlon's solution just shifts the question back a step, prompting us to ask why it's inappropriate to highlight further damage to a relationship that has already been damaged by the blamer.

R. Jay Wallace (2010) identifies a different source of inappropriateness. On his view, hypocritical blame demonstrates a partiality that is inconsistent with the equal moral standing of persons. If Tom is going to blame Daisy for her unfaithfulness, then he should have already blamed himself for *his* unfaithfulness. To ignore his own faithfulness is to make an exception of himself: to excuse himself, for no good reason, from the interpersonal sanctions that go along with wrongdoing. And this violates what would seem to be a fundamental commitment of morality, namely that we apply the same moral standards to everyone.

Macalester Bell (2013) turns a skeptical eye toward the idea that hypocrisy undermines the standing to blame. On her view, blame has a five-fold purpose: when it's functioning properly, blame (i) signals relational damage, (ii) gives notice to wrongdoers, (iii) motivates the target to change, (iv) educates and motivates members of the moral community, and (v) defends one's moral values. Perhaps hypocritical blame would be inappropriate if hypocrisy somehow clouded the blamer's perception of the wrongdoing; but Bell points out that similar wrongdoing in the past doesn't necessarily compromise one's moral vision, and in some cases can even enhance it. She also argues that blame can serve its five-fold purpose even when the blamer is himself guilty of wrongdoing. Moreover, we can acknowledge the blamer's moral failings without inferring that he has lost his standing to blame. Finally, she argues that we all have *responsibilities of reproach*: "special responsibilities within the domain of criticism" (2013, 279). To forswear blame in cases of hypocrisy would be to shirk these responsibilities of reproach. On her view, blame is not a privilege for the morally pure, but a useful tool for moral communication.

For some recent defenses of the inappropriateness of hypocritical blame, see Roadevin (2018) and Fritz and Miller (2018). Todd (2019) also defends a non-hypocrisy condition on blaming, and argues that a proper understanding of this condition will lead to a unified general account of the standing to blame.

RECOMMENDED READING

Coates, D. Justin, and Neal A. Tognazzini. 2013. "The Contours of Blame." In *Blame: Its Nature and Norms*, edited by D. Justin Coates and Neal A. Tognazzini, 3–26. Oxford University Press.

Todd, Patrick. 2019. "A Unified Account of the Moral Standing to Blame." *Noûs* 53: 347–74.

Tognazzini, Neal, and D. Justin Coates. 2021. "Blame." In *The Stanford Encyclopedia of Philosophy*, edited by Edward N. Zalta, Summer 2021. https://plato.stanford.edu/archives/sum2021/entries/blame/.

WORKS CITED

Bell, Macalester. 2013. The Standing to Blame: A Critique. In *Blame: Its Nature and Norms*, edited by D. Justin Coates and Neal A. Tognazzini, pp. 263–81. Oxford: Oxford University Press.

Eshleman, Andrew. 2014. "Worthy of Praise: Responsibility and Better-than-Minimally-Decent Agency." In *Oxford Studies in Agency and Responsibility, Volume 2: "Freedom and Resentment" at 50*, edited by David Shoemaker and Neal Tognazzini, 216–42. Oxford University Press.

Fitzgerald, F. Scott. 1995 [1925]. *The Great Gatsby*. New York: Scribner.

Fritz, Kyle G., and Daniel Miller. 2018. "Hypocrisy and the Standing to Blame." *Pacific Philosophical Quarterly* 99: 118–39.

Roadevin, Cristina. 2018. "Hypocritical Blame, Fairness, and Standing." *Metaphilosophy* 49: 137–52.

Scanlon, T. M. 2008. *Moral Dimensions: Permissibility, Meaning, Blame*. Harvard University Press.

Talbert, Matthew. 2019. "Moral Responsibility." In *The Stanford Encyclopedia of Philosophy*, edited by Edward N. Zalta, Winter 2019. https://plato.stanford.edu/archives/win2019/entries/moral-responsibility/.

Wallace, R. Jay. 2010. "Hypocrisy, Moral Address, and the Equal Standing of Persons." *Philosophy & Public Affairs* 38: 307–41.

THE TROUBLING CASE OF ROBERT HARRIS

THE PARADOX OF BLAME FOR EXTREME EVIL

In "Responsibility and the limits of evil" (1993 [1987]), Gary Watson offers a critical discussion of P. F. Strawson's theory of moral responsibility. (For more on Strawson's theory, see Chapter 38.) One important question that arises in this discussion involves *excuses* and *exemptions*: Under what conditions are people excused (or exempted entirely) from being morally responsible for their actions? Watson highlights a paradoxical feature of our blaming practices that arises when we consider extreme evil. On the one hand, extreme evil would seem to warrant the most severe forms of blame; but on the other hand, it can sometimes seem as though extreme evil disqualifies the evildoer from blame entirely. This paradox is poignantly (and tragically) illustrated in the case of Robert Harris (Watson 1993 [1987], 131ff.).

Watson quotes at length from a *Los Angeles Times* article (Corwin 1982) that profiles Harris, a convicted murderer who (at the time of the article) is imprisoned and awaiting the death penalty. Watson quotes at length because "it is very important here to work with realistic and detailed examples" (1993 [1987], 134n14). We, unfortunately, won't be able to look at all of those details in this chapter. So instead of quoting directly from the article, I will instead quote from Susan Wolf's (2011) summary. She summarizes the newspaper article as one

DOI: 10.4324/9781003126119-44

that depicts Harris's behavior and character in a way that makes clear that Harris is a horrible human being, nearly monstrous in his indifference to human life. No sane human being could fail to adjust his or her attitudes toward Harris in a way made appropriate by Harris's "impairment." ...

After describing the man Harris has become by the time he has committed the brutal murders for which he was eventually executed, Watson's article provides an account of Harris's childhood and adolescence. They are also brutal, and heartbreaking. Reading it, one thinks, "no wonder Harris grew to be so full of rage and hatred of his fellow man." Beyond this, reactions differ—but some people who read this, including me, are inclined to modify the attitudes their introduction to the crime and character of Robert Harris initially inspired. That the possibility of any kind of relationship with Harris is, probably permanently, impaired is beyond question. That one's attitudes toward him should include distrust and defensiveness, if not also an absence of good will, is not in doubt. But something else is in doubt, which in my ordinary way of speaking I would express as the question of whether one can justifiably blame him. Suspecting that one cannot, I would say that I neither blame him nor judge him to deserve blame.

(Wolf 2011, 333–34)

Wolf aptly describes the paradox generated by extreme evil. On the one hand, the more evil someone's deeds, the more we are inclined to blame (and perhaps punish) them. On the other hand, once the depth or extent of evil reaches a certain limit, we start to wonder if the individual committing the deeds is even part of the moral community at all. And presumably a reactive attitude such as blame can only be appropriately applied to a member of the moral community. For example, one reason why it would be inappropriate to blame your tire for going flat is that your tire is not a part of the moral community; it would be a kind of category mistake to react to any inanimate object in the same way that you react to fellow human persons. Similarly, it would be a kind of category mistake to react to a plant, or even an animal, as though they were a member of the moral community. So, to the extent that someone's engaging in extreme evil makes us doubt whether that person is a member of the moral community, we should also doubt whether blame is the appropriate attitude to take toward the person.

As Watson emphasizes, reactive attitudes such as blame are morally significant ways of communicating with each other. When we target someone with blame, we are typically letting them know that they have violated some sort of moral demand or expectation, and we are typically inviting them to respond in a way that sets the stage for excuse or recompense for that violation. Unfortunately, if someone is not capable of understanding the communication that the reactive attitudes are supposed to deliver, then those attitudes seem to lose their point. "At these outer limits [of the moral community], our reactive attitudes can be nothing more (or less) than than a denunciation forlorn of the hope of an adequate reply" (Watson 1993 [1987], 134).

The Harris case is even more complicated than this, because he is not just a perpetrator of extreme evil but also a *victim* of extreme evil. We had reasons to doubt whether Harris was an appropriate target of blame even before we learned about his formative experiences, but the additional information exerts even stronger pressure to modify our attitudes. So the knowledge of his formative circumstances adds another layer of complication and puzzlement to an already complex story. As Watson says (1993 [1987], 137), "Those misfortunes affect our responses in a special and non-evidential way. The question is why this should be so." Harris-type cases also highlight some of the implications of *moral luck* (see Chapter 44). The recognition of Harris's tragically bad luck "infuses one's reactive attitudes with a sense of irony" (1993 [1987], 139).

RESPONSES

Watson is more interested in showing how cases like that of Robert Harris cause trouble for a Strawsonian theory of moral responsibility, and less interested in settling the question of whether and to what extent Robert Harris is indeed blameworthy for his crimes. His claim is primarily that it's not clear how we should react to Harris: "we are unable to command an overall view of his life that permits the reactive attitudes to be sustained without ambivalence" (Watson 1993 [1987], 138).

Much of the ensuing discussion of individuals such as Robert Harris has focused on the issue of *moral ignorance*, asking whether a lack of moral knowledge excuses one from responsibility. Recall an example from Chapter 18: If I unintentionally detonate a bomb by flipping a light switch, I'm not responsible for the bomb going off because I wasn't aware that the switch was connected to the bomb. Ignorance gets me off the hook. It's more complicated in cases of *moral* ignorance, however; sometimes we feel reluctance to excuse someone from moral responsibility on the basis of a lack of moral knowledge. Vogel (1993), for example, contrasts the Harris case with a fictional case from Susan Wolf involving the son of an indulgent wealthy dictator (Wolf 2013 [1987]; see Chapter 48). Vogel uses this contrast to argue that the deprivation and abuse that Harris experienced as a child are what make it unfair to expect him to have turned out differently (on this point, see also Mason 2015, 2019). On Vogel's view, different sources of moral ignorance (e.g., extreme deprivation in contrast to exorbitant privilege) can generate different judgments about whether an individual is culpable for his or her ignorance.

Greenspan (2003) connects discussions of the Harris case with discussions of psychopathy more generally. (See also Chapter 38.) Identifying and diagnosing psychopaths is a complicated and difficult business, but one core characteristic of psychopathy is an *emotional deficit*: psychopaths suffer from a lack of various emotions, including the empathy that's required for seeing the well-being of other people as a source of moral reasons. In other words, psychopaths lack access to an important source of moral motivation. Greenspan argues that, despite these impairments, we are nevertheless justified in holding psychopaths responsible and making them the target of our blaming practices.

RECOMMENDED READING

Rudy-Hiller, Fernando. 2018. "The Epistemic Condition for Moral Responsibility." In *The Stanford Encyclopedia of Philosophy*, edited by Edward N. Zalta, Fall 2018. https://plato.stanford.edu/archives/fall2018/entries/moral-responsibility-epistemic.

Watson, Gary. 1993 [1987]. "Responsibility and the Limits of Evil: Variations on a Strawsonian Theme." In *Perspectives on Moral Responsibility*, edited by John Martin Fischer and Mark Ravizza, 119–48. Ithaca, NY: Cornell University Press, 1993.

Wolf, Susan. 2011. "Blame, Italian Style." In *Reasons and Recognition: Essays on the Philosophy of T.M. Scanlon*, edited by R. Jay Wallace, Rahul Kumar, and Samuel Freeman, 332–47. Oxford: Oxford University Press.

WORKS CITED

Corwin, Miles. 1982. "Icy Killer's Life Steeped in Violence." *Los Angeles Times*, May 16.

Greenspan, Patricia. 2003. "Responsible Psychopaths." *Philosophical Psychology* 16: 417–29.

Mason, Elinor. 2015. "Moral Ignorance and Blameworthiness." *Philosophical Studies* 172: 3037–57.

Mason, Elinor. 2019. *Ways to Be Blameworthy: Rightness, Wrongness, and Responsibility*. Oxford: Oxford University Press.

Vogel, Lawrence. 1993. "Understanding and Blaming: Problems in the Attribution of Moral Responsibility." *Philosophy and Phenomenological Research* 53: 129–42.

Wolf, Susan. 2013 [1987]. "Sanity and the Metaphysics of Responsibility." In *Ethical Theory: An Anthology*, 2nd ed., 330–39. Chichester: Wiley-Blackwell.

PROBLEMS WITH PRE-PUNISHMENT

TROUBLE IN THE PRE-CRIME DEPARTMENT

The year is 2054 and crime in Washington, D.C. is virtually non-existent. This is because it's been eliminated by the Department of Pre-crime, a law enforcement unit that periodically receives and then acts upon reliable reports of future crimes. These reports, which come from a group of clairvoyants, provide the who, the what, and the where of crimes that have yet to happen. Members of the department, led by Detective John Anderton, apprehend the (pre-)perpetrators before they can commit their crime. These detainees are then imprisoned for the crimes they *would have* committed, were it not for the pre-crime intervention. Anderton believes strongly in the system—until one day the clairvoyants predict that *he* will be the next one to commit murder.

You may recognize this as the plot of the movie *Minority Report*. The thought experiment that the movie is based on traces back to a short story by Philip K. Dick (1956), but the general idea shows up even earlier, in chapter V of Lewis Carroll's (1871) *Through the Looking Glass*:

> "It's a poor sort of memory that only works backwards," the Queen remarked.
> "What sort of things do *you* remember best?" Alice ventured to ask.

DOI: 10.4324/9781003126119-45

"Oh, things that happened the week after next," the Queen replied in a careless tone. "For instance, now" ... "there's the King's Messenger. He's in prison now, being punished: and the trial doesn't even begin till next Wednesday: and of course the crime comes last of all."

Whether it shows up in science fiction or a fairy tale, the idea of pre-punishment raises lots of interesting questions. Perhaps the most obvious question about pre-punishment is simply whether it could ever be morally justified. The answer to this question will at least partly depend on how reliable the predictions are, so let's suppose that they are 100% reliable. (As we saw in Chapter 8, the presence of infallible prediction seems to threaten free will; but let's set aside that worry for now.) The answer to the moral justification question will also partly depend on answers to more general questions about the purpose and grounding of punishment. For example, is primary aim of punishment to give wrongdoers the harsh treatment that they deserve as a result of their wrong actions? Or does punishment have some other primary aim, such as the rehabilitation of the wrongdoer or the betterment of society? We won't try to settle such questions here. We'll just use the word "punishment" to refer to whatever types of harsh treatment are appropriately administered to wrongdoers, while also noting that these different justifications for punishment might support different answers to questions about *pre*-punishment.

With these caveats in mind, our more specific question is this: Could we (as a society) ever be morally justified in punishing someone for crimes that he hasn't committed, but would certainly commit if he weren't prevented from doing so? There seem to be strong considerations pointing in different directions.

On one hand, pre-punishment seems obviously unjust, simply because it's always unjust to punish someone for a crime that they haven't committed. It's obviously wrong, for example, to imprison someone for a crime that someone else committed. And it seems that the best explanation of this fact is the more general principle that it's wrong to punish someone for a crime that they didn't commit. (Although we are staying neutral on the primary aim of punishment, it's worth noting that if harsh treatment is deserved in virtue of bad behavior, then it seems impossible for that harsh treatment to be deserved before the behavior has taken place.) We might also say, following Saul Smilansky (1994), that pre-punishment fails to respect the moral autonomy of human persons. The key difference between the time leading up to the crime and the time following the crime is that, prior to the crime, it remains in principle possible for agents to exercise their autonomy in a way that affects their moral status. This in-principle possibility must be respected, which precludes the moral permissibility of pre-punishment.

On the other hand, it does seem as though an inerrant prediction of future crime does provide us with an opportunity that we shouldn't pass up. It would seem that we are not only permitted, but might even be *obligated*, to intervene to prevent certain wrongdoing. Some instances of wrongdoing might be preventable simply by adjusting the circumstances; but there will be other cases in which preventing the wrongdoing will require some sort of harsh treatment of the pre-wrongdoer—containment or restriction of movement at the very least. Especially if the primary aim of punishment has to do with societal benefit, it seems that many of those societal benefits are best achieved by engaging in pre-punishment. (Although these considerations raise an additional puzzle, namely that it seems the crime still has to happen in order for the pre-punishment to be justified! So perhaps the alleged societal benefits aren't available after all; perhaps the flaws in the Department of Pre-crime run deeper than anyone realized.)

RESPONSES

One "response" to this thought experiment is to wield it in an argument against compatibilism. For example, Smilansky (2007) argues that compatibilism is a radical view—more radical than it might seem—because compatibilists are forced to endorse pre-punishment. He treats the impermissibility of pre-punishment as an assumption of common sense, and then argues that compatibilism, in virtue of denying this commonsense assumption, is a radical view.

The compatibilist might object to this argument by trying to appeal to Smilansky's own (1994) principle cited above: she might say that compatibilists, like anyone else, can appeal to the in-principle possibility of a significant exercise of moral autonomy as all the justification they need for refraining from pre-punishment. This, in effect is Kearns's (2008) response to Smilansky: on at least some compatibilist views, the pre-criminal is able to refrain from committing the crime even if it's determined that he commit it. So we have to respect that ability, which precludes pre-punishment. (And this compatibilist notion of ability has to be a live option at this stage in the dialectic: to insist on an incompatibilist understanding of ability in an argument against compatibilism would beg the question.)

Kearns also notes that pre-punishment, if it occurs, will often be a cause of the crime being punished. We can see this by looking at the counterfactual relation between the pre-punishment and the crime: it will often be true that, had the person not been pre-punished, he wouldn't have committed the crime. (Recall from Chapter 27 that we evaluate counterfactuals by inspecting the nearest possible world in which the antecedent is true and observing whether the consequent is also true in that world.) If someone is pre-punished in the actual world, then their life is going to go very differently for them in the nearest world in which they are not pre-punished. It's plausible to think that this significantly different world will *not* include the crime. So whatever societal benefits are supposed to justify pre-punishment, they are outweighed by the potential for pre-punishment to cause the crime itself. The compatibilist can simply point to that potential as a reason for not engaging in pre-punishment. (See Sorensen 2006 for an argument against pre-punishment that appeals to a causal relationship going in the other direction, from crime to verdict.)

Beebee (2008) also objects to Smilansky's argument, pointing out that it's the predictability that's doing the work in allegedly justifying the pre-punishment, not the determinism. This can be shown by imagining an indeterministic time travel case in which we travel into the future and witness a crime being committed. That knowledge of the future crime would seem to justify pre-punishment even if determinism is false. (The pre-criminal would be *able* to refrain from committing the crime, but we know they *won't* refrain because we already saw what happened.) So whatever considerations the libertarian uses to rule out pre-punishment in this time travel case can also be used by the compatibilist in a more ordinary deterministic case.

Beebee also questions whether the resistance to pre-punishment really is enshrined in common sense. (For example, in some legal systems someone can be punished for merely planning a crime.) Greene (2021) builds on this point in some interesting ways.

Smilansky published replies to both Kearns (Smilansky 2008a) and Beebee (Smilansky 2008b). Robinson (2010) argues that Smilansky is wrong to claim that compatibilists are committed to the moral insignificance of the time at which the crime occurs. Todd (2013) shifts the focus to *divine* pre-punishment, arguing that consideration of divine pre-punishment has implications for the debate over the apparent conflict between human freedom and divine foreknowledge (see again Chapter 8).

RECOMMENDED READING (OR VIEWING)

Beebee, Helen. 2008. "Smilansky's Alleged Refutation of Compatibilism." *Analysis* 68: 258–60.
Kearns, Stephen. 2008. "Compatibilism Can Resist Prepunishment: A Reply to Smilansky." *Analysis* 68: 250–53.
Smilansky, Saul. 2007. "Determinism and pre-punishment: The Radical Nature of Compatibilism." *Analysis* 67: 347–49.
Spielberg, Steven. 2002. *Minority Report*.

WORKS CITED

Carroll, Lewis. 1871. *Through the Looking Glass*. Kindle edition. Public Domain.
Greene, Preston. 2021. "The Real-Life Issue of Prepunishment." *Social Theory and Practice*. https://doi.org/10.5840/soctheorpract2021413123.
Robinson, Michael. 2010. "A Compatibilist-Friendly Rejection of Prepunishment." *Philosophia* 38: 589–94.
Smilansky, Saul. 1994. "The Time to Punish." *Analysis* 54: 50–53.
Smilansky, Saul. 2008a. "Prepunishment for Compatibilists: A Reply to Kearns." *Analysis* 68: 254–57.
Smilansky, Saul. 2008b. "More Prepunishment for Compatibilists: A Reply to Beebee." *Analysis* 68: 260–63.
Sorensen, Roy. 2006. "Future Law: Prepunishment and the Causal Theory of Verdicts." *Noûs* 40: 166–83.
Todd, Patrick. 2013. "Prepunishment and Explanatory Dependence: A New Argument for Incompatibilism About Foreknowledge and Freedom." *The Philosophical Review* 122: 619–39.

THE UNFORTUNATE FAWN

A TRAGIC THOUGHT EXPERIMENT

The thought experiment we begin with in this chapter is, unfortunately, a disturbing one. It comes from William Rowe:

> Suppose in some distant forest lightning strikes a dead tree, resulting in a forest fire. In the fire a fawn is trapped, horribly burned, and lies in terrible agony for several days before death relieves its suffering. So far as we can see, the fawn's intense suffering is pointless.
>
> (Rowe 1979, 337)

The reason why Rowe paints such a disturbing picture of suffering is that it serves to set up the *problem of evil*. This label typically refers to the problem (or set of problems) that theists encounter when trying to reconcile the existence of God, as traditionally conceived (omnipotent, omniscient, and morally perfect), with the existence of evil. In philosophical contexts, the problem of evil typically involves attempting to respond to the *argument from evil* against theism. (For additional related discussion of the problem of evil, including a proposal for a novel response to the problem, see Pendergraft forthcoming.)

One particularly powerful formulation of the argument from evil appeals to the idea of *gratuitous* evil, because gratuitous evil is what seems to generate the most tension with the traditional conception of God. (The word "suffering" is often used to capture most of the evils that are relevant to the problem of evil.) We are all familiar with

DOI: 10.4324/9781003126119-46

various kinds of suffering that lead to (and are often required for) some greater good. Surgery to repair a broken bone involves quite a bit of suffering, but that suffering is necessary for full healing. Even activities as simple as going for a run or lifting weights follow the same pattern: suffering that contributes to a greater good. The existence of weightlifting doesn't present any problems for belief in God, because we can all see how it is a good thing that the world contains certain kinds of pain-inducing physical activities. (Your own mileage may vary with weightlifting in particular, of course.) What *does* create a problem for belief in God is the existence of suffering that seems pointless or gratuitous (e.g., the fawn's suffering mentioned above). The argument from gratuitous evil is one way of regimenting this idea.

The argument from gratuitous evil asserts a *theological* premise (about the type of world that God, as traditionally conceived, would create) and an *empirical* premise (about the way the world is):

(1)   If God exists, then gratuitous evil doesn't exist.
(2)   But gratuitous evil does exist.
(3)   Therefore, God doesn't exist.

Premise (2) seems, at least at first glance, to be true. Examples abound, unfortunately, so it doesn't take very much looking to identify instances of evil that appear to be gratuitous. But let's look a little more closely at premise (1). The idea, which is an old one (it goes back at least as far as Hume), is this: Suppose that God is omnipotent, omniscient, and morally perfect. Gratuitous evil could occur only if there's some evil that God is unable to prevent, or that he's unaware of, or that he takes pleasure in. But omnipotence, omniscience, and moral perfection rule out these possibilities. Thus we have (1): if God (as traditionally conceived) exists, then gratuitous evil doesn't.

The most popular responses to this argument attempt to cast doubt on (2), the empirical premise, by claiming that the existence of some set of sufficiently valuable goods entails, and thus justifies, the existence of some set of evils. (More precisely, some proposition involving the goods will entail some proposition about the evils.) These *greater-good* strategies have been implemented in various ways, but they typically involve arguing that some apparently gratuitous evils are not in fact gratuitous because they are constituents, prerequisites, or necessary consequences of some goods that are valuable enough to justify permitting those evils.

Speak (2013, 206) offers a helpful way of analyzing greater-good strategies, pointing out that they will typically endorse both an *impossibility proposition* and a *value proposition*. The impossibility proposition tries to identify some goods that are impossible to bring about without also bringing about (or at least allowing) some evils, and the value proposition will claim that a state of affairs including both the goods and the evils is more valuable than a state of affairs including neither the goods nor the evils. (If this type of value proposition is true for some goods, then we will say those goods are *valuable enough* to justify the evils.) If these two propositions are true, for some set of goods and evils, then it follows that God has a sufficient reason to create a world that includes those evils; in other words, they are not gratuitous.

One reason why we are considering the problem of evil is that the most popular way of implementing a greater-good strategy involves an appeal to free will. What makes free will (arguably) valuable enough to justify evil is not the mere ability to choose between options, but to choose between good and bad options; i.e., the ability to make choices that have moral significance, and for which one is morally responsible. Let's call this valuable type of freedom *significant freedom*.

A greater-good appeal to freedom will typically have something like the following structure (including an existence proposition in addition to the impossibility proposition and the value proposition):

(4) Significant freedom exists.
(5) Significant freedom would not be possible without evil.
(6) Significant freedom is valuable enough to justify the existence of evil.

The theist is just going to have to assume that free will exists, but that's an assumption that most people would grant. And it should be relatively easy to see why (5) is plausible. Significant freedom includes the freedom to choose the bad, i.e., to bring about evil with one's choices. So if significant freedom exists, then evil will exist too.

What about (6)? This is probably the most controversial element of the free-will response to the argument from evil. What (6) is saying is that our human ability to choose between good and bad is so valuable that a world with significant freedom and evil is better than a world with neither significant freedom nor evil. One way to evaluate this question of whether

(6) is plausible is to imagine these two worlds and then run a mental comparison between them. Our own world has both free will and evil, and it contains a lot of good and a lot of bad. What about a world with neither free will nor evil? We could imagine a world populated with nothing but artificial intelligences that never cause any harm; kind of like a maximally sophisticated simulation of a human society, programmed so that nothing is harmed. To many it has seemed that the actual world is more valuable than any such simulation world; but it is admittedly difficult to come up with a compelling argument in support of that intuition.

RESPONSES

Despite the intuitive plausibility of the value proposition in (6), not everyone is convinced. Laura Ekstrom, for example, argues that if we really try to engage in a clear-eyed comparison between the value of free will and the tremendous disvalue of all the evil in the world, it's not at all clear that the balance is positive: "It seems to me that, as soon as we try [to conceive of the totality of pain and suffering in the world], and begin to pile it on to the scales, our weighing device simply breaks under the strain of it all" (Ekstrom 2016, 77; see also Ekstrom 2021). Given the choice, Ekstrom would gladly abandon free will: "I can say in an instant that I would greatly prefer to live in a world without murder, rape, theft, persistent physical pain, the abuse of children, and wrongdoing and victimization of all sorts, even if that world lacked deserved praise and blame and even if our sense of ourselves as agents facing … an open future were incorrect" (Ekstrom 2016, 77).

Whether or not you would endorse (6) or join Ekstrom in rejecting it, it's worth considering a couple of alternative responses to the argument from evil. One venerable response is the *soul-building* response, sometimes known as a *developmental* response. According to John Hick (1977), the most valuable kinds of goods are available only to those who have undergone a character development process—the soul-building process. The ultimate aim of this process is a state of moral perfection that cannot be achieved in any other way (Speak 2013). As Hick envisions it, the soul-building process includes exercising free will in the face of hardship and temptation; and Hick endorses a libertarian view of free will. But some have argued that a version of Hick's view can be developed even if one rejects a libertarian view of free will (cf. Pereboom 2016; Byerly 2017).

An alternative response tries to cast doubt on the empirical premise in a more literal way by adopting some version of *skeptical theism*. According to skeptical theism, we should be reluctant to affirm the existence of gratuitous evils because we should be reluctant to think that we have a handle on all of the possible reasons that God might have for bringing about evil. To assert that a particular evil or set of evils is gratuitous requires confidence in the claim that God could have no reason for permitting those evils, and such confidence is simply not warranted for limited beings such as ourselves. (For a helpful introduction to skeptical theism, see McBrayer 2010.)

RECOMMENDED READING

Plantinga, Alvin. 1977. *God, Freedom, and Evil*. Grand Rapids, MI: William B. Eerdmans.

Speak, Daniel. 2013. "Free Will and Soul-Making Theodicies." In *The Blackwell Companion to the Problem of Evil*, edited by Justin P. McBrayer and Daniel Howard-Snyder, 205–21. Chichester: Wiley Blackwell.

Tooley, Michael. 2021. "The Problem of Evil." In *The Stanford Encyclopedia of Philosophy*, edited by Edward N. Zalta, Fall 2021. https://plato.stanford.edu/archives/fall2021/entries/evil.

WORKS CITED

Byerly, T. Ryan. 2017. "Free Will Theodicies for Theological Determinists." *Sophia* 56: 289–310.

Ekstrom, Laura W. 2016. "The Cost of Freedom." In *Free Will and Theism: Connections, Contingencies, and Concerns*, edited by Kevin Timpe and Daniel Speak, 62–78. Oxford: Oxford University Press.

Ekstrom, Laura W. 2021. *God, Suffering, and the Value of Free Will*. Oxford: Oxford University Press.

Hick, John. 1977. *Evil and the God of Love*. 2nd ed. New York: HarperCollins.

McBrayer, Justin P. 2010. "Skeptical Theism." *Philosophy Compass* 5: 611–23.

Pendergraft, Garrett. Forthcoming. "Toward a Reactive Attitudes Theodicy." In *Theological Determinism: New Perspectives*. Cambridge: Cambridge University Press.

Pereboom, Derk. 2016. "Libertarianism and Theological Determinism." In *Free Will and Theism: Connections, Contingencies, and Concerns*, edited by Kevin Timpe and Daniel Speak, 112–31. Oxford: Oxford University Press.

Rowe, William L. 1979. "The Problem of Evil and Some Varieties of Atheism." *American Philosophical Quarterly* 16: 335–41.

43

DO SOCIAL AGENTS EXIST?

A PUZZLE INVOLVING THE WAY WE TALK ABOUT GROUPS

We often talk about groups or organizations performing actions. We say that the class met outside, that the band marched in the rain, that the movers unloaded the truck. We say that a team won a game, that an orchestra played a symphony, that a corporation bought back some of its stock. Some of these actions are merely *joint actions*: they involve multiple people, but the collective action is just the sum total of the individual actions. For example, when the band marches in the rain, that action simply consists of each individual band member marching in the rain. And some joint actions don't even require multiple actors; for example, one mover could unload the entire truck by himself, depending on what's in it. Some of these collective actions, however, go beyond a mere collection of individual actions. When a corporation buys back some of its stock, that involves lots of individual actions, but there's no single action that counts as the buying back of the stock; it's not as though the buyback consists of a bunch of employees buying back some shares. Let's call these actions, which seem to be essentially collective, *social actions*.

Even though we talk about social actions all the time, they are a puzzling phenomenon. An individual action occurs when an agent forms and then executes an intention, which is itself the result of beliefs, desires, and other psychological states of the agent (see Chapter 32).

DOI: 10.4324/9781003126119-47

The problem is that we talk about collectives (e.g., corporations) as agents, but those collectives don't appear to be capable of engaging in some of the essential steps of performing an action (such as forming an intention). We seem to be faced with a dilemma: we either have to acknowledge that much of the way that we talk about groups is mistaken, or we have to try and make sense of the idea of a genuine *social agent*.

When we're analyzing a concept, it's usually better, if possible, to avoid saying that most of the way we talk about that concept is mistaken. So let's see if we can make sense of the idea of a social agent.

One particularly helpful attempt to do this comes from Frederick Stoutland (2015). A social agent, according to Stoutland, is not just a plural agent (i.e., a group of people doing something together), but a *collective* agent: not a "they" but an "it" (at least in American English). And the social actions that social agents perform share numerous characteristics with individual actions. For example, they are intentional under at least one description, which implies that they are done for a reason; and they often bring about unintended consequences, which means that they are *not* intentional under other descriptions. Suppose that Congress passes a law designed to reduce the deficit (a farfetched possibility, to be sure). On Stoutland's view, Congress intended to reduce the deficit: reducing the deficit was their reason for passing the law. But there will also be unintended consequences of this action, such as increasing unemployment or angering certain constituencies. Thus the action would not be intentional under a description that focuses on those consequences (e.g., "Congress increased unemployment last month").

It's not enough, though, merely to pick a plausible example of social action and demonstrate that the way we talk about that action closely resembles the way we talk about individual actions. We need some reasons to think that the way we talk about the plausible examples can extend to social agency in general. And one way to provide these reasons is to neutralize the main objections to the generalized way of talking about social actions.

RESPONSES

Perhaps the strongest objection to genuine social agency is that social agents cannot exist because the attitudes essential to agency can only be ascribed to individuals. Some who raise this objection have argued that social attitudes are merely a special kind of individual attitude. Most of these philosophers want to preserve the genuineness of social *action* while maintaining that there are no social *agents*. For example, some of these individualists will try to avoid ascribing attitudes to groups by packing social content into individual attitudes: an action becomes social when the individual agents who perform the action have attitudes with shared content.

But Stoutland (2015) offers two reasons why this proposal won't work. First, social *actions* (unlike joint actions) cannot be divided into individual actions performed by individual agents, which suggests that social *attitudes* are not divisible either. Second, at least two crucial types of individual attitude—beliefs and intentions—can't have shared content. Beliefs that relate to action cannot have shared content because they must belong to the actor: someone else's belief cannot rationalize your action. (Your belief *about* someone else's belief could be a reason for your action, but their belief itself could not be a reason for your action.) An intention cannot have shared content for a similar reason, namely that an intention must refer to the agent who forms it. Thus it would seem that the existence of social action implies the existence of social attitudes that we can ascribe to social agents. (See Bratman 1993 for an alternative account of social intentions. For an extended recent treatment of social beliefs, see Lackey 2021.)

According to Stoutland, most philosophers resist ascribing intentional attitudes to social agents because they hold an entrenched view about the role of such attitudes in action. According to this standard story, agential attitudes explain actions because they cause bodily movements that correspond to their content: my intention to take a drink of coffee explains my action of raising the cup because it causes the movement that raises the cup. Clearly there cannot be any genuine social agents on this view, because there is no such thing as a social body (much less a social brain or social nervous system). However, we have independent reasons to reject this picture of the intentional attitudes. For starters, attitudes are not events but *states*; they are not concrete particulars but more like properties. And states, like properties, can't cause actions. They can, however, be *causally relevant* to actions, which Stoutland defines as follows: a property or state is causally relevant to an outcome just in case the outcome would have been different had the property been different (or absent). So a tree's being rotten is causally relevant to its falling over in the storm, and an agent's beliefs are causally relevant to her actions.

This view applies straightforwardly to social agents, since social agents can be in states that are causally relevant to actions. For example, Congress can be in a state that is causally relevant to its passing a law designed to reduce the deficit: had the state been different, the outcome would have been different. The fact that social agents can be in states that are causally relevant to actions suggests that we can also ascribe intentions, beliefs, and other agential attitudes to these agents.

But even if agential attitudes are legitimately ascribable to groups, there is a second reason why some individualists reject genuine social agency. These individualists claim that actions must be "subjectively understandable": the agent performing the action must have a collection of beliefs and intentions that give her an understanding of what she's up to. And surely social agents cannot have *that*. But here Stoutland appeals to Anscombe's notion of *practical knowledge*, according to which agents understand what they do simply by matching their actions to their intentions (Anscombe 1957, 33–46 *passim*; see also Schwenkler 2012). On this account, a social agent could in principle have practical knowledge (and thus a type of subjective understanding) of what it's doing.

More generally, Stoutland notes that contemporary philosophy of action happily accepts a wide range of *action* descriptions, but is much less happy to accept a range of *agent* descriptions. He endorses this pluralism about action description, but also advocates for pluralism about agent description. Perhaps the ontology of agency includes not just individual agents but social agents as well.

These questions about whether social agents exist (and, if so, what they might be like) have important implications for various questions, including questions about responsibility for corporate actions and responsibility for state actions. See Sepinwall (2016) for a discussion of corporate responsibility and Lawford-Smith and Collins (2017) for a discussion of state responsibility.

RECOMMENDED READING

Lawford-Smith, Holly, and Stephanie Collins. 2017. "Responsibility for States' Actions: Normative Issues at the Intersection of Collective Agency and State Responsibility." *Philosophy Compass* 12: 1–8.

Sepinwall, Amy J. 2016. "Corporate Moral Responsibility." *Philosophy Compass* 11: 3–13.

Smiley, Marion. 2017. "Collective Responsibility." In *The Stanford Encyclopedia of Philosophy*, edited by Edward N. Zalta, Summer 2017. https://plato.stanford.edu/archives/sum2017/entries/collective-responsibility.

Stoutland, Frederick. 2015. "The Ontology of Social Agency." In *Philosophy of Action: An Anthology*, edited by Jonathan Dancy and Constantine Sandis, 164–76. Malden, MA: Wiley Blackwell.

WORKS CITED

Anscombe, G. E. M. 1963. *Intention*. Ithaca, NY: Cornell University Press.

Bratman, Michael E. 1993. "Shared Intentions." *Ethics* 104: 97–113.

Lackey, Jennifer. 2021. *The Epistemology of Groups*. Oxford: Oxford University Press.

Schwenkler, John. 2012. "Non-Observational Knowledge of Action." *Philosophy Compass* 7: 731–40.

PART V

MORAL LUCK

Many of the questions we've been considering have to do with *control*—what kinds of control are required to secure the practical, moral, and social goods that we care about, and whether we can have those kinds of control in light of various potential challenges. In this last part we'll consider various dimensions of one final challenge, which to some is the most pervasive and troubling challenge of all: *moral luck*.

We'll start (Chapter 44) by looking at the general problem of moral luck, as crystallized by Thomas Nagel. In Chapter 45, we'll look at a sentiment, *agent-regret*, that often results from being a victim of bad moral luck.

One type of moral luck is luck having to do with the circumstances or situations we find ourselves in. Proponents of *situationism* (Chapter 46) take this type of luck so seriously that they question whether our character makes much of a difference at all to the way we act. Another type of moral luck also has to do with circumstances, but focuses on the *antecedent* circumstances that lead up to a moment of choice. Consideration of antecedent circumstances leads naturally to concerns about determinism, but it also leads to questions about whether and to what extent someone's *personal history* makes a difference to their freedom and responsibility. We'll consider some of these questions about the importance of history in Chapter 47.

DOI: 10.4324/9781003126119-48

The next two chapters extend the discussion of antecedent luck by looking at various kinds of bad luck having to do with formative circumstances. JoJo, son of Jo (Chapter 48) has lost some (if not all) of his moral capacities due to a decadent upbringing, whereas Huck Finn (Chapter 49) struggles to reconcile feelings of human sympathy with the flawed moral principles he picked up from his cultural and social context.

In the 50th and final chapter, we'll close by letting our imaginations run as wild as a herd of pigs.

44

IS ANYTHING REALLY UNDER OUR CONTROL?

THE PARADOX OF MORAL LUCK

Imagine two truck drivers, Lonnie and Mace, who also happen to be identical twins—as similar as they can possibly be while still being different people. (Alternatively, we can imagine two possible worlds. World A contains Lonnie (but not Mace) and world B contains Mace (but not Lonnie). Lonnie and Mace are identical in every way, and they have identical histories, except for the differences described below.

Both Lonnie and Mace, unfortunately, are a bit negligent about keeping up with the maintenance on their trucks (which are identical, and have been driven in identical conditions). As a result, the brakes are shot. One day they set out on one of their routes and, sure enough, their brakes go out while they are trying to stop for a red light. But—here's where their stories diverge—the consequences of their brake failure are different. Lonnie is alone on the road, and he is able to pull off to the side and slow down without doing too much damage to his truck or anything else. Mace, however, is not so lucky. His truck hits another car and kills the driver.

The puzzle here is what to say about the relative moral responsibility (and by extension, blameworthiness and liability to punishment) of Lonnie and Mace. On the one hand, it seems pretty clear that Mace should be punished (or is at least blameworthy) for killing the other driver. On the other hand, if we focus on what's under their

DOI: 10.4324/9781003126119-49

control, Lonnie and Mace are no different. They were both negligent about their maintenance, and it's only a matter of luck (good luck in Lonnie's case, bad luck in Mace's case) that that their respective brake failures produced wildly different outcomes.

The article that set the terms for the debate over moral luck was Thomas Nagel's "Moral Luck" (1979 [1976]), which was originally written as a reply to Bernard Williams (1981 [1976]). Nagel defines moral luck as follows: "Where a significant aspect of what someone does depends on factors beyond his control, yet we continue to treat him in that respect as an object of moral judgment, it can be called moral luck" (1979 [1976], 26).

This definition applies to Mace: significant aspects of the traffic accident (including most notably the presence of the other driver) depend on factors beyond his control, yet we continue to treat him as an object of moral judgment. Generalizing these considerations, we can express the problem of moral luck as an inconsistent triad:

(1) We are typically morally responsible for our actions.
(2) A significant aspect of what we do depends on factors beyond our control.
(3) If a significant aspect of what we do depends on factors beyond our control, then we are not morally responsible for our actions.

These propositions cannot be true at the same time; pick any two of them and you have an argument against the remaining one. You might think that the solution is simply to reject (2), which does seem to be the least plausible member of the set. But if we really think about all of the various factors that affect what we do and yet are beyond our control, we can get ourselves into a frame of mind in which (2) starts to look more plausible. For example, we might start to focus on just how many of the situations in which we find ourselves depend on factors beyond our control. We can think about how, even though our choices are the result of our character, that character was formed in ways that we didn't have any control over. We can think about how minute changes in causes can produce wildly different effects.

Here's how Nagel summarizes the case for (3):

> [The existence of luck is] opposed by the idea that one cannot be more culpable or estimable for anything than one is for that fraction of it which

is under one's control. It seems irrational to take or dispense credit or blame for matters over which a person has no control, or for their influence on results over which he has partial control. Such things may create the conditions for action, but action can be judged only to the extent that it goes beyond these conditions and does not just result from them.

(Nagel 1979 [1976], 28)

If their influence is significant enough, then it seems that the relevant factors outside our control do indeed take away our responsibility.

Nagel groups these factors into four different categories, corresponding to four different kinds of luck:

There are roughly four ways in which the natural objects of moral assessment are disturbingly subject to luck. One is the phenomenon of constitutive luck—the kind of person you are, where this is not just a question of what you deliberately do, but of your inclinations, capacities, and temperament. Another category is luck in one's circumstances—the kind of problems and situations one faces. The other two have to do with the causes and effects of action: luck in how one is determined by antecedent circumstances, and luck in the way one's actions and projects turn out.

(Nagel 1979 [1976], 28)

We have already briefly considered the first two kinds of luck: *constitutive* luck and *circumstantial* luck. The we way we are constituted is largely a matter of luck. We can shape our "inclinations, capacities, and temperament" to a certain extent, but even that shaping is motivated by values that, at least at the beginning, are simply given to us. Similarly, we can shape our circumstances—the "problems and situations" we face—to a certain extent, but many of the details (and the influence of those details) are outside of our control. Nagel mentions an example that should trouble any of us who have ever thought, "There but for the grace of God go I":

Someone who was an officer in a concentration camp might have led a quiet and harmless life if the Nazis had never come to power in Germany. And someone who led a quiet and harmless life in Argentina might have become an officer in a concentration camp if he had not left Germany for business reasons in 1930.

(Nagel 1979 [1976], 26)

The third kind of luck—"luck in how one is determined by antecedent circumstances," or simply *antecedent* luck—is one we have already encountered as the threat from determinism (See Part II). Even if we have some control over the immediate causes of our actions, if we trace those causes back far enough (before we were born, for example), then our control goes away completely.

The final kind of luck is "luck in the way one's actions and projects turn out," sometimes called *outcome* luck, or *resultant* luck, because it has to do with the results of our actions. The truck driver example we began with is an example of resultant luck, as is an example of attempted murder that Nagel mentions:

> To take another legal example, the penalty for attempted murder is less than that for successful murder—however similar the intentions and motives of the assailant may be in the two cases. His degree of culpability can depend, it would seem, on whether the victim happened to be wearing a bullet-proof vest, or whether a bird flew into the path of the bullet—matters beyond his control.
>
> (Nagel 1979 [1976], 29)

(For an argument that there is an additional type of moral luck, *transformative* luck, see Herdova 2019.)

If we look at our actions, and remove all of the elements that are affected by any of these four kinds of luck, it seems that nothing remains for which we can be responsible.

RESPONSES

How should we respond to this rather bleak picture of our moral life? Nelkin (2021) provides a helpful taxonomy. The first strategy ("denial") tries to argue that moral luck doesn't exist; it *appears* that moral luck exists (indeed, it appears that we are surrounded by it), but that appearance is illusory. In later work, Williams (1993) could be construed as adopting this strategy. Zimmerman (2002) is another notable example of this strategy.

An alternative strategy ("acceptance") acknowledges the existence of moral luck but tries to find a way to revise our theory and practice of moral responsibility judgments so that they are consistent with moral luck. This procedure is exactly what compatibilists about moral responsibility and determinism seek to do (see Chapter 18), although they are focused on antecedent and constitutive luck. Perhaps compatibilist efforts to deal with antecedent and constitutive luck can be somehow combined with libertarian efforts to deal with circumstantial and resultant luck. This type of strategy, in effect, tries to show how we can sensibly reject the claim in (3) above. (But see Levy 2011 for an argument that no such strategy can succeed.)

RECOMMENDED READING

Nagel, Thomas. 1979 [1976]. "Moral Luck." In *Mortal Questions*, 24–38. Cambridge: Cambridge University Press.
Nelkin, Dana K. 2021. "Moral Luck." In *The Stanford Encyclopedia of Philosophy*, edited by Edward N. Zalta, Summer 2021. https://plato.stanford.edu/archives/sum2021/entries/moral-luck.

WORKS CITED

Herdova, Marcela. 2019. "Transformative Moral Luck." *Midwest Studies in Philosophy* 43: 162–80.
Levy, Neil. 2011. *Hard Luck: How Luck Undermines Free Will and Moral Responsibility*. Oxford: Clarendon Press.
Williams, Bernard. 1981 [1976]. "Moral Luck." In *Moral Luck: Philosophical Papers 1973–1980*, 20–39. Cambridge: Cambridge University Press.
Williams, Bernard. 1993. "Postscript." In *Moral Luck*, edited by Daniel Statman, 251–58. Albany, NY: SUNY Press.
Zimmerman, Michael. 2002. "Taking Luck Seriously." *The Journal of Philosophy* 99: 553–76.

THE UNFORTUNATE TAXI DRIVER

A PUZZLE ABOUT REGRET

In Chapter 44, we explored some implications of the apparent reality that our actions are infused with moral luck. In this chapter we explore another dimension of luck, which has been called *agent-regret*. To illustrate agent-regret, Bernard Williams (1981 [1976]) uses the example of a cab driver who unintentionally runs over a child with his car. (We can imagine that the driver isn't at fault; perhaps the child suddenly ran out in front of his car, and he didn't have enough time to react.) Everyone who observes the accident will rightly feel some sort of regret, in the sense that they wish the accident wouldn't have happened. But the driver will experience an additional layer of regret. Even if he fully recognizes that he wasn't at fault—that the unfortunate outcome was a result of extremely bad luck—he will also experience a type of regret stemming from his particular involvement in the accident. (Nagel 1979 [1976], 29 points out that the bad luck experienced by the driver isn't necessarily bad *moral* luck; in order for the driver's bad luck to be moral, he would have to be guilty of some fault, such as negligence.)

This additional type of regret is what Williams calls agent-regret, in the sense that the driver regrets that he was the agent through which the accident occurred.

Here is how Williams characterizes agent-regret:

> But there is a particularly important species of regret, which I shall call "agent-regret," which a person can feel only toward his own past actions

DOI: 10.4324/9781003126119-50

(or, at most, actions in which he regards himself as a participant). ... "Agent-regret" is not distinguished from regret in general solely or simply in virtue of its subject-matter. There can be cases of regret directed to one's own past actions which are not cases of agent-regret, because the past action is regarded purely externally, as one might regard anyone else's action. Agent-regret requires not merely a first-personal subject matter, nor yet merely a particular kind of psychological content, but also a particular kind of expression.

The sentiment of agent-regret is by no means restricted to *voluntary* agency. It can extend far beyond what one intentionally did to almost anything for which one was causally responsible in virtue of something one intentionally did. Yet even at deeply accidental or non-voluntary levels of agency, sentiments of agent-regret are different from regret in general, such as might be felt by a spectator, and are acknowledged in our practice as different.

(Williams 1981 [1976], 27–28)

Williams then elaborates on the difference between the driver who runs over the child and a spectator who merely observes the accident:

Doubtless, and rightly, people will try, in comforting him, to move the driver from this state of feeling, move him indeed from where he is to something more like the place of a spectator, but it is important that this is seen as something that should need to be done, and indeed some doubt would be felt about a driver who too blandly or readily moved to that position. We feel sorry for the driver, but that sentiment co-exists with, indeed presupposes, that there is something special about his relation to this happening, something which cannot merely be eliminated by the consideration that it was not his fault. It may be still more so in cases where agency is fuller than in such an accident, though still involuntary through ignorance.

The differences between agent-regret and regret felt by a spectator come out not just in thoughts and images that enter into the sentiment, but in differences of expression. The ... driver may act in some way which he hopes will constitute or at least symbolize some kind of recompense or restitution, and this will be an expression of his agent-regret.

(Williams 1981 [1976], 28)

(As Williams notes, however, a willingness to offer restitution doesn't always imply agent-regret.)

These remarks from Williams are suggestive but somewhat cryptic, in part because it seems that all of the distinctive features of agent-regret can show up in cases that don't involve agent-regret. The basic idea, however, seems to be a type of regret—represented by a set of beliefs, emotions, and dispositions to act—that is most naturally the result of moral fault. But, in cases of agent-regret, the beliefs, emotions, and dispositions are all present (and arguably *should* be present, at least initially) despite the absence of fault.

Agent-regret, then, is an appropriate response to being related to an unfortunate event in a certain way. But—and here's where the puzzle, or at least part of the puzzle, arises—it is also appropriate to respond to someone who is experiencing agent-regret by trying to persuade them to *stop* experiencing it. (As Williams says, people will "rightly" try to help the driver feel more like a spectator, but he shouldn't feel that way "too blandly or readily.") What sort of phenomenon is this that it is (morally) appropriate to experience but also appropriate to be talked out of?

RESPONSES

Some answer the question above by saying that agent-regret is an *irrational* phenomenon. It is perhaps understandable that we feel it sometimes, but it is always irrational. For example, Scanlon (2008, 150) argues that it is not appropriate for the cab driver to feel guilt, but it *is* appropriate for him to apologize to the parents of the child. Sussman (2018) argues against this type of response, using as his starting point the impulse to say "I'm sorry" even when we're not at fault. On his view, agent-regret is a rational interpersonal response to bad luck.

Kamtekar and Nichols (2019) go beyond the thought experiments to consider some actual testimonials of individuals who feel agent-regret, along with some of the psychological research involving these individuals. In so doing, they take the puzzle described above and divide it into two separate puzzles, the *agent* puzzle and the *observer* puzzle:

> First, why do these agents feel guilt (or something in the neighborhood of guilt) when they could hardly be held morally responsible for what happened? Are the agents' feelings appropriate even though the agents themselves aren't at fault or blameworthy? Second, in addition to this *Agent Puzzle*, there is also an *Observer Puzzle*: why do observers judge both that agents should not feel guilty and that if they do not feel guilty, they are deficient in some way?
>
> (Kamtekar and Nichols 2019, 182–83)

Their explanation invokes the familiar Aristotelian conditions on voluntary action: a control condition and an epistemic condition (see Chapter 18). The basic idea behind their account, which is sophisticated and empirically informed, is that when we are looking back on an accidental injury that we have brought about, we focus on the control condition but tend to ignore the epistemic condition. The cab driver couldn't avoid running over the child because he didn't know what was going to happen; but *had* he known, he could have easily done something that would have prevented the accident. Because he failed to satisfy the epistemic condition, he wasn't at fault; but he ignores this fact when looking back and considering the various things he very easily could have done differently. But this reaction isn't irrational, because the relevant cognitive mechanism is operating as it should. Our cognitive mechanisms aren't perfect, so there will be false positives and false negatives; but these misfires don't render the outputs of the mechanisms irrational.

This explanation might resolve the agent puzzle, but what about the observer puzzle? Kamtekar and Nichols argue that false positives can be a good indicator that a mechanism is functioning as it should. The reason why it seems appropriate for others to experience agent-regret is that agent-regret indicates a likelihood that an agent will also experience regret when they actually *are* at fault. If, conversely, they didn't experience agent-regret in response to accidental injury, then we might wonder whether they would experience regret in situations where they are in fact at fault.

RECOMMENDED READING

Kamtekar, Rachana, and Shaun Nichols. 2019. "Agent-Regret and Accidental Agency." *Midwest Studies in Philosophy* 43: 181–202.
Williams, Bernard. 1981 [1976]. "Moral Luck." In *Moral Luck: Philosophical Papers 1973–1980*, 20–39. Cambridge: Cambridge University Press.

WORKS CITED

Nagel, Thomas. 1979 [1976]. "Moral Luck." In *Mortal Questions*, 24–38. Cambridge: Cambridge University Press.
Scanlon, T. M. 2008. *Moral Dimensions: Permissibility, Meaning, Blame*. Cambridge, MA: Harvard University Press.
Sussman, David. 2018. "Is Agent-Regret Rational?" *Ethics* 128: 788–808.

HOW IMPORTANT IS CHARACTER IN EXPLAINING BEHAVIOR?

DIFFICULTIES IN PROVIDING AN EXPLANATION OF EXTREME WRONGDOING

When something horrible happens, we often want an explanation. For example, when we hear of the crimes committed by Robert Harris (see Chapter 40), one natural reaction is to ask for an explanation: How could someone engage in such shockingly evil behavior? These questions become perhaps even more urgent when we consider large-scale horrors. For example, how could so many people participate in the literally unbelievable atrocities of the Holocaust? One sort of answer appeals to the character of the perpetrators: these horrific things happened because there was something deeply twisted within the character of the people who brought those things about.

Daniel Goldhagen (1996) provides an example of this type of explanation. On his view, there was something particularly evil about the individuals who perpetrated the Holocaust. It's not just that Hitler was evil, but that the atrocities he oversaw were only made possible by a host of accomplices who were already caught up in an eliminationist anti-Semitic mindset.

Hannah Arendt (2006 [1963]) proposes an alternative explanation. After observing Adolf Eichmann's trial in Jerusalem, she concluded that although the Holocaust itself was certainly evil, most of its perpetrators were not themselves evil. Eichmann in particular didn't appear

DOI: 10.4324/9781003126119-51

to be motivated by particularly evil motives. Instead, her diagnosis was that he was mostly *thoughtless*; he simply accepted, without reflection, the totalitarian ideology of the system he was in and then acted accordingly. In support of this conclusion, she points to his selective memory, his trite way of speaking, and his lack of ethical independence. Rather than trusting his own moral judgment concerning his actions, he simply carried out his orders.

The same explanation, she claims, applies to most of the perpetrators of the Holocaust. Amos Elon sums up Arendt's view in his introduction to *Eichmann in Jerusalem*:

> Evil comes from a failure to think. It defies thought for as soon as thought tries to engage itself with evil and examine the premises and principles from which it originates, it is frustrated because it finds nothing there. That is the banality of evil.
>
> (Elon 2006, xiv)

Thus we have two competing explanations of the evils of the Holocaust. If Goldhagen is right, then those evils trace back to an evil worldview embraced by a critical mass of German citizens; if Arendt is right, then those evils trace back to a lack of reflection and lack of resistance on the part of those citizens. Both explanations attribute the evil to a kind of character fault, but the severity of the fault differs greatly. According to Goldhagen, the character flaw leads to a dehumanizing belief in anti-Semitism. According to Arendt, the character flaw is merely a kind of thoughtlessness and unreflective acquiescence. This thoughtlessness doesn't always cause problems, but in this particular case it led to truly disastrous consequences. (Thus Arendt's explanation includes an appeal to a type of moral luck; see Chapter 44.)

We are, of course, simplifying these explanations for the sake of comparison. But the contrast is a useful one, because it represents the general dispute between those who explain wrongdoing (or rightdoing) primarily in terms of character, and those who explain it primarily in terms of circumstances.

RESPONSES

Stanley Milgram, a social psychologist at Yale in the 1960s, was also interested in explanatory questions involving the perpetrators of the

Holocaust. (His interest, like Arendt's, was partly generated by the Eichmann trial.) So he performed a series of experiments (Milgram 1963, 1974) in which he investigated human tendencies toward obedience to authority, particularly when obedience would require a violation of one's moral principles.

In one of Milgram's experiments, subjects were given the role of "teacher" while a confederate played the role of "learner." (The subjects didn't know about the confederate, and they thought that the choice of roles was random.) The subject sat down at the teaching apparatus while the confederate posing as the learner went into another room and hooked his microphone up to a device that could play pre-recorded clips. (Neither individual could see the other.)

The teaching apparatus was an array of switches that were labeled with increasing electrical voltages. The bulk of the experiment consisted in the teacher asking questions of the learner. If the learner answered correctly, then the teacher simply proceeded to the next question. But if the learner answered incorrectly, then the teacher was instructed to administer an electric shock before moving on to the next question. The teacher was instructed to begin at the lowest voltage and then work his way up the switches, increasing the voltage by one increment each time the learner answered a question incorrectly.

Perhaps this description of the experiment is already making you uncomfortable. What's *really* surprising, however, is what happened as the subjects (the teachers) worked their way up through the increasing voltages. The learner (who, again, wasn't really being shocked but instead was playing pre-recorded responses) missed quite a few questions, and as the voltage amounts increased, he communicated quite a bit of distress. The pre-recorded responses included complaints of heart troubles, pleas to stop the treatment, and screams of agony. Eventually the learner just went silent. If the teacher indicated that he didn't want to administer the shock, or that he wanted to quit the experiment, he was asked to continue by someone in a lab coat (also a confederate of Milgram's) who was observing the experiment. This overseer didn't use any coercive or overbearing tactics; he simply asked the subject to continue, and if they resisted then he would calmly say things like, "The experiment requires that you continue."

So: given that the administration of these shocks was causing the learner a great deal of distress (at least as far as the subject could tell), and that the overseer had no real authority apart from appearing to be the person in charge of the experiment, how many of the subjects would you estimate completed the entire experiment by administering all of the shocks, up to the highest amount of voltage? (Remember that before they made it to the highest voltage, the learner had gone silent after repeated complaints of pain and anguish.) How far up the shock board do you think *you* would go? As it turns out, a disturbingly high number—*two thirds*—of the subjects administered shocks all the way up to the maximum voltage.

Milgram's proposed explanation of these disturbing results was that we are predisposed to obey authority figures, even to the point of doing things that we would otherwise disavow. In other words, his claim was that the best explanation of why the subjects were willing to cause so much suffering was that they were in a situation in which they were enabled and encouraged to do so by an authority figure.

These findings, then, support Arendt's "banality" claim: the primary problem that led to the horrors of the Holocaust was a failure of reflection, coupled with a default disposition to obey authority. If this banality claim is correct, then we should expect to find this phenomenon show up in other contexts as well: bad behavior that traces back to cognitive failures rather than explicitly moral failures. (In some cases the agents would also be blameworthy for these cognitive failures, but the blame for the outcome would far outweigh the blame for the cognitive failure.)

Unfortunately, this is exactly what we find. For example, in 2004, someone called various fast-food restaurants posing as a police officer and ordering restaurant employees to engage in various kinds of misconduct. In the most egregious incident, an 18-year-old female employee was strip-searched and sexually abused at the hands of an assistant store manager and her fiancé, all because someone claiming to be an authority figure was giving them orders over the phone (see Stossel and Vargas 2006).

On a more mundane level, Heath (2008) has argued convincingly that much of the bad behavior in the business world can be explained by features of the environment—in particular, a tolerance for "techniques of neutralization" in which immoral (or even criminal) behavior is rationalized by describing it in a way that eliminates the conflict with moral or legal norms. (For example, stealing office supplies might be rationalized by describing it as "borrowing" or claiming that nobody will ever miss them.)

Harman (1999) and Doris (2002) generalize these observations, arguing that there's no such thing as a global character trait that can be attributed to individuals independently of context. (The generalized view that circumstances, or situations, are more relevant to explaining behavior than character is often called *situationism*.) If true, this radical thesis would spell trouble for various normative ethical theories, but especially ethical theories that appeal to the notion of *virtue* as a development of certain character traits through training and practice. (For critical discussions of situationism, see Annas 2005; Sabini and Silver 2005; Adams 2006, chs. 8–9.)

The debate over situationism is far from over, but even if the radical thesis is false, the challenge for free will and moral responsibility remains. Many people would argue that some sort of reasons-responsiveness is essential for moral responsibility (see Chapter 18); but if circumstantial and situational features play a significant role in explaining our behavior, then that would seem to undercut our reasons-responsiveness. (We would be responding to features of the situation, rather than responding to reasons.) See Herdova and Kearns (2017) and McKenna and Warmke (2017) for an attempt to address this challenge.

RECOMMENDED READING

Annas, Julia. 2005. "Comments on John Doris's 'Lack of Character.'" *Philosophy and Phenomenological Research* 71: 636–42.

Herdova, Marcela, and Stephen Kearns. 2017. "This Is a Tricky Situation: Situationism and Reasons-Responsiveness." *The Journal of Ethics* 21: 151–83.

McKenna, Michael, and Brandon Warmke. 2017. "Does Situationism Threaten Free Will and Moral Responsibility?" *Journal of Moral Philosophy* 14: 698–733.

Miller, Christian B. 2017. "Situationism, Social Psychology, and Free Will." In *The Routledge Companion to Free Will*, edited by Kevin Timpe, Meghan Griffith, and Neil Levy, 407–22. New York: Routledge.

WORKS CITED

Adams, Robert Merrihew. 2006. *A Theory of Virtue: Excellence in Being for the Good*. Oxford: Clarendon Press.

Arendt, Hannah. 2006 [1963]. *Eichmann in Jerusalem: A Report on the Banality of Evil*. New York: Penguin Books.

Doris, John M. 2002. *Lack of Character: Personality and Moral Behavior*. Cambridge: Cambridge University Press.

Elon, Amos. 2006. "Introduction." In *Eichmann in Jerusalem: A Report on the Banality of Evil*, vii–xxiii. New York: Penguin Books.

Goldhagen, Daniel Jonah. 1996. *Hitler's Willing Executioners: Ordinary Germans and the Holocaust*. New York: Vintage.

Harman, Gilbert. 1999. "Moral Philosophy Meets Social Psychology: Virtue Ethics and the Fundamental Attribution Error." *Proceedings of the Aristotelian Society* 99: 315–31.

Heath, Joseph. 2008. "Business Ethics and Moral Motivation: A Criminological Perspective." *Journal of Business Ethics* 83: 595–614.

Milgram, Stanley. 1963. "Behavioral Study of Obedience." *Journal of Abnormal and Social Psychology* 67: 371–78.

Milgram, Stanley. 1974. *Obedience to Authority: An Experimental View*. New York: HarperCollins.

Sabini, John, and Maury Silver. 2005. "Lack of Character? Situationism Critiqued." *Ethics* 115: 535–62.

Stossel, John, and Elizabeth Vargas. 2006. "Fast Food Nightmare." *20/20*. ABC News Productions.

THE INDUSTRIOUS
PHILOSOPHER(S)

THE IMPORTANCE OF HISTORY

To what extent do facts about your personal history make a difference to your freedom? Answers to this question vary widely. At one
extreme, someone might say that your history almost completely determines your freedom: early on in your development as a human
agent (and then only at select times after that), you were faced with
choices that were crucial for forming your character (see Chapter 29).
Maybe these choices took place in relatively mundane circumstances,
and maybe you weren't even aware of their importance. But, on this
view, your freedom consists almost entirely in the results of those past
choices.

At the other extreme, someone might say that history is irrelevant
to freedom. On this view, whether or not an action of yours is free
is a function of a time-slice or snapshot of your mental and physical
states and capacities at the time of action. For example, someone might
say that as long as you are appropriately sensitive to reasons, or that
your beliefs and desires are sufficiently aligned, then your choice is free
choice (see Chapters 18, 35, and 36). We can call this a time-slice or
snapshot view, since it holds that the essence of a free action consists of a
mental and physical snapshot of an agent. (We could also call it a "struc-
tural" view, since it emphasizes the structure of the agent's psychology
at a particular time; or we could simply call it a "non-historical" view.)

DOI: 10.4324/9781003126119-52

Of course, nobody is forced to adopt one of the extreme views; someone could endorse a hybrid view according to which the right kind of snapshot and the right kind of history are both necessary for free action. But, if we place these views on a continuum running from one extreme to the other, the site of the most conflict has perhaps been at the border between a hybrid view and a no-history snapshot view.

One of the participants in this dispute, Alfred Mele (1995, 2006), has devised a case in which two philosophers, Ann and Beth, differ only in their histories:

> Ann is a free agent and an exceptionally industrious philosopher. She puts in twelve solid hours a day, seven days a week, and she enjoys almost every minute of it. Beth, an equally talented colleague, values many things above philosophy for reasons that she has refined and endorsed on the basis of careful critical reflection over many years. Beth identifies with and enjoys her own way of life, and she is confident that it has a breadth, depth, and richness that long days in the office would destroy. Their dean wants Beth to be like Ann. Normal modes of persuasion having failed, he decides to circumvent Beth's agency. Without the knowledge of either philosopher, he hires a team of psychologists to determine what makes Ann tick and a team of new-wave brainwashers to make Beth like Ann. The psychologists decide that Ann's peculiar hierarchy of values accounts for her productivity, and the brainwashers instill the same hierarchy in Beth while eradicating all competing values—via new-wave brainwashing, of course. Beth is now, in the relevant respect, a "psychological twin" of Ann. She is an industrious philosopher who thoroughly enjoys and highly values her philosophical work. Largely as a result of Beth's new hierarchy of values, whatever upshot Ann's critical reflection about her own values and priorities would have, the same is true of critical reflection by Beth. Her critical reflection, like Ann's, fully supports her new style of life.
>
> Naturally, Beth is surprised by the change in her. What, she wonders, accounts for her remarkable zest for philosophy? Why is her philosophical work now so much more enjoyable? Why are her social activities now so much less satisfying and rewarding than her work? Beth's hypothesis is that she simply has grown tired of her previous mode of life, that her life had become stale without her recognizing it, and that she finally has come fully to appreciate the value of philosophical work. When she carefully reflects on her values, Beth finds that they fully support a life dedicated to philosophical work, and she wholeheartedly embraces such a life and the collection of values that supports it.
>
> (Mele 2006, 164–65)

Mele then claims, and invites us to agree, that the difference in histories implies a difference in freedom: Whereas Ann is free, Beth is unfree because her autonomy was violated.

If Ann and Beth do indeed differ in freedom and in history but not in their snapshot properties, then Mele's example supports a hybrid view according to which history matters to freedom. As he puts it, "autonomy is in some way history-bound" (Mele 2006, 165).

RESPONSES

Mele is himself agnostic on whether free will is compatible or incompatible with determinism, but many compatibilists have felt the need to join him in endorsing a historical condition on freedom. This is because without such a condition it seems that compatibilism is vulnerable to a manipulation argument. In Chapter 20 we saw a representative example of such an argument:

(1) If an agent is manipulated into performing some action, then that agent is neither free nor responsible for the action (even if the action satisfies compatibilist conditions for acting freely).
(2) There is no freedom-relevant difference between manipulated agents and causally determined agents.
(3) Therefore, if an agent is causally determined to perform some action, then that agent is neither free nor responsible for that action (even if the action satisfies compatibilist conditions for acting freely).

Consider Beth, as described above, who has been manipulated into being an "exceptionally industrious philosopher." It seems that Beth is not free, but it also seems that Beth satisfies compatibilist conditions for acting freely. (Whatever those conditions may be, we can suppose that the brainwashers in the story are capable of revising Beth's hierarchy of values in a way that satisfies them.) This is the case in support of premise (2). In response, many compatibilists have felt the need to add a historical condition that allows us to distinguish between Ann and Beth. Both Ann and Beth satisfied compatibilist conditions at the time of action, but only Ann had the right kind of history; thus Ann is free but Beth is not. If this response works, then the compatibilist can set aside manipulation concerns and focus on arguing that a deterministic history can be the right kind of history.

Vargas (2005) provides some reasons why this response might not work. The main problem is a tension between satisfaction of a historical condition on responsibility and satisfaction of the *epistemic* condition on responsibility. (See Chapter 18 for a brief explanation of the epistemic condition.) In short, the epistemic condition says that we can only be responsible for an outcome if we could have been reasonably expected to foresee that outcome. But the more (and the farther) our responsibility for some present outcome traces back to some prior decision, the less likely it is that we could have been reasonably expected to foresee the outcome. This is perhaps not a fatal flaw (Vargas himself adopts a kind of historical condition in Vargas 2013, ch. 9), but it does show that there is work to be done in formulating a theoretically satisfying historical condition. Perhaps the most active defender of a non-historical approach is Michael McKenna (2004, 2012a, 2012b), although he remains officially agnostic on whether compatibilists should ultimately endorse a historical condition.

In more recent developments on the manipulation argument front, Matt King (2013) tries to make the case that the manipulation argument as it stands can be reversed to function as an argument against *in*compatibilism. Taylor Cyr (2016) argues that King has not successfully made the case, but then (Cyr 2020) tries to make a similar case of his own, presenting a manipulation argument that targets libertarianism in general.

RECOMMENDED READING

McKenna, Michael. 2012a. "Moral Responsibility, Manipulation Arguments, and History: Assessing the Resilience of Nonhistorical Compatibilism." *The Journal of Ethics* 16: 145–74.
Mele, Alfred R. 2006. *Free Will and Luck*, chapter 7. Oxford: Oxford University Press.
Vargas, Manuel. 2005. "The Trouble with Tracing." *Midwest Studies in Philosophy* 29: 269–91.

WORKS CITED

Cyr, Taylor W. 2016. "The Parallel Manipulation Argument." *Ethics* 126: 1075–89.
Cyr, Taylor W. 2020. "Manipulation Arguments and Libertarian Accounts of Free Will." *Journal of the American Philosophical Association* 6: 57–73.

King, Matt. 2013. "The Problem with Manipulation." *Ethics* 124: 65–83.

McKenna, Michael. 2004. "Responsibility and Globally Manipulated Agents." *Philosophical Topics* 32: 169–92.

McKenna, Michael. 2012b. "Defending Nonhistorical Compatibilism: A Reply to Haji and Cuypers." *Philosophical Issues* 22: 264–80.

Mele, Alfred R. 1995. *Autonomous Agents*. Oxford: Oxford University Press.

Vargas, Manuel. 2013. *Building Better Beings: A Theory of Moral Responsibility*. Oxford: Oxford University Press.

JOJO, SON OF JO

SUSAN WOLF'S DICTATORIAL THOUGHT EXPERIMENT

In Chapters 35 and 36 we encountered two general frameworks for conceptualizing the way human psychology works. One framework conceives of a hierarchy of (sometimes conflicting) desires, whereas the alternative framework conceives of two different (and sometimes sharply opposed) sources of motivation. Both frameworks agree, however, that moral responsibility arises from features of our psychology that go beyond basic desire satisfaction. Susan Wolf (2013 [1987]) has described views that share this commitment as "deep-self" views, and characterizes them according to the type of control that they require for responsibility. On a deep-self view, "the key to responsibility lies in the fact that responsible agents are those for whom it is not just the case that their actions are within the control of their wills, but also the case that their wills are within the control of their selves in some deeper sense" (332). At the simplest level of description, then, a deep-self view requires that responsible agents exercise the right kind of control over their wills.

Wolf wants to argue that deep-self views are missing something important about moral responsibility, so she proposes a counterexample. She asks us to consider the fictional case of JoJo:

> JoJo is the favorite son of Jo the First, an evil and sadistic dictator of a small, undeveloped country. Because of his father's special feelings for

DOI: 10.4324/9781003126119-53

the boy, JoJo is given a special education and is allowed to accompany his father and observe his daily routine. In light of this treatment, it is not surprising that little JoJo takes his father as a role model and develops values very much like Dad's. As an adult, he does many of the same sorts of things his father did ... He is not *coerced* to do these things[;] he acts according to his own desires. Moreover, these are desires he wholly wants to have.

(Wolf 2013 [1987], 334)

Now consider JoJo's evil and sadistic actions (i.e., those actions of his which involve "many of the same sorts of things his father did"). It seems that these actions are in control of JoJo's will, and that his will is in control of his deep self, which would mean (at least according to deep-self views) that he is morally responsible for those actions. But most of us also feel an intuitive resistance to saying that JoJo is fully responsible for all of the heinous acts he commits. (For example, we would probably be inclined to blame or even punish JoJo less severely than someone who performed similar acts but had a more typical upbringing.) Perhaps our intuitions are wrong on this, and JoJo really is fully morally responsible. But it's also possible that our intuitions are pointing us toward an additional element of our moral psychology that is also relevant, and perhaps even required, for moral responsibility. Wolf explores this latter possibility, arguing that more than just deep-self control over our wills is required. She proposes that we add a "sanity" condition to our account of responsibility, where sanity involves the right kind of connection to truth (including moral truth). To be sane, in Wolf's sense, is to have "the minimally sufficient ability cognitively and normatively to recognize and appreciate the world for what it is" (335).

What does it take to cognitively *and* normatively recognize and appreciate the world for what it is? The commonsense notion of sanity refers primarily to the cognitive recognition of reality: avoiding delusion and other distortions of one's perceptions of oneself and the surrounding physical (and social) world. For example, a human person who believes that he's a cat is suffering from a delusion, and thus fails to appreciate reality in various important ways. *Normative* recognition involves roughly the same idea, but with respect to *moral* reality rather than physical or social reality. (Normative reality might also include aesthetic or other dimensions.) For example, one feature of moral reality is the fact that all human persons have equal dignity and are worthy of equal respect. JoJo fails to grasp this feature of reality, and thus fails to normatively appreciate the world for what it is. So there is a sense in which JoJo is insane, and that's the reason why we are hesitant to claim that he's responsible for his actions.

Wolf's view is thus a "sane deep-self view":

> The conception of responsibility I am proposing, then, agrees with the deep-self view in requiring that a responsible agent be able to govern her (or his) actions by her desires and to govern her desires by her deep self. In addition, my conception insists that the agent's deep self be sane, and claims that this is *all* that is needed for responsible agency. By contrast to the plain deep-self view, let us call this new proposal the *sane deep-self view*.
>
> (Wolf 2013 [1987], 335)

Being a responsible agent, on this account, requires not only the right kind of control but also the right kind of connection to reality.

RESPONSES

Wolf's thought experiment is interesting in its own right, but even more so when compared to some of the other examples discussed in other chapters. First, note that JoJo's insanity—his failure to grasp important elements of normative reality—is a species of moral ignorance. Both Robert Harris (Chapter 40) and Huck Finn (Chapter 49) also suffer from moral ignorance, but these three different instances of ignorance come from different sources and have different implications for moral responsibility. The details of Harris's situation (including his crimes and his tragic upbringing) suggest that he is no longer a member of the moral community. JoJo also had an unfortunate upbringing, but the fact that it was characterized by indulgence rather than abuse seems to render him slightly more capable of overcoming his ignorance. His normative capacities are stunted, but they are arguably not broken in the way they might be as a consequence of severe abuse. (Vogel 1993 contrasts Harris with JoJo along these lines.) Thus, it would seem that JoJo's ignorance is not so severe that it excludes him from the moral community entirely. He's arguably not responsible for his bad behavior, but at the same time he's not a psychopath.

His moral ignorance is more severe than Huck Finn's, however: JoJo's ignorance prevents him from doing the right thing, whereas Huck's does not (at least when it comes to helping Jim escape).

Even if we grant, however, that JoJo isn't morally responsible for his actions, we might still wonder whether he's *blameworthy* for them. For example, as discussed in Mason (2015), Zimmerman (1997, 2008, ch. 4) and Rosen (2003, 2004) argue that moral ignorance renders someone blameless. Mason, in contrast, wants to argue that there's an important sense in which he *is* blameworthy.

On Mason's (2015) view, there are three types of blame-relevant attitudes: ordinary blame, objective blame, and the objective stance. (See Chapter 39 for more on blame; see Chapter 38 for more on the objective stance.) The shift from ordinary to objective blame occurs when we recognize that the wrongdoer is not a part of our moral community, so we do not judge them in reference to the shared values of our moral community. We do, however, judge them as an agent in general, and this judgment can recognize that, in virtue of their actions or attitudes, they have fallen short of an objective standard. On Mason's view, objective blame is what allows us to respond appropriately to "moral outliers": ordinary blame is not appropriate, since they are not a part of the moral community, but we can respond with the full weight of objective blame. But objective blame is continuous with the objective stance, so additional knowledge (e.g., of someone's formative circumstances) can push us toward the objective stance. Mason illustrates this slide toward the objective stance by contrasting JoJo with his father, Jo:

> Compare JoJo to his father, Jo. Let's imagine that Jo was raised in a fairly liberal society, and engineered a bloody coup in order to make himself dictator. Jo is a moral outlier, and our objective blame has full force. Our attitude to JoJo should be subtly different. Our objective blame of JoJo is undermined by considering his formative circumstances. Of course, this makes very little difference to anything practical: as I said, we should hold him accountable just as we do Jo. The point is that we can see JoJo as a product of his environment in a sense relevantly different from the sense in which we are all products of our environment, and so we see JoJo as less of an agent when we see him in that light.
>
> (Mason 2015, 3055)

If we are prompted by knowledge of formative circumstances or other details to see someone as less of an agent, then we are licensed to take (more of) an objective stance toward them. Due to the differences in upbringing, we are led to take more of an objective stance toward JoJo than toward Jo, and still more of an objective stance toward Harris than toward JoJo. We don't take a completely objective stance, however, even toward Harris; to take a purely objective stance is to cease judging someone as an agent at all.

RECOMMENDED READING

Mason, Elinor. 2015. "Moral Ignorance and Blameworthiness." *Philosophical Studies* 172: 3037–57.

Rudy-Hiller, Fernando. 2018. "The Epistemic Condition for Moral Responsibility." In *The Stanford Encyclopedia of Philosophy*, edited by Edward N. Zalta, Fall 2018. https://plato.stanford.edu/archives/fall2018/entries/moral-responsibility-epistemic.

Wolf, Susan. 2013 [1987]. "Sanity and the Metaphysics of Responsibility." In *Ethical Theory: An Anthology*, 2nd ed., 330–39. Chichester: Wiley-Blackwell.

WORKS CITED

Rosen, Gideon. 2003. "Culpability and Ignorance." *Proceedings of the Aristotelian Society* 103: 61–84.

Rosen, Gideon. 2004. "Skepticism about Moral Responsibility." *Philosophical Perspectives* 18: 295–313.

Zimmerman, Michael J. 1997. "Moral Responsibility and Ignorance." *Ethics* 107: 410–26.

Zimmerman, Michael J. 2008. *Living with Uncertainty: The Moral Significance of Ignorance*. Cambridge: Cambridge University Press.

HUCK FINN DOES WHAT HE THINKS IS WRONG

A PUZZLE ABOUT DOING WHAT'S RIGHT (EVEN WHEN YOU THINK IT'S WRONG)

One way to describe *weakness of will* is to say that you know you ought to do one thing, but you do a different thing instead. As we have seen, various puzzles arise when we look more closely at this phenomenon (cf. Chapter 33). Perhaps even more puzzling, however, is a kind of case in which someone acts against their better judgment, but their judgment about what they ought to have done is mistaken. Suppose you believe that you ought to do one thing, but you do a different thing instead; unbeknownst to you, however, you were mistaken about what you ought to have done, so the thing you did was actually the thing you ought to have done.

In Mark Twain's *The Adventures of Huckleberry Finn*, the title character ends up in this type of situation. He has escaped from an abusive father, and while he's on the run he encounters a slave, Jim, who has also escaped and is also on the run. (Huck is acquainted with Jim, but doesn't get to know him very well until they spend time together on the run.) Huck aids Jim in his escape to freedom, but at the last minute begins to wonder if he's doing the right thing. In fact, his conscience is telling him that he's doing the *wrong* thing:

> Well, I can tell you it made me all over trembly and feverish, too, to hear him, because I begun to get it through my head that he *was* most

DOI: 10.4324/9781003126119-54

free—and who was to blame for it? Why, *me*. I couldn't get that out of my conscience, no how nor no way. It got to troubling me so I couldn't rest; I couldn't stay still in one place. It hadn't ever come home to me before, what this thing was that I was doing. But now it did; and it stayed with me, and scorched me more and more. I tried to make out to myself that *I* warn't to blame, because *I* didn't run Jim off from his rightful owner; but it warn't no use, conscience up and says, every time, "But you knowed he was running for his freedom, and you could 'a' paddled ashore and told somebody." That was so—I couldn't get around that noway. That was where it pinched. ...

(Twain 1983 [1884], 91)

Huck wrestles with his conscience for a while before things come to a head:

My conscience got to stirring me up hotter than ever, until at last I says to it, "Let up on me—it ain't too late yet—I'll paddle ashore at the first light and tell." I felt easy and happy and light as a feather right off. All my troubles was gone.

(Twain 1983 [1884], 92)

As it turns out, shortly after Huck's resolution to turn Jim in, an opportunity arises. Here's what happens as he finds himself on the verge of telling someone about Jim:

I tried to, but the words wouldn't come. I tried for a second or two to brace up and out with it, but I warn't man enough—hadn't the spunk of a rabbit. I see I was weakening; so I just give up trying ...

(Twain 1983 [1884], 93)

When it came down to it, Huck couldn't bring himself to betray the man whom he had come to know and regard (even if only subconsciously) as a fellow human worthy of dignity and respect. According to Huck's own moral judgment, he was doing the wrong thing; but as matter of moral fact he was doing the right thing.

RESPONSES

Jonathan Bennett diagnoses Huck's predicament as a struggle between sentiment and principle—"between *sympathy* on the one hand and *bad morality* on the other" (Bennett 1974, 123). Because Huck's morality consists largely of false moral principles, his is a bad morality. This bad morality tells him that he should turn Jim in (indeed, should have turned him in right away), but his sympathy for Jim as a friend and fellow human pushes him strongly in the other direction. In this case, sympathy wins out, but in other cases the bad morality might win out. (Bennett discusses Heinrich Himmler as an example of an individual who experienced the same struggle, but with a tragically different result). As Bennett notes (1974, 131), Huck's experience of the conflict between his sympathy and his bad morality leads him to give up on morality altogether. He's not interested in undergoing any similar struggles in the future, so he simply jettisons one of the sources of the struggle.

The possibility that Huck is overlooking is the possibility of revising his principles in light of their conflict with his sympathies. Bennett describes how this process might go:

> This is sometimes a pretty straightforward matter. It can happen that a certain moral principle becomes untenable—meaning literally that one cannot hold it any longer—because it conflicts intolerably with the pity or revulsion or whatever that one feels when one sees what the principle leads to. One's experience may play a large part here: experiences evoke feelings, and feelings force one to modify principles.
>
> (Bennett 1974, 132)

The process that Bennett aptly describes is sometimes called *reflective equilibrium*. When, upon reflection, two different sources of normative input deliver different verdicts, equilibrium requires that one of them be revised. In Huck's case, his moral principles and his sympathies deliver different verdicts. His solution was to restore equilibrium by discarding one source of normative input entirely. What he failed to recognize was that he could have also resolved the conflict by revising rather than rejecting his moral principles. (Bennett also provides an example of "revising" our sympathies: When a mother sees her child tearfully protesting an unpleasant but necessary medical procedure, her sympathies will push her to accede to the child's wishes; but in this case her moral principles should temporarily silence the sympathies.)

Although Bennett is complimentary of Huck's sympathies, which he describes as "broad and kind" (1974, 132), he doesn't seem to think that Huck is praiseworthy for doing what he did. We might say that it is just a matter of good moral luck that Huck does the right thing in this situation. (See Chapter 44 for a discussion of moral luck.)

Nomy Arpaly (2003) offers a slightly different perspective on the Huck Finn case. She thinks that Huck is praiseworthy for helping Jim escape (and especially for refraining from turning him in when the last opportunity arose). As she describes the case (2003, 76–78), Huck's morality *does* change over the course of his interactions with Jim, even though Huck isn't aware of, and wouldn't be able to articulate, the change. He gradually starts to perceive Jim differently—as a human person worthy of dignity and respect—and these perceptions influence his judgments. So in the end he is acting for moral reasons even though he isn't aware of them or the role they are playing in his mental life: his morality has become less bad. (For a recent discussion of Arpaly's perspective on this case, see Markovits 2010.)

Arpaly then generalizes the point to cover a wide range of cases in which people can seem praiseworthy even though their moral principles are questionable:

> They are praiseworthy because, despite any character-building imposed on them by their misguided selves or others, some of their moral common sense, much of their moral goodness—that is, their responsiveness to moral reasons—remains intact.
>
> (Arpaly 2003, 79)

Most of the examples we have considered in this book have involved bad behavior. The Huck Finn case, and the more general cases that Arpaly is envisioning, offer us a welcome opportunity to critically examine our reactions to good behavior as well.

RECOMMENDED READING

Alvarez, Maria. 2017. "Reasons for Action: Justification, Motivation, Explanation." In *The Stanford Encyclopedia of Philosophy*, edited by Edward N. Zalta, Winter 2017. https://plato.stanford.edu/archives/win2017/entries/reasons-just-vs-expl.

Arpaly, Nomy. 2003. *Unprincipled Virtue: An Inquiry Into Moral Agency*, chapter 3. Oxford: Oxford University Press.

WORKS CITED

Bennett, Jonathan. 1974. "The Conscience of Huckleberry Finn." *Philosophy* 49: 123–34.

Markovits, Julia. 2010. "Acting for the Right Reasons." *The Philosophical Review* 119: 201–42.

Twain, Mark. 1983 [1884]. *The Adventures of Huckleberry Finn*. New York: Signet Classics.

A HERD OF WILD PIGS

CAUSAL DEVIANCE REVISITED

We have already seen how certain cases of causal deviance threaten our ability to explain what makes an action intentional (cf. Chapter 32). Even a set of attitudes (e.g., a set of beliefs and desires) that *would* provide one's reasons for an action under normal circumstances don't always rationalize that action in cases of causal deviance. The anxious mountaineer didn't actually intend to loosen his hold on the rope, but his beliefs and desires were of a sort that very well could have led to such an intention.

The mountaineer case was one in which the causal deviance occurred inside the head, so to speak: the mountaineer's mental states produced an action, but in a strange way (with a missing intention). Another set of related but distinct cases involves causal deviance *outside* the head: strange occurrences that happen in between an action and its consequences.

It is plausible to think that if someone tries to do something, and that trying causes the thing to happen, then the person did the thing intentionally. In fact, many action theorists—*causalists*—want to turn this intuitive thought into an analysis. Here's a simple version of the causalist analysis:

> **Causalism:** S performs action A intentionally if and only if A is caused by S's mental states.

DOI: 10.4324/9781003126119-55

Unfortunately for the causalists, there are counterexamples to this analysis. Davidson's anxious mountaineer is one such counterexample; a second one comes also from Davidson, who attributes it to Daniel Bennett:

> A man may try to kill someone by shooting at him. Suppose the killer misses his victim by a mile, but the shot stampedes a herd of wild pigs that trample the intended victim to death. Do we want to say the man killed his victim intentionally? The point is that not just any causal connection between rationalizing attitudes and a wanted effect suffices to guarantee that producing the wanted effect was intentional. The causal chain must follow the right sort of route.
>
> (Davidson 2001 [1973], 72)

Even though the man's killing of his victim was caused by his mental states (i.e., his trying to kill the victim, which led to the shooting), we feel some resistance when Davidson asks whether the man killed his victim intentionally. This resistance comes from a recognition that the causal chain from shooting to death was a deviant one.

RESPONSES (AND A BONUS PUZZLE)

The causalist response to this challenge is simple, but not easy. The solution is simply to add a qualifier: intentional action requires that the action be caused *in the right way*. The hard part is specifying what exactly counts as the right way. O'Brien (2012) argues that this task is not just hard but impossible. Her claim is that any sufficiently sophisticated treatment of causation "in the right way" will rule out *diverse but not deviant* causal chains. Consider a system, whether mental or physical, that has adapted, whether as a result of deficit or harm, to perform a characteristic function via an unusual pathway. The agent who employs this system can be doing something intentionally, but using an adapted system that fails to meet the conditions of a more sophisticated causal analysis. Thus O'Brien's challenge can be formulated as a dilemma: If the analysis is simple, then causal deviance will be a counterexample to the sufficiency component of the analysis ("If intentional, then caused"); whereas if the analysis is sophisticated, then causal diversity will be a counterexample to the necessity component of the analysis ("Intentional only if caused in the right way").

O'Brien thinks that her challenge is enough to motivate the search for a non-causalist theory of action, but she doesn't herself propose such a theory (although she does suggest that it will involve an appeal to the agent's *perspective* on the action, and on its causal chains). Shepherd (2014) argues that the causalist can meet O'Brien's challenge; he proposes a general theory of control that, he argues, enables the causalist to solve the problem of causal deviance.

This debate has practical implications for issues in moral and criminal responsibility. We often appeal to the mental states that caused an action as grounds for blaming and punishing (or praising and rewarding) someone. Thus, it would seem that a justified judgment of blameworthiness (not mention a justified instance of punishment) would require that we be able to determine exactly when someone's mental states caused a particular action in the right kind of way.

Speaking of wild (pigs), discussion of deviant causal chains in the context of moral and criminal responsibility can get pretty wild. The following thought experiment—our final thought experiment, at least for now—was presented by Don Harper Mills at a 1987 banquet for the American Academy of Forensic Sciences:

A medical examiner surveyed the body of Ronald Opus and concluded that he had died from a gunshot wound to the head. The victim had originally jumped from the top of a ten-story building, intending to take his own life. He left a note to that effect, indicating his despondency. But as he fell past the ninth floor, his life was interrupted by a shotgun blast through the window, which killed him instantly.

Neither the shooter nor the deceased was aware that a safety net had been installed just below the eighth-floor level to protect building workers. Ronald Opus would have failed to complete his suicide attempt the way he had planned.

Ordinarily ... a person who sets out to commit suicide and ultimately succeeds, even though the mechanism might not be what he intended, is still defined as a suicide. Because Mr. Opus was shot on the way to certain death nine stories below, and because his suicide attempt probably would not have been successful due to the safety net, the medical examiner felt that he had a homicide on his hands.

The shotgun blast had come from a room on the ninth floor that was occupied by an elderly man and his wife. They had been arguing, and he was threatening her with a shotgun. The man was so upset that when he missed his wife, the pellets went out the window, striking Mr. Opus.

When one intends to kill subject A but kills subject B in the attempt, one is still guilty of the murder of B. When confronted with the murder charge, the old man and his wife were adamant. They both said that they thought the shotgun was not loaded. The old man said it was his long-standing habit to threaten his wife with the unloaded shotgun. He had no intention to murder her.

Therefore, the killing of Mr. Opus appeared to be an accident; that is, the gun had been accidentally loaded.

The continuing investigation turned up a witness who saw the old couple's son loading the shotgun about six weeks prior to the fatal accident. It transpired that the old lady had cut off her son's financial support, and the son, knowing the propensity of the father to use the shotgun threateningly, loaded the gun with the expectation the father would shoot the mother. The case now becomes one of murder on the part of the son for the death of Ronald Opus.

Now comes the bizarre twist. Further investigation revealed that the son in fact was Ronald Opus. He had become increasingly despondent over the failure of his attempt to engineer his mother's murder. This led him to jump off the ten-story building, only to be killed by a shotgun blast passing through the ninth-story window. The son had actually murdered himself, and the medical examiner closed the case as a suicide.

(Campbell 2002, vi–vii)

Unfortunately, it's not clear exactly what to say about this case. But perhaps this state of puzzlement is an appropriate place to end.

RECOMMENDED READING

Duff, Antony. 2009. "Legal and Moral Responsibility." *Philosophy Compass* 4: 978–86.

Levy, Neil, and Michael McKenna. 2009. "Recent Work on Free Will and Moral Responsibility." *Philosophy Compass* 4: 96–133.

Shepherd, Joshua. 2014. "The Contours of Control." *Philosophical Studies* 170: 395–411.

WORKS CITED

Campbell, Andrea. 2002. *Making Crime Pay: The Writer's Guide to Criminal Law, Evidence, and Procedure.* New York: Allworth Press.

Davidson, Donald. 2001 [1973]. "Freedom to Act." In *Essays on Actions and Events*, 59–74. Oxford: Oxford University Press.

O'Brien, Lilian. 2012. "Deviance and Causalism." *Pacific Philosophical Quarterly* 93: 175–96.

INDEX